SO-AIT-327

CENTURIES
of HOLINESS

CENTURIES
of HOLINESS

Ancient Spirituality
Refracted for a Postmodern Age

ॐ

RICHARD VALANTASIS

continuum

NEW YORK • LONDON

2005

The Continuum International Publishing Group Inc
15 East 26 Street, New York, NY 10010

The Continuum International Publishing Group Ltd
The Tower Building, 11 York Road, London SE1 7NX

www.continuumbooks.com

Printed in the United States of America

Library of Congress Cataloging-in-Publication Data

Valantasis, Richard, 1946-
    Centuries of holiness : ancient spirituality refracted for a postmodern age / Richard Valantasis.
        p.   cm.
    Includes bibliographical references.
    ISBN 0-8264-1705-1 (hardcover : alk. paper)
    1. Christian life. 2. Spiritual life. 3. Holiness.   I. Title.
    BV4501.3.V35 2005
    248.4 – dc22

                                                        2004029332

Contents ....

Acknowledgments ⁓

I BEGAN MY CAREER as a spiritual director while I was chaplain to the American foundation of the Society of St. Margaret, an Anglican religious order of women dedicated to ministry to the very poorest in our urban centers. Among those sisters, too numerous to single out, I especially recognize Mother Anne Marie (of blessed memory), Sister Mary Gabriel and Sister Catherine Louise, a creative and dynamic novitiate team for over a decade, Sister Winifred (of blessed memory), a monk of extraordinary insight who embodied contemplative action — all the sisters in their own ways both challenged me to be a spiritual director and trained me in how to do it. Their holiness, based on a combination of the contemplative and the active life, has always been an inspiration to me. I gratefully dedicate this volume to the sisters past and present who continue their faithful ministry to the poor.

I owe an enormous debt to the Rev'd Daniel Handschy, who started to work with me while we were both studying at Harvard, but who during years of his own professional life has become a spiritual director to me, to his parish, and to many others as well. His intelligence and his driving curiosity guided many parts of this book.

The Rev'd Jennifer Phillips, co-rector with me at the simultaneously craziest and most profound Anglo-Catholic parish in the country, has been a constant companion in the spiritual direction of communities. Our mutual work and our long friendship have had a profound impact on this book. Her ability to preach a transcendent God poetically holding on to an immanent divine presence, while I insisted on an immanent God discursively and stubbornly embodied in the community, has kept my theology in check for many years. Alas I have reverted in this book.

The Rev'd Victoria Sirota and Dr. Robert Sirota have been part of a seeking coterie of friends and companions over many years. Their energy and enthusiasm, and the intensity of their faith, were before me as I wrote these pages — I wanted not only to include the fruits of their knowledge but also to speak to the wonder of their faith.

Professor Margaret R. Miles led me on the way to the academic study of asceticism and pushed me to apply that tradition to contemporary parish life. She also convinced me that the genre of this book should be elements of the spiritual life organized into "centuries," a collection

11

of one hundred essays, like those of the early church ascetics. She and her husband Owen Thomas have been important conversation partners and models of religious practice.

My wife Janet, as the editorial, intellectual and spiritual companion that she is, has been with me from the beginning on this project. Like the three old men at the coffee house in my dream that you will hear about shortly, Janet has urged me for years to write this book. Her prodding and encouragement, as well as her excellent editorial reading, have played a vital part in its production.

Finally, all my students at Iliff School of Theology, St. Andrew's Episcopal Church and St. John's Cathedral (both in Denver), Saint Louis University, and Harvard, have queried and challenged and contested and embraced parts of this book as it has been taught over the years in various forms. I especially thank those in the 2004 Lenten program in my home: Lucy McGuffy, George and Betsy Hoover, George Magnuson and Carrie Doehring, Ginny Chase, Beth Taylor, Steve Kick, Sally Brown, and Mary Boland. In intense and often provocative discourse with them over the years, I have learned to translate the ancient traditions into language and concepts accessible to them. In the process they have transformed me and I hope I have them.

Introduction .... ༄

THIS BOOK IS FOR those who yearn for a spiritual life that has depth and intellectual challenge. It is a thinking-person's guide to the religious life written for the smart seeker who yearns for a mind, body, and spirit fully attuned to God, fully alive, fully enfleshed, fully interactive with other believing people from a wide variety of religions, fully connected to the wider world in which humans live, fully engaged with the physical universe, fully committed to service to the poor and disenfranchised of the world, and, of course, fully postmodern. It is not a book for the merely pious who wish to find the same answers and methods rehearsed in the traditional manner.

I present here one hundred provocative and short essays for you to consider in the construction of your own spirituality. I trust you to be able to think and to consider for yourself how it is that you need to create a religious life, a spiritual self, that makes sense in the context of your own life. It is not a prescription for an ideal spiritual life, nor do I give you specific advice on how you should create an appropriate spirituality. Rather, I present independent, and yet highly coordinated, small units as elements to help you think through the religious life.

Yes, I said "think through" your religious life. These one hundred essays intend to make you think. They are full of rich symbolism and language that should spur your mind to new ways of conceptualizing your religious life. The mind is not tuned out of this process but fully integrated into the realities of daily living. My intent is to deepen your faith by sharpening your mind and expanding your horizons in developing practices both intellectual and concrete for the living of your religious commitments. So I explore the ambiguities and complexities of living a religious life by delving deep into the well of the Christian tradition.

Although in an appendix I have offered a suggested pattern of reading these essays for various seasons of the church year or for a retreat, I have not presented them in any order in the body of the book. To put them into an orderly progression from one to one hundred would have resulted in a proscription for a spiritual life, and I do not want to do that. Rather, they are simply things to ponder, prose poems to read, or essays to be read poetically, in order to explore aspects imported from the Christian tradition that may speak to the postmodern world. There is an interplay here: I move from the premodern spiritual world of the Christian tradition to the postmodern realities of our current world, and back again. The movement from pre- to postmodern intentionally draws new meanings for old ways of living the religious life. It is precisely this interplay that makes these teachings trustworthy—they do not simply come from me but from my own intellectual and spiritual searching through the wonderful reservoir of the ancient Christian tradition of spiritual direction and formation.

But now, let me step back a few steps and talk about the larger frame that has informed the writing of this book. I know that there is in each person an ultimate yearning for holiness. It may be called by any number of different terms today, but the ancient spiritual masters in Eastern Christianity were certain about how to name it. The ancient theological tradition called it "divinization," a troublesome term intended to articulate the capacity of every person to become holy, godlike, attuned to God, and united to the divine in every aspect of being. The yearning is for divinization, that is, a personal holiness that unites every aspect of human existence, a social holiness that sanctifies every relationship, and a cosmic holiness that finds God gloriously revealed in the physical universe. This book was written for those who yearn for a kind of holiness in which the mind is engaged, the body completely cooperative, social relationships transparent, and the wonders of the physical universe applauded. Yearning and holiness define the project.

The quest for this kind of holiness, for a lively relationship with God, has probably been a preoccupation of humans since the beginning of their ability to be reflective. Opening one's eyes to the splendor of a sunset, or watching crashing waves of a turbulent sea, or standing among the majestic mountains or forests in their pristine beauty, or searching the stars at night in their glory and astonishing regularity, humans have realized that there is more to the universe in which they exist than meets the eye, or that the universe and human life within it is far more mysterious than the imagination can grasp. Also exploring the depth of emotions and experience, or delving into the depths of interpersonal relationships, or soaring in the mind and spirit to heights of meditation and contemplation, the human person comes to know that life is mysterious and gracious, deep and complex. And in social relationships, when seekers meld together into a corporate body in a worship service, or singing a hymn, or dancing to the religious rhythm of an initiation ceremony, or sitting quietly together in meditative chant, the thinking person comes to know the transformative relationship of social gatherings and the mystery of interaction that characterizes them. There are divine forces at work infinitely more powerful and mysterious than any person knows, and these forces became fascinating, and continue to fascinate those who yearn for holiness. This is how I imagine the beginnings of the awareness of the divine impulse in the world, and the human awakening to the divine presence within the world, and then within the self. This is how I understand the yearning that characterizes the postmodern religious age. It is a pattern of wonder and awe that seems to recur through the history of religious thought, even to our own day.

The wonder at the physical world, the exploration of the mind in individual experience, and the excitement of social gathering are all human endeavors focused upon the splendor and magic of the universe. These experiences are guides to the mystery and glory of God. People respond to that mystery and glory by wanting to know more, to experience the mystery more deeply, to understand and orient their lives to be in harmony with it, and to live their lives consistent with the mystery and wonder that they have experienced. Brave souls step out of the wonder to experiment with the means of living in the mystery perpetually. This is the mystique of the ancient monks in the desert of Egypt, women and men who moved out to live fully into the mystery, who created new paths for others to follow in experiencing the mystery of the divine order of the universe. These early Christian professional ascetics were pioneers of the human spirit and mediators of the divine presence to the social world of their day. Their pioneering spirit was compelling. As these early pioneers of the spirit advanced, they brought others along their way, pointing and modeling new patterns of thought and action. Their quest for the divine became a highly desired way of living. Their yearning for holiness compelled others to follow the paths they trod. This book continues their pioneering quest to articulate the intimate union of human and God in personal and communal daily living.

Over generations of the process of these quests, guides to the wonders of God began to develop ways of helping others to engage with the mystery of God and to relate that mystery to daily living. Gradually the spiritual sciences, if I can call them that, were systematized and codified so that they could more easily be communicated to future generations. Spiritual direction as a social function was born to effect that communication, so that each generation could pass on to the next the ways, both successful and unsuccessful, to live fully into the divine presence. These systems of spiritual direction often contained the very same advice across wildly different religions: fasting, incantation, meditation, prayer, regulation of sexual intercourse, patterning of social relationships, and the cultivation of specific ways of understanding the symbolic universe, the systems of thought that explain the meaning and significance of events. The various contexts in which these practices — such as fasting or abstaining from certain foods — created different meanings for the practitioners, but often the practices themselves seem remarkably the same. The meaning was not oriented to the specific practice but to the way the particular practice led the seeker to know the mystery of God in daily living. Spiritual directors often use the same practice to effect different ways of knowing God.

In this book I explore the Christian tradition but I do so with an awareness that there are other religions, other traditions, outside Christianity that have developed in parallel fashion, and often influenced Christian spiritual formation. I know the same practice may be useful in a variety of social and religious contexts. I am keenly aware that in the postmodern context, spiritual practice may indeed be a means of forging conversation among the rapidly expanding groups of religious combatants within Christianity and between Christians, Muslims, Jews, Buddhists, Hindus, Native Americans, and people of many other religious traditions. The yearning for holiness, or its cultural and religious equivalent, is not restricted to Christians alone. In this book I speak from within various Christian traditions, hoping to build bridges of communication with people from other religious traditions, as well as to open postmodern Christians to ways of experiencing God that will bridge the divide between Eastern and Western Christianity.

The traditions of spiritual advancement play an important role in an individual's or a community's ability to become holy, to seek and to find God, to develop as a person capable of relating fully to God. Those ancient spiritual traditions, however, are being lost and forgotten. Those fortunate enough to have had a good spiritual formation as a child and young adult have not come to the fore in promulgating their reflective knowledge to future generations. Those unfortunate enough to have received spiritual formation through abusive or manipulative religious communities actively work against the systems of their own abuse and dysfunction. Still there is a yearning for something more, something authentic and historically connected, something that replicates in the postmodern world the deep and life-giving spiritual formation of the past. The great proliferation of spirituality books attests to this. Although there is this great interest in spirituality, and even in the historical texts of spirituality, the deep and long traditions of spiritual formation, particularly as they relate to practices, seem to be waning. The current interest in spirituality, in other words, seems not to engage the long memory and history of the spiritual arts that have been developed over generations.

The rejection of certain parts of the spiritual tradition is understandable. The traditional anthropology, the understanding of the human person and human existence written into the tradition of Christian theology, emphasized the sinful depravity and unworthiness of the person before a distant and imperial God (at least in the theology of some early Christian leaders). The devaluation of the human person has been detrimental to human beings and their well-being. It does not resonate with postmodern values regarding the human person and the created universe. Consequently, the arts of guiding the soul simply dispensed with the traditions perceived to have been forged in old, defunct, and now useless understanding of the human person and the human predicament. Spiritual directors began to present a truncated version of the spiritual arts in order to circumvent the destructive parts of the spiritual tradition.

The need, however, was not for excising aspects of the tradition of their problematic parts, but rather for engaging with the underpinning of the ancient thought in order to translate it into a more appropriate postmodern mode of thinking and experiencing. The devaluation of the human person was based on a hierarchy of being that maintained that the spirit was higher on the ladder of being than anything physical. That hierarchy demanded that the spirit and the mind of the person subject and discipline the body. The physical aspects of human existence were devalued and rejected in favor of the spiritual. The devaluation of the physical, as well as the hierarchy of being, no longer resonates with postmodern thinking. The underlying hierarchy of being needs to be jettisoned and translated.

The hierarchy of being led to other problems. The older tradition promoted now inappropriate images of the cosmos based on a hierarchy of heaven and earth that replicated the hierarchy of spirit and body. The physical world was subordinate to the spiritual world and was to be subdued by the spiritual world, just as the body of the person was to be subdued by the mind and spirit. That subjugation of the physical world, that mastery of the physical world by the superior human forces acting on their higher order in the universe led to the devastating abuse of the environment, the squandering of natural resources, and the pollution of earth, air, and seas. The idea that the physical universe is lower on the hierarchy of being was an exceptionally destructive spiritual concept. Thus these old systems were circumvented and forgotten, if not discarded as useless, and for justifiable reasons.

Nevertheless, the old spiritual tradition — when properly translated into a postmodern context — still holds a wealth of information about human spiritual growth and godly development. It is incumbent upon us in the twenty-first century to retain the history and the memory of the past without necessarily replicating it. This means that the tradition, even in its destructive history, must be taken seriously and translated into new concepts. It is important to note that the tradition cannot simply be read and applied, because it does indeed come from a world other than our own, a world often inimical to our own values and needs, and one detrimental to the future of the physical environment.

So the need is for a retrieval of the past and for an appropriate translation of the old knowledge into postmodern modalities. The tradition can be translated into language and images that speak to our postmodern way of thinking and living without having to adopt the worldview or the hierarchy of being implied in the ancient traditions. This book intends first to retrieve, then to translate, that ancient knowledge and tradition into a language and set of metaphors and reflections that will assist postmodern seekers after God to pursue their goal in a way consonant and connected to the vitality of the ancient tradition.

While this book values the spiritual tradition, I do not treat tradition as a precious thing that must be replicated in the present exactly as it functioned in the past. I believe I am being faithful to the tradition itself in treating it as a dynamic and changing phenomenon. It is only in the rigid religious battles of the twentieth and twenty-first centuries that tradition has been rarified and made to be an unchanging pattern of religious thought and practice that imposes itself on each subsequent generation. Rather, the earlier concept of tradition presented itself as the best of the past that could be of use to future generations, a kind of treasury of good things of the past that people might find useful. As one Orthodox theologian described it, tradition is the action of the Holy Spirit making available the wisdom of the past in a new idiom and a new time. This is the way that I understand the tradition, and I treat tradition in this book as a living and changing process that enables each subsequent generation of people to plumb its riches, while living solidly in their own era. It is a dynamic tradition that insists upon its own transformation and interpretation in each succeeding generation, and that fluidity and mutability brings the riches of the past to bear on the complexities of the present moment. The spiritual tradition, though never really rigid and solidified, comes to the reader of this book refracted through the lens of my own knowledge and experience of the postmodern world.

This book actually began in my youth. For whatever whim of God or human, I have had a deep interest in asceticism — the ancient arts of spiritual formation and direction — from my youth onward. And curiously enough, I have had wonderful spiritual guides throughout my life. These guides took me aside to explain the richness of the ascetical and theological traditions of the Greek Orthodox Church in which I was reared. Priests, aunts, elders of the parish community — each in their own way fed the fire of my interest by passing on to me the richness of their own understanding. The world came to life for me, not as a place far distant from God but as a place where God was ever-present and waiting to be discovered. They guided me to understand God as both my companion in daily living and the purpose of all my activity. More than that, however, I understood that if I wanted to know and understand things divine, I had to work at it. In short, I needed to become an ascetic whose goal was to discover the incarnate and immediately present God and to conform my life to that discovery. They taught me the active engagement of my self with the divine impulse and presence all around me. This has been an important learning for me. Having moved now into the Episcopal Church, where I have been a priest for over thirty years, I have tried to transmit the same sense of God as constant companion and as ultimate goal to those among whom I have ministered. These early learnings have followed me and continue to inspire me. They became part of a way of living the spiritual life that has animated my ministry as a priest and, more especially, my daily life as an intentional Christian. It is now time for me to retrieve and pass on that which was given to me.

The immediate context for my writing began in a recurrent dream after the death of my brother, Michael — a death that left me to be the last of my immediate family's elder generation. The dream was this: I was sitting at a Greek coffee house, like the ones I knew as a child, where the elders gathered to commune with one another in the traditional way of Greek men. Three elders were sitting at a table across from me: each with one elbow on the table, the other on his knee, leaning forward to drink Greek coffee from the small cups that lay on the table. Sitting across from them, I was eager to hear their wisdom. They said to me, with no guilt or condemnation, "You are the last of the line."

I puzzled over this statement. The elders were calling me to do something, but I was not sure what it was. Over the course of the official forty-day mourning period for my brother, I considered the dream over and over again. I was not the last of the Valantasis family name, because I have two nephews. I am not the last of my mother's family, because we have a plethora of cousins bearing that family name. Of what was I the last of the line? I came to understand that I am among the last of Americans trained in the old system of ascetical formation in the Orthodox tradition, an Orthodox tradition that has undergone its own diminishment and transformation in the North American context. Those gifts spurring me on to wonder and curiosity about the things of God should not die with me but should be passed on to future generations. The asceticism that I learned as a child, and that I have studied for these many years as an academic, needed to be passed on to future generations.

But how should it be passed on? To teach it as I learned it as a child would be to present to my contemporary readers a false asceticism, a false spirituality that would be precious and old-fashioned. It would be teaching an asceticism from fifty years ago, which, as we all know, was a very different world with very different understandings of social life and responsibility. The way I learned the spiritual tradition cannot be replicated in contemporary times because the world has changed, and so have I. I am more critical, and I understand the world from a more postmodern perspective than from a modern one (I'll explain postmodern perspectives on spirituality in a while.) That ancient tradition that was passed on to me in my own North American context of a half century ago must be made to reflect the postmodern context in which we all live today. It is not precious like a relic but engaged as a dynamic system of thought and action capable of responding to every generation's own hurts and joys, needs and desires, successes and failures, as well as to all the new knowledge that has emerged in the time between when I learned these systems and when I must now live them.

So I decided to read a Western spiritual classic by Adolphe Tanquerey, a Roman Catholic ascetical theologian who systematized the ascetical tradition, and to translate that ancient tradition into a medium more appropriate to a twenty-first-century audience. In a sense, I used Tanquerey's *The Spiritual Life: A Treatise on Ascetical and Mystical Theology* (translated by Herman Branderis; Tournai, Belgium: Desclée, 1930) as a way of reminding myself of the full extent of the tradition, and as an opportunity to rethink and reconsider the principles of spiritual formation and spiritual development in my own context for my students, my co-parishioners, my colleagues and friends, and for the many people to whom I have been spiritual director over the past three decades. My retrieval and reinterpretation of the tradition, however, were not simply to make it applicable to my contemporary situation. I wanted as well to pass on the Eastern Orthodox ascetical tradition as I have received it and as I have developed it through my life as a spiritual director. In other words, the material of this book reflects both a more Eastern perspective on ascetical theology and a retrieval of that tradition for a postmodern context.

Already I am in a bind. This is a book of postmodern ascetical theology. (You will notice that I have discreetly slipped from the language of spirituality to that of asceticism.) But if I use "Postmodern Asceticism" or "Postmodern Ascetical Theology" as a title, no one would buy the book. Most people, even intelligent and well-educated seekers, would not understand the phrase "ascetical theology" and others, less oriented to critical thinking, would not like to see the word "postmodern," because it stands for the enemy of true spirituality in the minds of some (albeit falsely traditionalist) religious people. But I could not write the book without using those phrases. Ascetical theology is the traditional term for describing spiritual formation and the religious development of the individual person. It is the term that both the Eastern and Western churches used until modern times to name what we call "spirituality," that is until historical amnesia wiped out the ancient ascetical tradition. Asceticism originally referred, in the Greek language, to the training of an athlete, but in religious language, it simply refers to the spiritual workouts necessary to develop a holy and religious life. Asceticism refers to the disciplined practice of the religious life, and it emphasizes the fully integrated person (mind, body, and spirit) working toward the attainment of holiness.

Now the more difficult term. If "asceticism" sounds too arcane, then "postmodernism" sounds too contemporary. Postmodernism commands attention precisely because it refers to our current religious and intellectual frame of reference, even for those who claim not to be postmodernists at all. Postmodernism constellates around a number of particular attitudes and is not in itself a consistent philosophical or theological framework. As a set of attitudes, it has had an enormous influence on every aspect of twenty-first-century living and thinking. Although this book is not the place to explore postmodernism completely, I will state the postmodern elements that I embrace in the context of this book. The postmodernism in which I write about spirituality/asceticism maintains the following:

- that there is no consistent or universal narrative that explains all religious experiences and phenomena, but rather widely divergent and often conflicting narratives, each with an important story to be told;

- that other religions besides Christianity have validity and importance, bear the truth, and are worthy of respect;

- that Christian religious formation has a theology of its own, but that religious formation is not valid in only one religious tradition; in fact, often religious practices transgress denominational and faith boundaries;

- that the image of isolated individuals operating on their own is a false view because all people are connected to others, and all are connected and interrelated in the universe;

- that gender, race, and class play an important role in understanding spiritual direction;

- that spiritual formation applies not only to individuals but also to groups of people, and (in some way I cannot fully explain but will consistently explore) to the universe itself.

In this sense, then, this book presents a postmodern ascetical theology without any embarrassment or fear, because it brings the best of the past and ancient tradition to bear on the complexities and challenges of the twenty-first-century postmodern situation.

So having rejected the title "Postmodern Ascetical Theology," what does my current title suggest? I present here a "century," that is, a "hundred," independent items pertaining to the question of spiritual formation. (In the tradition, both the entire collection of one hundred essays as well as each essay is called a "century.") Each individual century articulates a specific concept or practice retrieved from the ancient ascetical tradition but thoroughly explored from the postmodern perspective. Each century, that is, retrieves an element from the tradition and translates it into postmodern modalities. The centuries function as fragments for the construction of a postmodern spiritual practice.

The tradition of providing small snippets of ascetical teaching numbering a hundred goes back to the very beginning of the popularization of asceticism. The first centuries of ascetical theology were written by Evagrios Pontikos (346–99 C.E.) who is in many respects the originator of the entire ascetical system used in Eastern and Western monasticism alike. In the Anglican tradition, a synthesis of ascetical theology and the "new" sciences was developed in the centuries of Thomas Traherne (1636–74). Both Traherne and Evagrios, among the many others who composed ascetical centuries over the past two millennia, recognized that people must put together their own practices in order to live the religious life. There can be no universal pattern imposed on all, so they wrote in centuries to provide provocative small units for seekers to consider as they progress toward the goal. Postmodernity recognizes the fractured and decentered nature of the self and society, and such a presentation of small units, of a century of direction, directly addresses the postmodern self, society, and world. It is a medium particularly important to our contemporary way of living and thinking. The fragments considered in these centuries assist the seeker in constructing a personal spiritual life responsive to the various communities in which the seeker lives, and resonate with the physical universe that gathers up all existent beings.

But both Evagrios and Traherne lived and wrote in a time of conflicting knowledges. This is why the choice of centuries seems so appropriate to the postmodern context. Evagrios was writing in the early church when conflicting models of philosophical and religious asceticism were being contested by various factions of the church and of Greco-Roman society. He wrote in the clash of Christian and Roman culture, in a period when Christianity was engaging with Greco-Roman intellectual and spiritual traditions, while at the same time articulating a particularly Christian mode of thinking and living. Evagrios opened the door to the deepest knowledge of the ascetical life in a language that fused old and new and profoundly influenced monastic asceticism since. Traherne was writing in a similar clash of cultures and knowledge. He wrote in the Renaissance, when new and conflicting views of science and religion challenged the hegemonic systems of the Middle Ages, and clashed with even some of the perspectives of the Reformation. His ascetical theology sparkled with the fiery conflict of emerging knowledges and their incorporation into new ways of living. The genre of the centuries emerges precisely from these clashes of cultures and knowledges in order to set the stage for a different way of articulating the religious life more resonant with the problems and joys of emerging knowledges and understanding. In other words, the fragments were employed as a way to gather the old knowledge into new systems that work in new environments.

My "centuries" emerge from the same sort of conflicts in the postmodern period. Twenty-first-century religious people live in a fractious religious environment. Tradition is used by one side to argue that no doctrine or practice should ever change, but by the other side to argue for radical change and transformation into new and challenging ways of thinking and living. Not only is tradition contested, but also contested is the very way of understanding religious realities: fundamentalism, liberalism, liberation theology, literal interpreters of the Scriptures, modernism, postmodernism, systematic and constructive theologies all contend with each other to stake out the one true path for all people living in the postmodern world. Yet there is no one such path, as every spiritual director in every generation has adamantly affirmed. In our own day, there can be only elements that individuals, groups, and societies piece together in order to attain the holiness for which they yearn. No one any longer can prescribe the one, true, and singular spiritual practice that applies to every person on the globe. That is a postmodern reality. That is indeed our reality. The centuries that follow in this book speak to that reality.

The "holiness" in the title refers to the centrality of sanctification to spiritual formation. The holiness of the tradition, the sanctification of self, society, and cosmos that were so important to the ancient ascetics, articulates in a historically contingent way a deep desire of postmodern people. The integrity, unity of purpose, and profound orientation toward God, which here I call divinization (again retrieving a concept from the Eastern Christian tradition), together with the transformation of societies and nations, and the respect for the sacredness of the environment, the earth, and even the universe itself, all are subsumed under the rubric of "becoming holy." Centuries of holiness, then, refers both to the ancient, centuries-old ascetical tradition and to the genre of the book, united in the seemingly trans-historical desire of religious people to become holy, to be sanctified, to become divinized.

Now the subtitle makes sense: "Ancient Spirituality Refracted for a Postmodern Age." This book does not simply present the ancient tradition uninterpreted. The ancient tradition is refracted; that is, it is passed through the prism of the postmodern context. The results of that refraction have been written down for the benefit of those who wish to pursue their own path of spiritual direction. The resulting spirituality combines the ancient and the postmodern in creating something very different, and very new.

There are some things that the reader should know about how this book was written. First, I have presented the teaching in as impersonal a way as I can. In other words, I do not present anecdotes or my own personal experiences as part of the ascetical theology. This is the way I was taught: asceticism is a set of principles to consider that may or may not apply to one's life situation at any particular point in time. This is not a spiritual director telling a seeker what the seeker must think and experience, but rather a presentation of principles that should be considered. To this end, I have avoided using any masculine or feminine pronouns in the text — they distract from the refraction of the tradition and from the potential applicability of the teaching to each seeker.

Second, I have stepped out, for the most part, from using explicitly Christian language to refer to God. This does not mean that this theology is non-Christian or even post-Christian. The language reflects the fact that ascetics have often been able to talk across religious and denominational lines, and that in antiquity they even may have lived together in the same monasteries. Indeed, some monasteries embraced both orthodox and heterodox believers, as well as pagans and other religious practitioners who were following the same religious practices. The specifically Christian language that remains seemed necessary to speak to my immediate audience, which I envision to be Christian, although I hope the language is sufficiently inclusive to appeal to others.

The language and metaphors of these centuries are intentionally bold. The conceptual boldness challenges the modalities of thinking of postmodern Christians and American and English-speaking practitioners of religion. I have retrieved an early Christian concept of the restoration of all things in God; in Greek it is called the concept of the *apokatastasis*. This concept rests upon 1 Corinthians 15:28, which presents Paul's vision of the restoration and subjection of all things to Christ, who in turn restores all things to the rule of God, until God encompasses all things in everything: "When he makes all things subject to him, then also the Son himself will make all things subject to the One who subjected all things to him, in order that God would be all things in everything" (my translation). This restoration was highly contested in the early church because it was so bold in predicating the sanctification and divinization of all people, societies, and even the physical universe. The vision revolves around an active and engaged process of subjecting everything in creation to the divine will and bringing everything in creation into the divine presence. The final restoration confounded the moral and intellectual boundaries set up by bishops and theologians — boundaries intended to demarcate clearly the divine from the human, the Creator from the creation. While theologians and bishops tried to suppress such dangerous thinking, the ascetics were putting it into practice. Early Christian ascetics were forging new ways of understanding the divinization (in Greek *theosis*) of seeking people who desired alone and with others to become holy, to become godlike, and in the end to disappear into God.

In addition to bold language, the concepts presented in these centuries are dynamic. It is not easy to describe states of being and ways of living in dynamic language, because the language itself tends to sound static. For example, I rely heavily on the concept of a "goal" for the religious life. This "goal" translates the Greek ascetical concept of a *skopos* — more than a simple and future thing to be achieved, an ascetic goal is an organizing principle that gathers fragmented elements into a cohesive process. The ascetic goals in this book emerge as moving targets, constantly shifting organizing principles to the religious life that give direction to disparate acts and thoughts while not precluding the final outcome. This is a very dynamic understanding of a goal, which cannot be confused with the more literal or business-oriented understanding as a static thing to be achieved. The language of the book consistently attempts to subvert static categories by placing them in dynamic relationship of past to future, of current states of being with emergent ones, and of foundational realities grounded in the present while always moving energetically to something not yet present.

The same dynamic language is evident in other terms as well. I use the word "eschatology" here to imply much more than the mere description of the end-times of history or the final state of human existence. In the context of this ascetical theology, eschatology refers to that final cause, that desired and imaged complete state of being that gathers and directs energy. Eschatology is something pulling seekers from the future that gives structure and meaning to the present. It is a compelling image of the future, a prolepsis, that draws together the elements of the present and thrusts them forward in time to make real the image that exists now only in the imagination. In this way, the references to eschatology stand as more navigational and dynamic realities in the midst of otherwise unrelated religious experiences and thoughts in the present. Eschatology exists as a directionality toward the future, moving to ever-increasing complexities.

The question of directionality also deserves some comment. The ascetical progress toward the goal of holiness, toward the eschatological divinized state, always exists as a relational and interactive process. The final goal and the hoped-for eschatological state continually change and shift as the seeker moves toward divinization. Divinization itself continually interacts with individuals, groups, and the environment to change directions and content. The end result, that is, remains evolutionary, following divergent paths that eventually meet in a future state that gathers together discordant and diverse streams of activity and thought not predictably related. In this I have been greatly influenced by the theology of Teilhard de Chardin, whose "omega-point" followed evolution to its most divine and holy final outcome. So the directionality of the religious life remains relational, interactive, and frequently unpredictable. In this sense, there is, as a good friend calls it, a sense of an "ascetic cubism," a simultaneity of elements existing at different times and in different dimensions existing simultaneously on the same canvass.

This ascetic foundation for such an "ascetic cubism" is built upon a dynamic interpretation of two Christian sacraments, at least as they were understood in the early church: baptism and chrismation. They require a little introduction before approaching the centuries themselves. The sacrament of baptism, understood dynamically, confers upon a seeker a divinization, a grace of divine union, that becomes both the reality and the final goal of a seeker's life. Baptism is not merely symbolic, or a mere ritual, but a process of continual conversion of self into the divine that sets the seeker on a road toward manifestation in daily life of the gift of divinization and union with God bestowed in the sacrament. Baptism in this ascetic system defines the beginning, the struggle of life, and the end of life all at once. Chrismation, on the other hand, is the sacrament of pouring oil over the newly divinized body, and marking it as God's own forever. Chrismation opens the body to the process of perceiving and understanding the reality of the divine status of the believer and the goal to divinize self, society, and the physical universe. Chrismation is the dynamic principle of making all things conform to God — all things pertaining to one's own individual life, all things pertaining to one's social and familial relations, all things pertaining to society as a whole, and all things that exist in the physical universe. Both baptism and chrismation describe dynamic processes of divinization.

These centuries were written to be performed in the mind. Although in the popular way of thinking, spirituality is something more related to emotions than to thinking, this was not the case in early Christianity. In fact, creative and energetic thinking has been considered a spiritual discipline through most of the history of Christianity. The mind, thinking and ruminating on the mystery of the divine presence in meditation, and the mind, creating appropriate theology — both were understood as gateways to the direct experience of God. Mind and experience, thinking and engagement, were connected practices leading to the sanctification and divinization of the person. It was considered a good thing to think boldly, creatively, energetically about the love of God and the yearning to become holy. So these centuries tease the mind into contemplation; into considering positions that challenge current orthodoxies and perspectives; into exploring the mystery of the physical universe as an arena for divine revelation; into a direct experience of God that confounds the categories; and, in the end, into sanctification and holiness.

The best way to perform them in the mind is to read them slowly and deliberately one century at a time. The centuries are not ordered in any particular progression. I have placed them in random order, although I have tried generally to present more basic concepts in earlier centuries, while later centuries move into more advanced thinking about the spiritual life. The distinction, however, between introductory and advanced thought depends entirely on the seeker and the communities to which the seeker connects. So my recommendation is that one century be read each day, ideally combining the reading with a time of reflection, meditation, and prayer. In reading the century, look for what challenges you, what confounds your assumptions, what excites the mind, and what may be most useful to you in the practice of your religious life alone and in community. Then turn those thoughts and reflections into conversations with the divine. You may jump around, finding topics of particular interest to you, or subjects you want to pursue more fully in response to some personal or community need. But the traditional way to read centuries is simply to take them one at a time, reading slowly and meditatively, taking the significant thoughts with you through the day and the week. I myself generally read such spiritual reading after reciting daily morning prayer and before I begin to do the work of the day, but that is not necessary for using this book.

After finishing a draft of these centuries, I assembled a group of interested people to read and reflect on them. They were assigned a selection of them for every week, and we gathered to discuss their responses one evening a week. This group insisted that the group reading and discussion actually was an important option. They could envision these centuries as the starting point for corporate and mutual spiritual direction and formation for people who live, or worship, or work together. And they wanted me to suggest this group reading as a helpful and productive way of engaging with the centuries. The conversations were deep and rich, full of the energy of people striving together for holiness in lives that were very different from one another. It was indeed a healthy and productive way to move toward new forms of spiritual direction and thinking — forms that would at once enhance individual lives but at the same time open doors for more social and corporate ways of living out the process of divinization in the world and in the physical universe.

For the convenience of these groups and individuals, I have selected some centuries appropriate to Advent, Lent, Eastertide, and two retreats. These suggestions will give some particular thematic cohesion to the centuries and provide a starting place for those who want to use this book either individually or in community for spiritual reading. These may be found in the appendix at the end of the book. They are merely a suggestion; they do not weave a narrative out of the material, but simply present some options for your assistance in reading the centuries.

So I present to you now the fruit of a lifetime of reflection on the practice of the religious life. It feels both like retrieving prior centuries and bringing them to bear on our postmodern living, and like the beginning of a new century when so many of the mysteries of God's divine presence and activity will be seen and known in ways never before imagined. These centuries bridge the centuries, and present fragments for the construction of a thoroughly postmodern spiritual practice. The goal is holiness, so take the centuries as an indicator of one way of seeing the path toward holiness, adjusting them as you need to suit the fabric and texture of your own holiness. Take your learning and experience out to your various interlocking communities and expand the horizon of your holiness to include others, and even the physical and intellectual universe in which we live. These centuries of holiness point a particular way in the hopes that in the end, as the scripture promised, God will be all in all (1 Corinthians 15:28).

CENTURIES
of HOLINESS

1 / Conversion .... ☙

S OMETIMES IN THE MIDST of living through the day, people suddenly experience a deep yearning for something that seems missing from their lives. The experience begins in the recognition, sometimes almost furtively perceived around the edges of one's life, that life as it is being lived seems not to be in right perspective. The luster, the glitter, the energy of living seem to have somehow gotten sidetracked in the mundane activities of moving from task to task, conversation to conversation, relationship to relationship in the day-to-day drudgery of living. Then the yearning comes. It is a yearning for meaningful conversation, not just exchanged words (or even e-mails); for rich and deep connection with others, not just the passing interaction at the office or at dinner; for the sense of being intimately related to the source of life, not just living off the resources of life. The yearning leads the person to convert the self from being just someone, to being a seeker, a yearning person, a person searching for the divine.

For all the talk of conversion in American society, conversion generally happens slowly over time. The recognition of shallowness, the understanding that something holy is missing from daily living, the desire for intimate and deep relationship with others, the hope for the restoration of the physical beauty of the natural environment lead to a yearning to connect with the divine that begins a process of conversion and transformation. No one can ever turn their back on such yearnings, nor reject them — once they have intruded into a person's consciousness; that is, once a person has become a seeker, there is no turning back. From then on it is forward movement only; the return to the drudgery becomes unthinkable.

Conversion takes on three particular environments. First, it is a conversion of oneself. Once the realization that there is more to life than meets the eye or, more properly, than feeds the mind and soul, there can be no satisfaction until seekers find that for which they yearn. That fullness of being is something that dwells within them, a presence of the divine that seems to be calling seekers inward, into the inner recesses of their being, where the mind meets the divine and finds fulfillment.

Conversion also seeks communities. The satisfaction of finding the presence of the divine within oneself turns seekers toward other people who similarly seem to have found a divine presence. Community is formed among those who have connected with a mysterious and wonderful interior sense of the divine presence, and among those who have banded together to become a living agency for the communication of the divine presence in the people around them. Communities awaken to the divine life within and to the communication of the divine life to all around them. Communities begin to perceive that, in addition to the existence of an interior divine presence, there seems to exist a divine impulse that gathers and directs communities of people into a new way of living, a different life, a divine presence tremendous and transcendent to themselves that compels and embraces their activity.

Finally, conversion seeks out the physical universe. Like an abused person, the environment has been severely beaten over generations of misuse and degradation, while at the same time scientists from a wide range of disciplines have begun to plumb the depths of the reality of the energy and complexity of material existence in the universe. This mysteriously complex and scientifically mystical world in which humans live also seems to manifest the presence of divine forces and divine impulses that has put all known creation into motion and allowed it to evolve and develop in the miraculous way that our world has. And this despite the fact that humans have been detrimental to the natural evolution and development of the physical environment. So, even the physical environment cries out for conversion and transformation, seeking to become the site where the divine presence and impulse may be seen and known in its glory.

Conversion engages all these dimensions — the self, society and community, and the physical environment. The self, society, and the cosmos become conversant with the divine presence that wells up within them; begin to move toward a manifestation and presentation of the divine impulse that seems to draw them forward; and move toward something unknown, something distant and unfamiliar, yet something for which they deeply yearn and without which they cannot live.

Conversion begins in this awakening to something more, something impinging, something erupting deep within the self, and deep within society, and deep within the physical environment that is at once irresistible and compelling. The awakening is to the presence of the divine. Sometimes this awakening can be dramatic, as one finding a completely new self, but most often it is something more subtle and elusive: a yearning, a sense of loss or of finding something is lost, or a still, soft sound that simply invites the person to hear an inner voice.

2 / Sanctification .... ⤳

ONE GOAL OF THE RELIGIOUS LIFE may be expressed as "sanctification." To sanctify life means to bring life, with all of its activities, into relationship with God. This relationship of daily life to God is not impossible because people know that God is ever-present and ever-active in the daily activities of the whole world. God's activity is the given reality, and sanctification involves making that reality a conscious and articulated part of daily life. When seekers bring the reality of God to mind throughout the day, they engage in the sanctification of life.

Since most twenty-first-century people have put God into a particular category distant from the mundane activity of work, or school, or play, it is difficult to imagine that God may be present. Slowly, as seekers begin to image the day as part of God's plan, their work, relationships, and activities become luminous with divine light. Seekers become incrementally capable of imaging everything they think and feel as revelatory of God not only to others, but to themselves. As seekers turn their minds to the memory of God in daily living, their days are sanctified, and God is made visible through their daily activities.

One place where the tradition has taught that God is never present is in anything sinful. At the logical level, if one says that God has no sin, then it may be assumed that God has no place in a seeker's sinful activity. From an ascetical perspective, however, that is not true. Sinful activities and thoughts may become occasions for the remembrance of God. Even though the seeker has sinned, or is about to sin, or even engages in sinful activity on a regular basis, still God does not go away. God does not abandon one to sin, but stands present with seekers even when they are not directed toward God. Thus God is present even at seekers' sinning. Seekers' greatest hope is that through the awareness of the presence of God, even when doing things that most offend God's ways, they may gradually separate themselves from sin and come more fully to the knowledge of the presence of God. It becomes difficult to continue to sin when the mind focuses on the reality of the presence of God. It is difficult to sin if a person images all human activity as in the presence of God. It is difficult to continue sinning if God is present, active, and engaged with seekers even when they seem most distant from God. This is the sanctification that cleanses from the effects of sinful actions. This knowledge of God, the remembrance of the faithfulness of God, sanctifies every activity, thought, and emotion of the day.

One of the ancient ways to achieve this sense of sanctifying daily life is through meditation on scriptural passages that have been selected precisely to address the issues of the day. For example, if troubled by the sense of abandonment, take the psalm that says, "Lord, you have been our refuge from one generation to another" (Psalm 90:1) and bring it to mind throughout the day. By employing the scriptural passage as a means of addressing issues that emerge during the day, one's own sense of abandonment is met by the scriptural passage that speaks of God's faithfulness and constancy. Or if the seeker is beset consistently by the same sinful thoughts or inclination, the seeker may recite the words of the man praying humbly in the temple, "God be merciful to me a sinner" (Luke 18:13). Here the sinful activity and state are brought into relationship with the divine majesty and presence. Their connection within one's life sanctifies life by providing the proper theological reference to the sinful state. The occasion of sin may also become thereby an occasion for the sanctification of life.

Sanctification is not difficult work. One does not need to withdraw from the world, or step back from living, or disengage from relationships in order to become holy. Rather, this holiness and sanctification emerge in the turning of the mind toward God throughout the day. The holiness and sanctification develop out of the constant remembrance of God. So what each one does during the day connects with the reality of God, and each activity of the day becomes revelatory of the presence of God.

3 / Starting Out ....

T HE FIRST SMALL STEP toward divinization seems to be the largest. A seeker has a vision of God, and the divine impulse propels the seeker to begin to move toward divinization. The possibilities of divinization engage the imagination; the task of divinizing the self, all the people in groups around the self, and the very physical universe itself, seems overwhelming. Where is a person to start? How does one take the first step toward the ultimate and eschatological divinization of every living being?

The overarching goal of the first step is simply to begin with something very small and insignificant. A theory of linguistic transformation says that if a person introduces one minor variant in speech, eventually that variant becomes a marker of a group, builds solidarity among a group of people, who begin to move the marker toward signifying a dominant group; thus eventually the minor variant becomes a marker of the dominant group. This is seen consistently in slang words that eventually get absorbed into the general speech patterns of a society. The same applies in the spiritual life. At the very beginning of the spiritual life, the seeker must introduce one small and insignificant variant into the seeker's life.

The first variant is actually the easiest. The normal routine of the day ought to be interrupted for a period of prayer and meditation. This does not need to be a lengthy session but simply a brief variant that interrupts the normal flow of the day. This will become like the grain of sand in the oyster, which eventually produces the pearl. That small interruption and irritant to the day establishes an anchor to the reality of divinization in the midst of a life otherwise not cognizant of or interested in divinization. In a sense, the very small moment of acknowledging the call of divinization and responding to it has achieved what will eventually be the complete reality for all existent things. So the seeker sets a short time every day for connecting with the reality of the interior divine impulse and lives that moment connected to that reality. This simple act should not be abandoned for any purpose. It must remain an irritant, an interruption, in order to be effective.

From this personal and individual first step follows the second: to connect with a community of people who also seek divinization. A community of seekers challenges the boundaries of individual lives and forces upon the seeker the experience that everyone is connected to every other person. Just as a person begins to pursue divinization by interrupting the patterns of the day for prayer and meditation, the seeker must also interrupt the perceived isolation of one person from another. The connectedness of all persons and their bonding into communities manifest on the corporate level the divine impulse and presence experienced on the individual level. The divine impulse permeates not only individual lives, but also the corporate lives of communities of seekers.

In the third step, the seeker connects with the created universe. From the brief interruption of the day for prayer, through the connection with a community of seekers, the person seeking divinization

recognizes that the entire physical universe eagerly groans and awaits
the final transformation and restoration to its divinely ordained glory.
That moment when the seeker stops daily to pray and to meditate connects the seeker with the divine presence that pervades the universe.
The seeker enters into communion with the physical universe through
the divine impulse that operates in both the individual and the cosmos. Community emerges not only from the seeker's connection with
other seekers, but also from the seeker's union and connection with
all the created universe.

The small first step, as enormous as it seems in the beginning, will
start to show evidence of just-noticeable differences. Small, incremental moves toward divinization will be evident in an ever slowly shifting
of priorities, of minute changes in patterns of thought and relationship,
in small changes of attitudes toward the physical universe. Divinization will be evident in the very small transformations that happen in a
person, a day, a relationship, an action that connects it ever so slightly
to the divine impulse that permeates all life. That small connection,
that moment of realization of the presence of the divine in a small
detail of the day, opens the way to the complete transformation and
divinization not only of the individual person, but also of every society
and community, and ultimately of the universe itself. It begins in one
small step that makes a just-noticeable difference in the way life is
lived. But like the theory of linguistic transformation, the small variant in patterns will eventually become a dominant way of speaking;
the small variant that begins with simply connecting with the incarnate divinity within the person will lead ultimately to the divinization
of all living things. It begins with a just-noticeable difference of a day
interrupted to acknowledge the presence of the divine.

4 / Incarnate Living ....

T HE CENTRAL DOCTRINE of Christianity is the doctrine of the incarnation of Jesus Christ. It articulates the position that Jesus is at
once fully human and fully divine in a union in which neither divinity
nor humanity is lost, but both are held together in a substantial unity.
It is a complicated doctrine and one that is difficult to understand,
especially since the councils of the church that set forth and ampli-
fied the doctrine worked out of a philosophical and theological world

that postmodern people can neither experience nor fully understand concretely.

The doctrine of the incarnation focuses attention on the simultaneous humiliation of God descending into human existence and the exaltation of humanity being made worthy to bear God. That is to say, the incarnation is a classic irony: two elements (humanity and divinity) that are by nature distinct and different, coexist harmoniously and effectively in one person. Jesus Christ, both fully human and fully divine, has one personality that manifests, but does not mix into one, the two primary components of his subjectivity. The incarnation holds together that which otherwise seems not to cohere as a unity. The Eastern church would immediately characterize the doctrine as a mystery that is to be contemplated, rather than as a doctrine to be memorized.

The incarnation of Jesus Christ implies a different way of living for those who have been baptized into his body. Just as the divine descended to become human, so also does the human ascend to become divine in Jesus Christ. The corollary in human terms is that just as people have been born human, they are made capable of manifesting the divine presence that is implanted at baptism. In other words, baptism achieves for the Christian the same sort of incarnation that was achieved by Christ. Humans become capable of expressing the divine life present within them, not by mixing the two into one so that the Christian becomes God, but by manifesting through the life of the Christian the divine life to which one has been joined by the sacrament of baptism. The Christian becomes a mirror image of Christ. Christ was divine and took on the human body; the Christian is embodied and takes on the divine life.

This incarnate living for the Christian becomes important because it has radical and important implications for everyday living. It is not that Christians, by virtue of their baptism, ought to exalt themselves over all other people, or to have such a superior self-understanding that they despise all other human beings, especially those who are not baptized. On the contrary, the Christian understands that there is a special mission of manifesting the divine life in the arena of worldly existence. Just as Jesus ministered to the sick, the friendless, and the needy, so ought the baptized Christian minister to the entire world as an extension or manifestation of divine life in the world. Incarnate living demands that Christians manifest the divine life of which they are a part in their daily thoughts and life. Christians are called, by virtue of their baptism, to restore the world to its original beauty, to restore all people to their inherent glory, and to manifest in the social, political, and religious arenas of human existence the very presence and activity of the living God.

There is also another mystery here. The incarnation of Jesus Christ changed the nature of the universe. It is not only that Jesus came to save sinners or to bring good news to the captives or to perform miraculous deeds or even to bring the thoughts of God to bear on a new social and political order. Yes, Jesus did all these things. But, according to classical Christian thinking, the nature of the ordered universe shifted in the incarnation. The incarnation of Jesus, by virtue of its cosmic dimensions, changed the way the world operated: the world was no longer distant and at enmity with God, but now the world was the place where God could be seen, known, experienced, and touched. The world, like the flesh of Jesus Christ, became the place where God may be seen and known. This means that everything in the world — every religious tradition, every scientific exploration, every medical breakthrough, every political situation, the environment, outer space — everything in the world has been altered by the presence of God in the physical universe. Christians experience the physical world with a kind of sacramental view that says that this world is part of the body of Christ because it is the very context into which Christ came in his incarnation. So questions of environmental protection, of conservation of the earth's resources, of distribution of the riches of the earth to all peoples who live on the earth, of connecting all the peoples of the earth for their mutual health and mutual development, and of providing the basic necessities of life for all people — these become central issues of primary importance to Christians. The world is not neutral and not evil, but central and groaning to manifest the presence of the divine.

5 / Bodies .... ᔓ

A T THE HEART of asceticism is body-work. Asceticism works the body in order to improve and to perfect it, at least this was the way it was understood in previous generations. Postmodern conceptions of the body, however, demand a different perspective. There are in fact a number of bodies that interconnect in the life of a person, and each of these bodies has an impact on the ascetical program of an individual and community.

The individual body, as it might be called, consists of the corpse and that which animates the corpse. The corpse is what might be viewed at a funeral, after the death of the person. It no longer has a life, yet the individual body, precisely as an animated being, is the site of much animation and vitality, as well as the site for the continuation of life and the production of social, intellectual, spiritual, and familial life. During the life of the person, that body is animated with sensation, intellect, emotion, tactility, and the many human traits that make individuals to be complete and particular personalities. The appearance of people and their personalities merge through their lives, and each person is understood as a unity that, at death, has been shattered and destroyed, leaving only the shell of life, even though that shell was extremely important and essential to the viability of the person. In common language and understanding, especially in the United States, the question of body would end here — one person in one physical container isolated from all others.

The social body, however, is that individual body refracted through the myriad people who have encountered and influenced it. From the past, the social body consists of all the relatives and progenitors whose stories and genes make up the new person. This information, both physical and social, influences the development of the person by linking what lives in the present with that which was from the past. It also includes all those formative relationships (for good or for ill) from parents, grandparents, aunts and uncles, neighbors, and community members. They become part of a person's social body by virtue of their continuing influence on the thoughts and reactions and emotional structures of the person. In addition to the past influences on the social body, there are also all the intricate social relationships in which a person participates — immediate family, work associates, the local people among whom one lives, the ornery neighbor, the troubled kids on the street corner, spouse, children, friends of children. All of these people enter the social body and become a part of the person — again, for good or for ill. They become a part of one's identity and one's being as a social person.

The social body and the individual body both look at the world through the eyes of a particular person. The conglomerate of all those individuals and particular people, seen from the perspective of the whole group, is the corporate body. The corporate body consists of all the various social groupings by which a person may be described. It is the corporation or school where one is primarily employed; or the neighborhood, city, state, province, country, or continent in which one lives; or the race, ethnicity, or cultural group of a person's origin; or one's religious connection with others as a Christian, or Muslim, Jew, Buddhist, or Hindu. Or it can simply be among other humans differentiated from other living beings; or as a living being existent in the universe as opposed to all other nonliving and existent things; or it may be simply as "cosmopolites," a member of the universe. These various corporate bodies form specific personalities, function in particular and often exclusive ways, think as a group in peculiar and identifiable patterns, and in every way function in the same way as an individual body, except that it is made up of many, many bodies and it is experienced as a corporate whole, as a complex body made of many units.

For Christians, this corporate body is taken very seriously. At baptism, a person dies and is raised with Jesus Christ and becomes thereby a part of his corporate body, the body of Christ, or the church. This corporate identity takes priority, at least in theological terms, over all other understandings of the body. This corporate body governs and regulates and defines the social and the individual body, because the body of Christ expresses the essence of human identity and the most holy context in which to live. In the postmodern context, in which the individual body is highly problematized in its isolated and distinct form, and the social body comes much more to the fore as a fuller understanding of the function of creating identity, the corporate body holds together all the complex elements in a very complicated and yet highly articulated way. The corporate body's construction and reconstruction of the social and individual bodies has emerged in postmodern theory as a central focus of attention. For postmodern Christians, this body of Christ that functions as the immediate context for the transformation of all things into Christ, that is, for the incorporation (literally) of all existent beings and things into the body of Christ, provides both the image and the energy to instantiate the image.

Christians should not be fooled, however, into thinking that their body of Christ is the only religion with a corporate body. Other religions also have means of articulating the corporate body of all practicing people and of imaging an eschatology that transforms, sustains, sanctifies, or in other ways works with the conglomerate of people in a particular faith.

Working these three bodies — the individual, the social, and the corporate — provides the central focus of ascetical striving. The seeker, no longer experiencing self as isolated from others both living and dead, now searches to understand self as a social entity and as part of a variety of corporate entities. All the bodies work in concert, but not necessarily in harmony, and they form the basic unit for ascetical struggle and advancement.

6 / Discernment ....

THE MOST CRITICAL ISSUE in postmodern religious formation is the question of discernment. How does a person know that what one does, or thinks, or feels is right, or holy, or of God? In times more certain of set standards and where a particular religious hegemony operated, the question of discernment was easier. The relative lack of opposing perspectives within the society or culture made it easier to set a standard or norm for the whole culture. Granted, as history now proves, women, people of color, slaves, and others who did not participate in the dominant male and patriarchal systems in the West contested views of hegemonic power. But still, people of older generations could establish some norms and be confident that most of the people in the society or culture would accept those norms. Such normative standards do not exist in a pluralist and postmodern religious environment. So how do seekers discern what is best or right to do? How does one distinguish what is godly and good from what is ungodly and detrimental?

In exploring this problem, some prior questions must be addressed. First, discernment is a communal process. Discernment can only occur in relationship to other people who have knowledge of the person and the situation. One seeks out the divine will both in isolation from others, and especially in conjunction with others. The difficulty, however, revolves around the tendency in postmodern society to associate homogeneously; that is, only with other people with whom they agree or share a common perspective. This homogeneity does not foster discernment, because insufficient diversity exists to make distinctions. The discerning community, then, must be large or constructed in such a way as to admit opposing and diverse opinions and perspectives regarding the situation. Discerning community must be diverse and potentially be willing to oppose community, so that the sifting of good and bad, holy and unholy, may be accomplished in the context where the proposed action does not simply replicate the perspective of a homogeneous group. In this way discernment is distinguished from the activation of a group's ideological stance. So discernment can only occur in the context of diverse and opposing perspectives within a diverse community of believers.

Second, discernment must be critical. This occurs on two levels: critical of the proposed action itself, and self-critical of motives and intentions. Discernment involves critical examination both from within and from without: from without by exploring the way in which the proposed action or event conforms with what the community understands as God's ways; from within by exploring the internal motivations that have led to the discernment. The example of the just war provides a point of analysis. The just-war theory supposes that some wars are just and others are not. The criteria for the just war must be met in order to justify the action of war. Meeting those criteria, however, cannot rest simply with the aggressor whose intention and motivation is to go to war to defeat a perceived enemy. The establishment of those criteria must be affirmed by people who oppose the war and disagree that the proposed war is just. Only in the confrontation of the two perspectives will proper discernment take place. Only where serious opposition exists, or where intentional opponents, who question the fact and who simultaneously question the motivation, intrude, can proper discernment happen. Discernment, then, remains a difficult task, neither easily nor quickly accomplished, but successful only in the context of vigorous and aggressive communal discourse. One might also say, with respect to war, that from a Christian perspective, even the perspective of the perceived enemy must be sought in order to discern the justness and appropriateness of war.

Discernment, then, involves community and critical evaluation. In this context, there are some resources available to the person discerning: the critical reading of scriptural passages that address, suggest, or engage the action; the critical engagement of the religious tradition to establish various ways that such issues have been examined in other contexts and at other times; the critical use of analysis both rational and emotional, and the exploration of the effects of the action on living beings; the prayerful engagement with traditions other than one's own, from other religious communities and other religious traditions; quiet prayer and intercessory prayer in the context of the liturgical or worshiping community of which one is a part; and many others. Once the discerning person establishes the communal context and the critical perspective, then the discerning person may employ these resources in order to understand not only the ways of God in the past, but also the new and different way God may be leading into the future.

Because God is a living God, present and active, discernment does not mean "doing things the way they've always been done." Discernment explores the way of God in new and different circumstances, so that the living God may be seen and known in new ways and in different circumstances. That is to say, discernment looks for the way of God in the present time, seeking to understand how present circumstances relate to past ones, and at the same time to project the presence of the living God into future circumstances. It is precisely the changing focus of daily living, and the new circumstances of the postmodern situation, that demand discernment. The old ways, good as they were, may not apply to new situations, while new circumstances demand a creative engagement with God to point an individual, a community, or even the world in the right direction.

7 / Restoration .... ᔐ

T HE EARLY CHURCH had a strong sense that human beings needed to be restored to an original beauty. The church believed that humans were marred and defaced by the exigencies of living in a corrupted world, a world that no longer saw or experienced God. It was the engagement in the fallen world, the world without knowledge of God and a world not oriented to doing the things of God, that had a deleterious effect on the human person. Baptism offered the person an opportunity to be completely sanctified to God, and chrismation offered the person the avenue of apprehension and attention to God through the sanctification of the senses. Baptism created a person newly restored to the life of God; chrismation made it possible continually to perceive and understand God through the senses such as sight, sound, and touch, which reside in the body. Baptism set the person apart for the work of God; chrismation enabled the embodied person to know God in the body.

The experience of living in the postmodern context seems to revolve around constant efforts at staying on course. Postmodern living seems to come in short snippets, sound bites, that direct attention to details without the prospect of seeing the larger picture. Most of postmodern decision making is made in the context of a constant flow of unrelated and overwhelming information unorganized and undigested. The postmodern context forces a kind of continual fragmentation and spinning out from a center. It is indeed a decentering experience. In this context, restoration, or the exercise of baptismal and chrismal sacramentality, demands not so much a removal from the fallen and decentered world, but an attentiveness to the larger picture, the wider context, the metanarrative that holds all the disparate parts together. Restoration does not look so much to create order, or to control the details, or even to simplify the constant flow of information, but rather to enable the person to stand in the midst of such decentering activity and to understand that somewhere in the flow is the revelation of God; somewhere in the constant snippets of human existence, God appears to bring sanctification and wholeness; somewhere in the disorganization and fragmentation of living, there is One who holds together the fabric of living. Restoration is not a restoration of the world, but the restoration of a way of knowing God in the midst of a culture and a postmodern world that moves much too quickly to know anything with certainty.

Correlative to the baptismal and chrismal restoration is the restoration of confession. Confession, the honest and critical evaluation of the self before God, assesses the process of restoration by asking a series of questions: "What prevents me from experiencing the revelation of God in my daily life? What hinders me from seeing God's presence within myself and in the people around me? What prevents me from fully manifesting the God within me in my work, my household, my play, and all my other activities? What stands in the way of my being attentive to God's presence in myself and others?" Such questions look to impediments to full restoration and point the way to explore further religious and personal growth. The knowledge from confession should not result in guilt, or a sense of failure, but in promise and the hope for the transformation of self and world through an honest evaluation of the impediments to that transformation. Confession is oriented toward growth, maturation, transformation.

So three sacraments come together to form a system for restoration: baptism sets a new course; chrismation provides the bodily access to the new course; and confession provides the constant evaluation that keeps the course. This makes "the course" sound as though it is set, permanent, pervasive, or the same at all times. It is not. There has never been "a course" for all Christians to follow, nor has there ever been only one way to live out the Christian life. "The course" shifts and changes according to the exigencies of living and to the variability of the human person. That is why confession is so important as a means of reevaluating and resetting a course. The postmodernists are correct in saying that there is no fixed and permanent set of metanarratives that give meaning to life: meaning and depth of living are continually renegotiated and recreated in the ever-moving flow of daily living. Humans must construct their reality every day, every minute of every day. The question in that construction revolves around whether God will be a part of it. Restoration is the theological framework for constructing meaning in the context of a decentering and constantly moving flow of life that inherently has no meaning. Restoration through baptism, chrismation, and confession provides the focus in God that is otherwise wiped away by the postmodern decentered self and world.

8 / The Memory of God

ONE WAY TO ARTICULATE a goal of human existence comes from a metaphor of the ascetical tradition: the remembrance of God. The concept is relatively simple: our task as humans is to remember that God exists and that God is present in the course of daily living. This means that, since Christians know that God exists and that God is forever present to them, they must bring the remembrance of that reality to bear in every moment. So the remembrance of God is a kind of recollection of God in every event of the day. As seekers bathe, eat, work, relate to others, commute to work, sit idle, watch television — whatever seekers do in the day — seekers remember that they are before God, in God's presence: bathing before God, eating before God, working before God, relating before God, commuting before God, sitting before God, entertaining themselves before God; all the day's activities are done before God. There is no place in which God is absent; there is nothing that happens that is separate from the presence of God. To remember God, then, is simply to recognize that God is present and active in all that is done.

Metanoia, or repentance, simply means that one turns from forgetting God to remembering God in the course of daily living. The Greek word simply means something like "changing the thought pattern." Repentance means to change the way of thinking and living from a way in which God is not perceived, to a way in which God is acknowledged as fully present. Repentance, at its most basic level, involves first of all a simple remembrance of God.

Sanctification results from the remembrance of God. It is difficult to perform actions known to be offensive to God if one performs them knowing of God's presence. Slowly, over the course of years, the memory of God transforms the way the Christian lives and the way the Christian understands the world. God's presence becomes slowly more manifest, and the believer becomes more "holy." The remembrance of God begins the process of sanctification, and results in holiness. Now, holiness is not understood here as sanctimoniousness — not at all. Holiness is understood in the root sense of someone or something totally unified and set apart for God's purposes. Holiness designates the singular orientation to God that permeates every activity, thought, emotion, and gesture of the day; it is the sign that sanctification of life through the remembrance of God is taking deep root in the person.

The remembrance of God also has communal ramifications. It is not simply that each individual brings the memory of God into each activity, but that the whole community, when gathered together for their common work (called liturgy) on the Lord's Day, comes together to remember that they are part of the body of God in the world. They come together to remember God. Although it is a pun, the "re-membering" is literally the gathering of the members, the parts of the body, that constitute the body of God in the world. The corporate body of Christ gathered together reminds seekers that they no longer function as individuals solely, but as part of a corporate body that enfleshes the work of God in the world. So Christians remember that they are part of God; they remember that God has called them and renewed them as a corporate body; they remember that God is present to them as a group; and they remember that they are called to live and work completely orientated as a corporate body to the presence of God. The Christian corporate body calls forth the memory of God in order to sanctify its own life and to manifest the holiness that results from consecrating each individual and corporate action and thought to the ever-living and ever-present God.

9 / Vision of God, Reign of God .... ᔑ

F OR MUCH OF Christian history, the world was considered a place of exile and alienation from God. Although the doctrine of the incarnation should have stemmed such a metaphoric distancing of God from the world, the impulse in the spiritual life remained one to keep God at a distance from the world and human endeavor. Such a perspective cannot work in a postmodern world, which does not operate under the same hierarchical cosmology.

Two elements intertwine in an incarnational way to produce a more unified view of human and divine relationship: the vision of God, and the image of the reign of God in the world. The vision of God, in the old metaphoric system, meant seeing the God who is beyond the world by people who were living in the exiled world. The vision of God was a way of importing a spiritual sense into a mundane and alienated world. What I mean by the vision of God, however, is more basic. The vision of God means simply "to see God."

The simple practice of "seeing God" at work in the daily events of a person's life — in the people with whom a person has contact, in the perceived enemies who seem to thwart a person's ambitions or desires, in the regular course of family life, in friends and neighbors — is an ancient practice of imaging God in the lives and people with whom one lives. It is based on the simple saying of Jesus, "anyone who receives you, receives me; and anyone who receives me, receives the One who sent me" (Matthew 10:40; Luke 10:16). This vision, this sighting of God, among the daily events and in the people ready-at-hand, transforms relationships. God is here, present, active, within the people who surround the seeker, in the events and situations that challenge, in the circumstances that bring both pleasure and consternation. The reality of God immanent and acting is a reality that is available only if a person opens the eyes to see that God is present. It is a question of looking, and finding, of being willing to experience God immediately and completely involved in the world.

The vision of God knits together God's reality with the person's and the community's reality. The vision of God joins the daily life of this person and community to the ongoing and persistent life and activity of God in the world and in human events. It is this, the involvement of God in human events, that raises the question of the creation of the reign of God among us.

Eastern Christianity historically has upheld this image of the recreation of the world to reflect the presence of God. The concept is a simple one. Since God is present in the world, one goal of human endeavor is to assist God in the transformation of the world to reflect the divine presence. God's presence in the world mandates the transformation of the world into the primary arena in which the ways of God are seen and known. It is in the "making God visibly present" that the theology of the vision of God and the theology of the rule of God combine. The physical, political, religious, social, and economic environments of the world become the arenas for manifesting the reality of the presence of God. These arenas are not separate, or secular, or neutral, or even inimical to the reality of God — they are the very stuff that reveals the immediate and immanent presence of God among, within, and around all creatures. One's attitude toward the poor, the sick, the disenfranchised, the abused, the hated, the feared, displays to others what God's attitude toward them is. In order to change the world, to make visible the rule of God, each one must individually and communally display the things of God before others.

One of the greatest disappointments of the church in the postmodern period is precisely this lack of vision. In the seemingly interminable infighting over women's leadership, sexuality, doctrinal purity, and biblical interpretation, the church has revealed itself as visionless, and I would argue, godless. While the churches have fought, wars have been waged, the environment has been destroyed, people with AIDS have died throughout Asia and Africa, societies have engaged in ethnic cleansing and other forms of genocide, famines have taken the lives of millions while others have grown obese in the luxury of seeming endless supplies of food. It is a disgrace, and it is a deeply religious problem; while the churches have tried to make themselves pure for God, the very world and people who are God's greatest concern have been left to languish and to suffer and to die. The vision of God and the rule of God are not only linked, they are inseparable in the postmodern context.

The ultimate goal of ascetical activity may simply be described as divinization, the gradual absorption and transformation of every person and every thing in the cosmos into God. At the end, the divine will be known and seen openly, directly, and in every way in each individual, in every community, and throughout the universe. Divinization entails the gradual and incremental manifestation of the inwardly dwelling divine principle in the individual, community, and universe. Ultimately, it is a mystery as to how this will be accomplished, but that mystery does not place it outside the realm of human, corporate, and cosmic yearning.

10 / Divinization

DIVINIZATION CONJURES images of pantheism and heresy to Western Christians, because there is a tendency and desire to distinguish carefully the human from the divine realms, without confusion and conflation. Western Christianity protects the sovereignty and dignity of God by carefully drawing a line over which humans and the cosmos cannot pass, a line that clearly distinguishes the human from the divine, God from humanity, and God from the created world. Eastern Christianity, however, discusses divinization from a decidedly different perspective, that is, from Christology. Just as the two natures of Christ, human and divine, become joined and unmixed and unconfused in one person, so does each individual and each community, as well as the cosmos, find itself made of two natures conjoined (yet unconfused) in one realm. The world, then, with all the individuals and communities, conjoined as it is with the divine nature, will ultimately become divine. Divinization articulates the gradual and complete sovereignty of God by the principle of the universe that all things will eventually evolve into their most divine nature and self. The scriptural phrase that "God will be all in all" (1 Corinthians 15:28) becomes a literal expression of the goal of all existent beings. To be divinized, then, is the fate of all existent beings and processes.

What that divinization will look like for each person and community, however, is not the same. Divinization does not imply a denigration of diversity and difference, but rather says that all difference will ultimately be shown to have the same divine nature and process as every other divergent and diverse being. Within the plurality of understandings of the divine, everything will eventually show forth its divine nature in its peculiarity and substantive difference, and God will be shown to be all in all.

Divinization, however, is not naive. To say that eventually all existent beings will manifest their divine principle does not mean that everything in existence already is divinized. Much of one's life, social relations, and relationships to the larger cosmos are marked by a suppression of the divine energy and by a repression of the divine impulse. Humans still pollute the water and the air. Humans still kill one another, and steal, and abuse, and denigrate others. There is much in the world that does not conform to the impulse toward the divine. But such realities only strengthen the resolve to take up the ascetic struggle toward divinization. Ultimately, the divinization of all will be successful, but that ultimacy demands struggle and hard labor in order to bring it about. Divinization as an eschatological image of the final state of every existent being organizes the work and focuses attention on what is a demanding and fully transforming picture of the final state of all things. Without this goal, effort loses its energy and its direction, but with it even failures and disorientation find meaning.

The postmodern situation demands that the theological anthropology be positive. Divinization becomes a functional category because the goal of human existence does not find its basis in the explication of the biblical narrative of creation. Humans are not aiming to return to Eden, to the state prior to the sin of Adam and Eve (Genesis 1), and to the purity of relationship that the biblical sources emphasize. Rather, humans are evolving to something higher, more aligned with the divine principle and energy that permeates all existent beings. Divinization does not look back to an idealized past, but forward to a future state whose contours cannot easily be imagined or imaged. That is the glory of divinization; it looks to a future locked in the imaginary of beings capable of imaging the divine impulse in infinitely varied ways with an unimaginably rich diversity of expressions, all of them fully manifesting the reality of God.*

11 / Revelation

O NE ASPECT OF the life of faith involves one believer revealing God to another. The revelation in this book does not have the cosmic drama described in the New Testament Book of Revelation — an apocalyptic tenor most often portrayed in the media as the eternal and

---

*I use the word "imaginary" in the sense of postmodern, post-Freudian psychology to mean a range of possibilities originating in the imaginative exploration of human desire that is presented to the mind as experientially real.

unchanging rules of God to which humans must submit. Rather, revelation is "apocalyptic" in the sense of the meaning of the Greek root of the word; it means to "remove the veil" or to "unmask." Revelation is removing that which prevents others from seeing God clearly and directly as immanent in the world and present in human activity. The goal of the Christian life is to remove the veil so that all can see and know God directly. Human existence, then, is revelatory.

But how does this happen? To become a revealer of God is to make God's presence evident in daily living, that is, to reveal or unmask the God present in human relationships, in human thought, in human activity, in politics, in society, in short, in everything that a person does through the day. Each moment, each action, each thought becomes a time when God may be known and understood as present, and the revealer makes that potentiality explicit and immediate.

To accomplish this, the revealer must have a clear sense of the constant presence and immediacy of God. The memory that God is, and that God is present, provides the Christian with a context, a meaning, a point of orientation that informs the activities of the day. When that memory becomes evident to others, and is manifest in the events of the day, the revelation of God is communicated to others. What the believer knows and experiences within becomes visible and obvious to others. The presence of God has been communicated, the veil has been torn away, and the vision of God has been made visible to others.

The feast of the Epiphany (based on Matthew 2:1–12), or "The Manifestation of Christ to the Gentiles" as it is known in the Eastern church, celebrates this sort of revelatory practice in the liturgical year. Those (here the Three Kings) who have knowledge of God, who have read the signs of God in the universe, act on the basis of their knowledge, follow the signs in order to pay homage to the reality and presence of God in the world. This describes precisely what the baptismal vocation of being a revealer of God entails: to know God and to make God known.

Revelation involves a mystery. The divine is present and active in human life, in social relationships, even in the physical universe. The mysterious presence, abiding as it does behind all existent beings, waits to be glimpsed and intuited by the seeker. As in the discovery of a deep secret, the divine yearns to become manifest and humans yearn to manifest the divine mystery. The manifestation of the divine mystery thus works in both directions: human to divine and divine to human.

Revelation at once points to the mystery and excites interest in pursuing it — both revealing what is known of the mystery and pointing to what of the divine presence and impulse still remains hidden. The divine yearns to be made manifest through the lives of seekers, and the seekers yearn to make the divine manifest.

Revelation also instantiates the divine presence. By showing the way to the divine, revelation makes known the divinity hidden in creation, in individual seekers, in seeking communities and societies, and in the physical universes created by the divine. Human beings, societies and cultures, and even the physical universe become revealers of the divine. They display the divine before the eyes of all and show the way for others to achieve the divinization that is the eschatological goal of all existent being. Even when revealing only in part, seekers put the hidden mystery in the minds and thoughts of all. Then the mystery, even if only partially revealed, begins to draw all things to itself toward the point where God will be all in all (1 Corinthians 15:28).

12 / Living in the Present

D O SEEKERS LIVE in the present or the future? In ascetical theology, the emphasis on pursuing the eschatological divinization — the divinization that results in the final restoration of all things so that God will be all in all (1 Corinthians 15:28) — seems to suggest that ascetics are to live primarily in the future state at the present time. Although the ascetic bridges the future eschatological state and the present, the orientation of the ascetic always remains toward living in the present. The eschatological purpose emerges from the present moment even as the seeker continually imagines and reimagines the final restoration of all things during the course of the seeker's life and based on the seeker's experience. The ascetic instantiates the future divinization in the present as best as it can be understood. The focus, then, is on living in the present.

The present moment is the moment that offers the opportunity for immediate apprehension of the presence of the divine. It is immediate precisely because it is not subject to the work of the imagination, but to the work of the senses. The future divinization relies upon the eschatological imaginary, but the present moment depends only on the ability of the ascetic to seek for the divine presence and to find it. The foundation of the future and eschatological divinization of selves, societies, and universes lies upon the apprehension and vision of the divine in the present moment. Only when the ascetic knows the divine, and responds favorably to the immediately present divine impulse, can the work of instantiating the eschatological state begin; it cannot begin before then.

This makes sense in the context of an incarnational point of view. The divine's unity with all existent beings locates the center of attention in the present moment. The ascetic, indeed the seeker of any sort, develops the skills of recognizing the signs of divine presence in the thoughts, emotions, reactions, deeds, relationships, and current events of the present moment. In seeking for evidence of the divine presence and impulse in the present state of one's being, relationships, and the physical universe, the ascetic becomes adept at finding and documenting, if not articulating, the apprehensible presence of the divine. Becoming adept at seeking and finding, the ascetic becomes capable of imagining ever more rich and profound ways of understanding the divine presence precisely in order to continually revise the image of the eschatological divinization of all things, which is the goal of ascetical effort. The imaginary, however, comes into play only on the basis of solid evidence of the divine impulse known in the present moment.

The ascetic, then, is called to live the present moment fully, not focusing on the future only nor living only for the future. The ascetic must not suppress the reality that new things will be instantiated in the present that have never been dreamed by any human person. The present moment, and living the present moment fully with the expectation of finding traces of the divine presence, lay the foundation for all other ascetical activities.

The present moment, however, is not always a good or positive one. The present moment includes more often than not times of frustration, war, quarreling, famine, death, grieving. These difficult times especially demand the effort of the ascetic, not to name them good, or even to acknowledge that they result from the divine impulse, but rather to find ways of knowing the divine through them, experiencing the divine presence while passing through these difficult and challenging events. The divine presence known even only as a companion in difficulty provides evidence of the way in which the eschatological divinization will come.

So in whatever manner the ascetic lives, the present moment is to be lived fully. The ascetic, that is, enjoys the present moment, and lives that life of enjoyment to the fullest extent possible. The enjoyment is the sign that the ascetic sees the presence of the divine always active, and that the presence of the divine fills the life of all existent beings.

13 / The Society of the Godly

W HO STANDS ALONE? Our postmodern, and especially our American mythology, paints each person as an isolated individual, fully empowered to be a self-sufficient actor in life, distant from every sort of connection with other people, especially those who would limit the capacity to think and act independently. It further assumes that, although each person stands in a line of those dead who have preceded, certainly no one is limited by their presence. In fact, the postmodern and American mythology creates the impression that each person, standing alone and independent of all others, exists completely separated from the social bonds that might influence or limit the isolated individuality of the person.

Religion, however, teaches something much more compelling and empowering: human social bodies comprise a complex matrix of relationships of people living and dead who have had a formative influence, either negatively or positively, on a person's way of thinking, living, relating, and conceptualizing the world. The easiest expression to invoke here is the "communion of saints." This belief among Christians articulates a long line of people who have been baptized into the body of Christ in their own generation, and who at death became part of the mystical body of the living and the dead who gather in the presence of the risen Christ. The community of the saints surrounds the living Christian, providing a deep context for living out Christian faith and commitments. The saints people the universe with exemplars, with speech patterns, with antique responses to antique problems, with visions of God transformative of their own times, with struggles to remain faithful to their life commitments under adverse circumstances, with graceful responses to the overwhelming love of God in their own day, and with a myriad of actions, thoughts, prayers, renunciations, affirmations, and godly relationships that transformed their lives and inform the lives of postmodern Christians. When a person is baptized

into the body of Christ, that person joins the many precedent generations of people in that mystical body. The baptized becomes one body
with those saints.

The connections, however, do not end with those saints of yesterday.
Each person has a complex matrix of ancestral and current figures that
influences a concrete way of living and being. Parents, grandparents,
aunts, uncles, neighbors, friends in youth, compatriots and enemies —
these people also have become a part of a person's social body. Their
stories, interactions, and involvements in a person's life become part
of the fabric of that person's identity. They are present in the deep
structure of human personality, speaking and interjecting thoughts at
unexpected times, appearing in sleeping dreams or in waking stories
about other times. They have become part of the person and form an
important element of the internal social body of the Christian person.
These influential people may have had a positive or a negative impact,
becoming part of the person's identity through negative, or positive, or
neutral influences. These extensions of the human social body function both in their death and in their living; they become a part of the
memory that informs and shapes one's identity. Those memories are
fully socialized in the identity of the person.

And the connections are not just in the past, or in memory. The
social body of the person is also built around current communities in
which a person participates. The social body expands to include people
with whom the person lives, works, worships, commutes, shops, stud-
ies, or simply passes on the street. These extensions of the social
body form a spectrum from the most intimate social connections
with family and church to the least intimate with commuters and
coworkers, with degrees of gradation throughout.

All of this is to say that the American mythology of an isolated individual does not in fact describe the religious person, who is indeed
connected to many other people both living and dead, both positive
and negative, both intimate and distant. The human person is a community of persons living in a variety of communities for work, leisure,
and worship.

God works through all these networks of people to create a fabric
of community held together in God. These networks materialize the
sorts of complex relationships, or presences and memory, that God
has with God's people. These networks make incarnate the manner
of God's own interaction and connection with each person — through
the community of the godly, God makes known the deep and abiding

intercommunion of God and human, God and world, God and cosmos that animates the Christian faith.

What is particularly lovely is that these interconnections in the social matrices that make up the human person can also include people from different religious traditions. As part of a person's social body, the Muslim, or Jew, or Buddhist, or Hindu, or animist becomes a part of the fabric of life characterized as infused with the divine. They participate in the Christian world and the Christian life. Likewise, through one's participation in another's social body, the Christian fully connects with Hinduism, or Judaism, or animism through the intricate connections that bind all humans to one another in their social bodies. Interreligious dialogue and communion are not just ideas, then, but extensions of each one's body into the matrix of another's social body. For Christians, this is a way of experiencing the fullness of God. Other religions express interconnection in other ways, but ultimately all humans are connected in their social bodies to one another in the present time, as well as extending far into the outer recesses of ancestral time. The hope remains that as social interconnectedness reaches into the future, humans may experience a greater degree of harmony and understanding based not so much on agreed theology or politics, but on the mystery of their interconnection in one another's social body.

14 / The Detriment of Idealization

WESTERN CHRISTIANITY HAS A TENDENCY toward idealization that proves detrimental to the religious life. That tendency may best be seen in the creation of a fully idealized Jesus, who is so completely perfect, so beyond emotion, so divinely oriented, that Christians cannot imagine a fully human person who had emotions, ate meals, took baths, laughed, enjoyed good food, paid attention to the scholars (both Jewish and Roman) who lived in his village, or had real struggles with religion. The idealized and perfected view of Jesus detracts from the theologically correct view of his complete humanity. The idealization creates a false impression based on the impetus toward making all religious figures perfect in every way. Mary the Mother of God and most of the saints display the same sort of idealization and perfection. Believers portray them as above the fray, beyond the exigencies of human existence, outside the realm of real human experience, and capable of feats of power, self-abasement, and faithfulness not granted to the regular and normative believer. The perfection of Jesus, the Mother of God, and the saints only emphasizes the imperfections, the insufficiencies, the weaknesses of the living baptized member of the body of Christ.

The purpose of such idealization was to set examples for imitation. The believer, compelled by the ideal and perfect Savior or saint, was impelled to attempt to imitate the actions, thoughts, emotions, and deeds of the idealized figure, while at the same time experiencing the reality that such actions, thoughts, emotions, and deeds were beyond the capacity of the not-very-perfect person. The imitation intended to lift the believer out of the realm of normative living, into a realm of complete, perfect, and ideal faithfulness in order to return to the mundane world transformed. The problem is that such a return only underscored the diminishment of the world, and the ineffectuality of human will and ability. The shadow of that perfection became most visible: just as the perfect saints are capable of miraculous feats of spiritual prowess, so equally is the imperfect person incapable of living out the life of faith in the context of daily living. The more perfect and idealized the religious figure, the more diminished and depraved the capacities of the believer struggling to live out the life of faith.

Incarnate theology has always valued both the mundane and the spiritual, the physical and the spiritual, the bodily and the intellectual, the visible and the invisible, the perfect and the imperfect. Although the tradition has tended to privilege the status of the perfect, the spiritual, the intellectual, and the invisible, in reality that privileging distorts the theology. There certainly are differences between the material and the spiritual, but difference does not necessarily imply a hierarchy or a devaluation of one member over the other. The tendency to value that which is perceived as most spiritual and most perfect has further distorted the reality of the incarnation that holds together these opposites in creative and holy union. The perfect, if such a category can exist in postmodernity, finds its completion in the imperfect. In fact, the perfect can only be perfect because of the presence of imperfection. The same applies to the spiritual and the physical: the contrast creates the category. The deep appreciation for what is perceived as the lesser of the dyads creates the possibility for idealization and for the image that perfection, though impossible to achieve, remains the highest expression of human religious aspiration.

In the postmodern context, the tables must be reversed. The idealization and perfection attributed to religious figures must be thoroughly integrated with their incarnate and normative behavior in order to underscore that the ability to reflect the divine presence in their lives emerged from the very concrete and mundane contexts in which they lived, prayed, worked, thought, and emoted. In the postmodern context, it is the ability to see the presence of God in the mundane realities of daily living that causes the surprise. It is the emphasis on the bodily, the physical, the practical, and the imperfect that best reveals the reality of God living and acting in the world. This emphasis turns attention away from an idealized world of saints and perfect people in order to focus attention carefully on the mundane and complex world that constitutes the primary arena for the revelation of God. Christian believers in the postmodern context direct their attention not to the perfect and idealized world beyond a world, but to the messy and compromised world that demands that God be seen and known concretely in the daily routines of living, working, praying, and dying.

The category of the perfect, which is beyond human capacity, has been an important one to Western religious thought and piety. It remains a very pervasive theological stance. Yet the detriment to such idealization stands. The detriment is that it turns attention away from the world in which humans live, to an imagined world where everything is perfect and in order. Such a turning violates the central theology of the incarnation and the significance of baptismal living, and at the same time produces Christian believers who do not trust in their own ability to live and to be fully in tune with God in the context of their daily life. The idealization produces weakness among believers, and such a weakness and incapacity for following the divine path detracts from the glory given to humans in baptism, and from the mission to repair the world that stands at the heart of Christian mission.

15 / Knowing the Mind of God

THE MOST COMFORTING ASPECT of the sort of religion that provides all the rules to be followed is that adherents to that religion never have to think about what is right or wrong. The religious leaders, whether bishops, imams, rabbis, ministers, monks, or priests, tell the laity what God's mind intends; that is, they relate the rules to be followed, and the practitioner either does them (and becomes good or holy) or refuses to obey them (and consequently becomes bad or sinful). This system of hierarchical knowledge of the divine may also be called magisterial knowledge of God because it arises out of agreed-upon rules established by a governing body of leaders who claim to speak for God. When they meet as a group, the magisterium — the conference of teachers of the divine way — discern, decide, and rule on what the divine mind is for the adherents of their religious group.

There have always been problems with a rule-oriented magisterial system for the knowledge of God. One need only point to the Holocaust of Jews in Germany during the Second World War to see that not all religious leaders were capable of knowing the mind of God — some opposed the Nazi ideology and struggled against it as supremely evil and denigrating of God, while others supported it as definitely God's will, with the sure knowledge that this is what God intended. Most people in Germany, and many people in other countries including those countries fighting the Nazis, followed the rules, and some even believed that the Holocaust was the mind of God. Other situations parallel the Holocaust of the Jews: the repression of indigenous and native peoples in South America by the Western ecclesiastical hierarchy; the pogroms between tribes of different religious traditions in Rwanda and Burundi; the oppression of blacks and mixed-race people in Southern Africa by white European settlers; the pogrom of the Armenians and the Smyrnians by the Turks; there are clearly many others.

The mind of God is never simply a set of rules to be followed mindlessly, but is a relationship of reflective people with a living God at once present in the moment and transcendent of all time. The history of Israelite religion, Judaism, Christianity, Islam, Hinduism and Buddhism all attest to the changing perceptions of the religious condition of humanity. None of these religions have stayed the same, following the same rules eternally without exercising some increment of discernment about the manner of understanding the mind of God in new contexts, under new circumstances, among different people, with different technologies and arts, and in ways that the ancestors or founders could never have predicted or envisioned. Just as the times change, so must the discernment about the mind of God shift and change to make manifest the ways of God in new and different times. The key here is discernment.

To discern the mind of God, then, is not simply to follow a path designated as eternal and unchanging, but to engage with God's mind in new contexts, seeking ways of understanding and acting in ways understood as consistent with the mind of God in new circumstances. But how may that happen, if there are no set rules? Although there are no immutable rules, some touchstones exist to assist in discernment. All the touchstones rest on the sure foundation that humans may understand the ways of God through the exercise of their minds, through the exercise of intellectual exploration and the sifting and analysis of human experience. God has so equipped human beings as to be able to reflect on their experience, to analyze relationships, to explore the past through memory, and to articulate a plan of action or belief. This noble human capacity, the inherent capacity of all humans to know and to understand God, stands at the center of discernment. Without the supreme confidence in the human capacity to know God, there can be no discernment, no knowledge of the mind of God.

16 / Communion

I T IS AXIOMATIC that all humans throughout the world and throughout history are connected to one another by a common humanity. Human beings have forever been cognizant of the presence of something both biological and intellectual that has linked them one to another: when modern or postmodern people look at a skull of a prehistoric person, the elements of a common humanity may be experienced; when they look upon a photograph of a running child, they recognize intuitively a human commonality with that child. This linkage of all humans to one another plays an important role both in enhancing human cooperation and sympathy and in curbing the otherwise animal-like tendency to human killing and hatred. The knowledge of a common bond both enhances and inhibits natural tendencies.

This commonality among persons may also lead to communion, to the deep sense of a shared experience, shared biological phenomena, significant common roots manifested in articulated common responses to tragedy and to joy, and to profound common self-reflection signified (at least in one sense) in the recognition of one's own self in the eyes of another person. This is communion. Communion (the Greek word used in the New Testament is *koinonia*) begins in the sense of a partnership, a business relationship, a cooperation in order to achieve mutual goals, but it quickly moves beyond the unity of two divided persons joining together for a common goal, to the two united into one in pursuit of common goals. In other words, communion moves from divided people joined in a common pursuit, to the unity of people under the aegis of common aims and pursuits. Partnership becomes full participation of one person in another, so that by communing with one another, believing people enter into a profoundly unitive state characterized by a lowering of the boundaries of separation and a heightening of commonality and cohesiveness. What begins as an exterior cooperation ends as a solidly interior union.

In the realm of religion, this communion takes on a rich and mystical sense, because it not only refers to the business practice transformed into united living, but it also refers to the union and unity that articulates the bond between humans and God. In communion with God, humans experience the gradual transformation from mere partnership to deep union with God. What begins in the process of daily living as a series of unrelated practices and adjustments to daily life to reflect the reality of God culminates in a deep union of each believer with the God whose presence dwells within. So as Christians manifest more and more the divine impulse to repair the world, a repairing that includes themselves, they become more and more united to God. The boundaries of separation, the limits of external partnership, fall away; and gradually, ever so gradually, the sense of a constant and abiding union with God begins to take hold and to be experienced within. And that abiding union becomes visible to others in the transparency of God's presence manifest in the patterns of daily living.

This communion links two important parts of the Christian life: the regular reception of the Communion of the body of Christ, and the commitment to serve others. Matthew's Gospel (25:40) presents a parable in which the king concludes, "in as much as you have performed it for one of these impoverished ones, you have performed it for me." Communion means that there is no longer a boundary between one and another, between human and God, between religion and social action. All are related, made one, united into the common thread of living that connects all actions, thoughts, emotions, and responses to God. So Christians seek out and find God in the sacraments during the liturgy in order to seek out and find God in the person next to them. The same union manifest in the sacrament becomes manifest in the deeds of mercy and attention to the needs of others in daily living. Communion makes them one and the same process.

17 / Hindrances .... ♌

I T IS AS IMPORTANT to understand the hindrances that stand in the way of a person's progress in faith as to understand the positive successes. The hindrances tell a person what prevents, or inhibits, or derails the attainment of the religious pursuit; hindrances inhibit the constant memory of God and make the effort toward manifesting the presence of God hollow and difficult. To understand hindrances means to know what ultimately thwarts the desire to achieve the goal.

Hindrances come from a variety of places. Some come from outside the person: a demanding job that is not satisfying, or colleagues who continually stand in the way of the exercise of holy living, or a large and complicated extended family that continually interferes in the life-decisions of a nuclear family, or even living in an urban project that continually bombards the person with loud music. These external hindrances become the easiest to control, because they are the most variable and changeable. It is possible to create a space within oneself to address the hindrances created by life-circumstances and to act differently, even to live differently, in an environment hostile to a holy life. This is difficult to achieve, but generally possible to attain.

The interior hindrances, however, are another matter altogether. These interior hindrances include a wide variety of factors resistant to the practice of the religious life. They are the resistance to daily prayer or to the discipline of regular attention to God, the frustration at failed efforts or results, the dissatisfaction with current practice, the boredom experienced as one levels out on the religious path, the gluttonous seeking after unhealthy experiences and excesses, the anger generated by living in a complex world, the ennui of continuing to live faithfully when there seems to be no concrete benefit, the yearning for apparent rather than actual goods, and many more. The seeker encounters them daily and regularly, and these experiences stop or hinder the progress toward the holy life that the seeker deeply desires.

The first step to countering the effect of these hindrances both internal and external is simply to know that they exist. Tabulate them. Understand their debilitating effect. Be aware of their effect, and subtlety, and complexity. And then forget about them. They are not to be dwelled upon as a subject or issue in themselves, but simply to be acknowledged for what they are — hindrances.

The second step to countering their effect is to begin to work around them by finding alternative ways of growing and developing that avoid the pitfalls and the debilitations they present. These alternate routes at once acknowledge the presence of hindrances, but also recognize that they will ultimately not remain successful in preventing progress.

The third step is simply to wait. Hindrances are not permanent, and they do not perform their destructive duty forever. They are temporary, and as the person seeks alternatives, and waits for understanding and direction from within, growth and transformation begin to happen in surprising ways.

In the ancient language of asceticism, these hindrances were understood as demonic attacks. They were always exterior forces that invaded the physical environment of the ascetic and grasped hold of the soul of the practitioner and seeker after holiness. These demons, however, performed an important function: they pointed the way toward the next phase of development for the ascetic. In other words, the hindrances told the seeker where the next place of growth and struggle needed to take place. Without them, the seeker lacked direction and focused attention in the process of growth. When the demons attacked, however, the ascetic knew precisely in what arena of life and in what dimension interiority demanded attention. For example, if the demon of fornication attacked, then the problem to be addressed was lust, and if the demon of gluttony attacked, then the problem was eating and food. The remedies were never direct, however, for the problem of lust was addressed by fasting and the problem of gluttony was addressed by obedience to superiors, for example.

Postmodern seekers understand their growth and development in the faith in the same way. Sensitivity to the hindrances profoundly redirects the seekers' progress by speaking clearly to them where the next hurdle stands. The irony is that the presence of hindrances of all forms indicates sure progress in the religious life, and they are to be welcomed wholeheartedly as definite signs of progress.

18 / Reality ⋯⋯⋯⋯⋯⋯⋯⋯⋯⋯⋯⋯⋯⋯⋯⋯⋯⋯⋯⋯ ꣠

I N GREEK ORTHODOX icons of Christ, there is an inscription written in the nimbus around Christ's head; it has three Greek letters,
an omicron, an omega, and a nu. This epigraph is pronounced *ho on,*
and means "the being" or "the reality." To Eastern Christians, reality does not consist of the visible and tactile ephemera of daily living,
but rather of the acknowledgment of the sacred underpinning of the
physical universe. The Eastern concept of reality is radically different
from the Western and Christian view, which was so influenced by the
Enlightenment that it establishes "the real" as composed of physical,
measurable, and visual stuff of everyday experience. The spectrum of
what is real shifts even more dramatically when other religions are included. Muslims, for example, rank the literary and theological world
of the Qu'ran as the basis of the real, while locating all other physical
and intellectual activity as subordinate to those Qu'ranic realities. In
religion, the definition of the real plays an important part in the formative process because it directs attention either toward or away from
various aspects of living and provides a system of values and factors
worthy of observation and attention.

In the postmodern religious context, the real takes on a very wide
and diverse perspective. The real is not limited to certain privileged
classes; in fact, postmodernity suspects the privileging of people or
phenomena. For the ascetical life, the interior and the exterior, the
sacred and the purely secular, the divine and the human, exist as categories and realities side by side, even in their apparent opposition and
contrariety. In an odd sense, postmodernity insists upon an important
theological point: all human existence and all divine activity are completely woven into one complex and often self-contradictory fabric of
existence that demands attention and cultivation. In postmodernity,
God cannot be placed hierarchically far above the world in a cosmic
structure of the universe, unobserved in the heavens and reflecting the
patriarchal cosmology of previous generations. Nor can the divine impulse be located merely in human activity, since world history reveals
the tyrannies and horrors of human genocide, of fascist regimes, impe-
rialist and capitalist oppression, and the general impulse to establish
destructive political and social hegemony. The structure of reality that
rests on this polarity is inconsistent with postmodern experience.

Reality must, therefore, be defined as a conjunction of elements.
It is at once both divine and human, both spiritual and secular, both

religious and opposed to religion, both visible and invisible, both tactile and beyond touch; this reality must recognize the ultimate unknowability and mystery of all human existence. Reality must include all the elements that in previous generations were kept separate, but which now must be conjoined even in their opposition, because the fabric of life defies simple polar characterizations; it demands respect for the complexity and richness of knowledge and experience.

Consequently, in the ascetical life there can be no easy division between the work of God and human effort, the plan of God and human intentions, because they are so interwoven as to become inseparably part of one fabric, one reality. The burden shifts from a reality based upon a sure knowledge of given elements (such as the priority of spiritual over physical, higher over lower), to a reality far less easily categorized. The human and ascetical projects shift as well. The human can no longer simply submit to a higher being, a divine plan given to the church or (more likely) the church's hierarchy; each must chart a path where one never clearly knows whether the plan works out a divine impulse, or some other impulse deeply embedded in the human person. It is the ultimate unknowability and insecurity about the divinity of human activity that creates the energy for bold and dramatic engagement with life, a life now teeming with energy, confusion, insecurity, and yet ultimate faith that God will be known in all things and in every way.

This confusion and contradiction in the category of the real actually reverts to a very early modality in the ascetic life. In earlier generations, ascetics needed to discern carefully because demons could appear as God, angels could be demonic manifestations, and what appeared to be good could just as easily be evil. The ascetic's discernment required sifting through the various elements of the experience to find the root reality of the phenomenon. So too in postmodernity, the sureties of previous generations and the practices of the church do not provide indisputable facts of authentic religious living, but rather force the practitioner to discern, to sift through the elements, and to try to understand and express that which ultimately is beyond both understanding and expression. This burden of discernment is both a blessing and a curse — a blessing in that it demands a level of introspection and analysis beyond the usual for most people, a curse in that the old religious truths can no longer simply be accepted without thinking and without reflection. The reconstruction of "the real" in postmodernity, therefore, places a great burden on the religious practitioner to live authentically, because there can be no artificial distinction between religion and other facets of human and cosmic existence.

19 / Divine Indwelling ....

HUMANITY AND DIVINITY are connected. Incarnational Christian theology has always emphasized the inherent connection between the two as resulting from the (mostly Neoplatonic) christological formulation of the two natures (human and divine) of Christ. Incarnational theology specifies that no distance between the divine and the human exists since all Christians by virtue of their union with the body of Christ participate as humans in the divinity, just as Christ, as God, participated fully in the human realm as God. God, the divine, dwells in the human person, so that the human person, transformed by the presence of the divine in the self, performs as a divine agent in the world. The transformative indwelling of God in human agency enables the seeker to function as God in the realm of human activity. The presence of the divine in the person empowers the person to become and to act as a divine agent in the human realm, in society, and in the universe.

With humans instantiating the presence and action of the divine in the human realm, it is possible to work toward the transformation and eventual divinization of all people and all things. Seekers need not wait for some future revelation to begin enacting the ways of God, or transforming the world according to the divine impulse, or recreating societies that reflect the justice, peace, and harmony intended for the universe and all existent beings within it. The divine indwelling empowers the seeker to act, to think, to live, to work as the divine transformative agent within every arena of human existence.

Some theologians find this formulation difficult and puzzling because no control over human agency in its divinizing effort exists as a surety. The objectors insist upon a clear distinction between human and divine effort, so that the things of God will not be confused with human efforts. Clearly, the divinity does not dwell fully in a single human being. The fullness of the divine does not reside solely or completely in one person. This means true empowerment finds its proper context when the divinity dwelling in one person meets and coordinates with the divinity in another. The context demands recognizing that the divine impulse dwells in a variety of different people, situations, societies, and universes. The recognition of the context retains, therefore, utmost importance. But the divinity present in one person also remains conditioned by its functioning in relationship and proximity to all the other divine agents in a society. The effort of one person connects with the efforts of others and their close connection works to mutual effort or correction. Both the context and the contingency function as instruments of discernment to some degree, because the coordinated work of individuals will either move in the same direction, with some common understanding, or in divergent directions that demand conversation. Discernment will follow upon both the agreement and the divergence.

The wonder of such an incarnational theology of divine indwelling revolves around the possibility of instantiating the divine impulse in so many different ways and by so many different means. Throughout the universe, a gradual and incremental activation of the divine impulse takes place in myriad contexts simultaneously. Through the work of an infinite number of independent agents all acting under the divine impulse, the transformation of existence begins to take shape. Moving and shifting along seemingly chaotic and independent pathways, patterns of transformation begin to become evident in individual seekers, in social groupings, and in the way the universe is treated, understood, and evolving. The incremental movement forward, meandering as it does along various trajectories, instantiates the divine so that slowly patterns of transformation may be observed and documented. Although the path of divinization remains diverse and multidirectional, the ultimate movement into full divinization becomes incrementally visible and obvious. Divinization, that is, begins to look like the equally complex process of the evolution of the human species. When evolutionary change occurs, it is not possible at any one point to say, "Look, here it is!" Major shifts in genetic and human evolution do not happen in an instant of time; only over millennia do changes become visible and calculable. All this is possible precisely because the divine dwells within the person, and within the societies in which people live, and in the universes in which all existent beings understand their evolutionary development.

20 / Reading the Signs ⁓

THE PURSUIT OF ASCETICISM demands a certain skill in reading signs. The various bodies — individual, social, corporate — all form texts to be read and interpreted in order to discover their significance and meaning. Thus everything has a significance, which may be read. Nothing is neutral.

Reading life as a text entails understanding what ideological or theological principles the particular life event displays. Congruently, the seeker searches for the theology implicit in certain thoughts and actions, and asks whether they are consistent with the ascetical values that the seeker has articulated and is pursuing. The seeker must establish whether or not the theology of an event or an encounter, of an emotion or a thought, advances or hinders the attainment of ascetic tasks.

A seeker may read the individual body by attending to the frequency of certain emotions or reactions, or by listening carefully to the inner dialogue that takes place in the mind, or by concentrating on the moments of particular joy or frustration, or by noting the frequency that one feels uncomfortable about a particular situation or circumstance. These all potentially hold important information about the underpinning and substructure of one's progress toward divinization. And they should be read for understanding of oneself, for adjusting the final and ultimate image of divinization that organizes and focuses attention, and for shifting one's ascetical strategy for development and growth.

The seeker may also read the social body as a text for information regarding the pursuit of ascetic goals. Memories of past associations as well as the implications of current social affiliations, dinner engagements, friends, the quality of relationships in the workplace, the depth of relationship with subordinates in the office as well as service personnel while commuting — these and all the other social interactions signify to the seeker the quality and depth of theological and religious commitments. The reading of the social body should become an opportunity for self-evaluation with respect to progress toward ascetical eschatological divinization.

Likewise reading corporate bodies plays an important role. Such issues as who is rejected and included, who is valued and despised, which social concerns are central and which peripheral, which social values are played out in reality and which in fantasy only — these as well as attitudes toward others, especially others of different race, sexual orientation, gender, social status, economic status, and ethnicity — all become important analytical points of understanding for the ascetic; and all relate important information to the seeker about the seeker's own advancement toward the ultimate divinization of everyone and everything. They are continually to be read critically for the information they provide on the real movement toward divinization.

Reading the signs, then, provides important data for the seeker to use in discernment. To read the signs structures an important form of discerning the value and importance of thoughts, relations, emotions, and every event of daily living with respect to the ascetical tasks. In reading the signs the seeker critically evaluates the reality of progress toward divinization. At the time of reading the signs the seeker discovers the weakest points in progress, adjusts the direction and the means to achieve the stated tasks, and begins to move in the new direction. Or, concurrently, the seeker discovers in reading the signs that the seeker indeed makes progress, and that the path selected indeed displays success in leading the person, society, and universe toward divinization.

To sift through the minutiae of a person's day, or the complexities of familial and other social relations, and the policies and attitudes of one's various corporate bodies requires serious and vigorous effort. The opportunities for self-deception are great, and so this discernment by reading signs should also include the reading of others who are parts of various corporate bodies different from the seeker's own. Seekers avoid self-deception only by the rigorous reading of the signs in the context of others similarly reading their signs. The discourse over the significance of the signs enhances the ability to read and tends to correct the possibility of self-deception.

21 / Mortification Reconsidered ⁓

SPIRITUAL THINGS receive greater praise and value than physical things. When a clear distinction between physical and spiritual stands as the normative understanding of the human condition, there is a tendency to arrange the elements in a hierarchy that says all things spiritual are better, more valuable, more highly regarded, than all things physical. When this hierarchy of value prevails, then the objective becomes to promote the spiritual things over the physical so that the person gradually becomes more spiritual and less physical. The body, the physical part of human existence, needs to submit to the person's spirit, or higher nature. As a result, there is a long tradition in Christianity of "mortification."

Mortification refers to the spiritual discipline of rendering the body dead to physical needs and desires. The tradition closely linked mortification with self-denial, a denial of the physical needs and responses of the body to the world around it, so that a comparable embracing of the spiritual realities could take place. Mortification through self-denial worked on the premise that given the hierarchy of spirit over flesh, of spiritual over physical, then any denial of the physical enhanced the presence of the spiritual. So if one fasted regularly and consistently in order to deny the body food, then one would be more susceptible and receptive to the presence of the spiritual food, which is grace. Mortification comprised a complete system for pummeling the body in order to augment the presence of the Spirit of God.

Most postmodern people, however, do not have such a negative view of their bodies. A theology that emphasizes the goodness of creation and the high value of the body as participating in the incarnate presence of God in the world cannot rest on a conception of a clear division of body and spirit, physical and spiritual. Postmodern bodies participate in the incarnate realities of God's presence in the world. So a postmodern understanding of how one conforms oneself to that incarnate reality must shift. Mortification, that is, must be redefined to encompass the theological reality of the incarnate life of the Christian that mirrors the incarnate reality of Jesus Christ in the world.

The redefinition requires a reorientation and reconfiguration of the problem. The problem that mortification addressed can be summarized in this question, "How can I be more receptive and responsive to God in my life?" This question raises the problem of making space in life for the presence of God, and therefore addresses a very positive question about conforming a person's life to the reality of God's presence and activity. The object, then, becomes not so much to pummel the body into submission to the spirit, but to transform the day-to-day life of the person such that the person may experience the presence of God more fully. Reconfiguring the problem in this way, the seeker's orientation turns more to what is known to be true: God is fully involved in the day-to-day lives of God's people. Then what is known to be true can be made consciously part of the day's activities and thoughts. The disciplines ought to revolve around bringing the memory of God into each event, of living and working in a state of awareness of the presence of God, of acting such that lives are lived with a fully engaged God. Metaphorically, this process can be described as living out the Christian life in the light of the sun, as opposed to living indoors or in the dark. The aim is to bring everything out into the sunshine so that the sun's warmth and radiance might illuminate it and penetrate it. This does not mean that everything in the night or indoors is bad, but that it simply has not yet been exposed to the sun's transformative presence.

Some specific practices that may assist in this transformation exist. One is the traditional "Practice of the Presence of God" where persons consciously place themselves in the presence of God, imagining God as really present in the moment, and attempting to hold on to that image while living. Another practice involves meditating on future activities at the beginning of the day, in order to see in the mind's eye the physical representation of God accompanying the seeker in the day's activities. This meditation soaks the day in the presence of God and sets up the day's experiences to resonate with incarnate divinity. Another practice is to stop throughout the day to recollect the mind to the realities of God's presence. This was known in older systems of prayer as "arrow prayers," prayers shot out throughout the day to infuse the day with conversation with God. But no matter what system or practice one employs, the purpose is to infuse the reality of God's incarnate presence into every moment of the day, to bring everything more and more into relationship with the God who is present and active in the world.

The most difficult shift that a religious person must make is a shift in worldview. In previous eras of history, people understood the reality of God as an essential part of the way they constructed their world. They simply took it for granted. People knew that God created the world and sustained and directly guided the events that took place in creation, and they paid attention to the reality of God in their daily lives. Slowly over the years since the Enlightenment, God has been removed from the description of the world in which humans live. The scientific view did not leave room for the divine imperative or presence. A rational understanding of the universe, especially after space exploration, left no place for imagining a God above the heavens, looking down from a distance and guiding the fate of the world.

22 / Worldview .... ↳

THE SCIENTIFIC VIEW really displaced — and this displacement should be applauded — the mythology of an anthropomorphized God and a three-tiered universe (heaven, earth, and under the earth), above which God presided. To a great degree, this mythologized worldview depended on the distance of God from the day-to-day world and upon a location of God far above the realm of human activity. Such a conception, although consistent with earlier worldviews, cannot be sustained in a postmodern world. Seekers must find other ways of conceptualizing the relationship and presence of God in the world and in the realm of human affairs and activities.

In the postmodern context, a fully anthropomorphized God residing far above the world does not work. The postmodern understanding of God conceptualizes God much more as a present God, incarnate in human activity, and fully integrated in human history. This integration does not mean that seekers have no sense of transcendence, although the whole question of transcendence has been problematized by recent critical theorists. Rather, the understanding of transcendence itself has shifted. God is present, and yet seekers know that God cannot be fully exhausted in that presence. This articulates a negative theology that recognizes the immanence of God, but also recognizes the limits of the human capacity to understand God's immanence. God cannot be fully apprehended in God's immanence, and yet the primary way of knowing God issues forth from the processes and events of daily living in which God is fully immanent.

The reality of the postmodern Christian must include a God fully present in human existence and in the created universe, and yet also not limited by such knowledge. The shift in the postmodern worldview must be toward envisioning God as fully immanent, present, active, and engaged creatively in the tasks and thoughts of human agents. Having given up on an anthropomorphized transcendent God, seekers must shift to different ways of understanding God's presence in the universe, so as not to fall into the mistake of saying that the scientific inability to represent God in the universe proves God's absence.

Another way to approach this problem is to think about the ability and availability of God to act in the present. Is this a living God, a God fully engaged with human life, human relationships, and the environment that God created? The reality of a living God, acting and engaged in a process of renewal of the world, must inform the ascetical worldview. In other words, seekers work in vain if they do not have the sense of engaging in a world in which a living God is in the process of making all things new, of renewing the world and restoring people and human relations to the full participation in the divine energy.

23 / Confession ....

THE FOUNDATION of a religious life fully integrated into the mainstream of living rests upon a solid self-understanding and self-knowledge. Understandably this sounds a lot like the ancient Greek aphorism, "Know thyself," and it is. Honesty about one's life and a clear self-understanding enables each person to discern what is good and what is bad about the self. In other words, the issue arising in self-understanding and self-awareness does not revolve around the self, but about the ability to discern.

In the ancient monastic ascetic literature, the spiritual masters speak about the demons that afflict the person seeking to become perfect. The monk gradually withdraws from the company of other monks into the seclusion of a hermit's life, in which only the interior dynamics of will and desire are seen. The monk's will is to become perfect, but the interior life reveals that there are many impediments to achieving that perfection. The monastic masters metaphorize these impediments as demons. They argue that the more one advances toward perfection, the more evident and debilitating the demons become. But the contest with the demons, which is the way the monks understand their relationship with them, remains a positive one. Without the demons, the monks would not be able to advance, because they would not know the weak areas of their lives that need to be addressed, or they would not understand the weaknesses and frailties — the sins — that prevent them from attaining their goal of perfection. For the monks, the demons stand as essential and vital agents of self-awareness and self-understanding.

Rather than the traditional and more problematic metaphor of "perfection," the postmodern quest is for the knowledge and understanding of the limits of one's capacity to be transparent to God. This knowledge and understanding emerges from an honest assessment of seekers' lives. The knowledge of where seekers are good, or successful, or capable of manifesting God through their daily lives, provides important information. Unfortunately, it is not as important as understanding the impediments. The impediments speak to seekers of the boundaries of their resistance to God and the limits of their capacity to conform their lives to the divine energy in the world in which they live.

Confession, whether to a minister or someone else, helps the person to understand the boundaries of growth and maturity. So seekers go to another to speak of the successes and places of great satisfaction in their lives, and they explore the failures, the bad habits, the detriments, and all other factors that keep them from being fully transparent to God. The honesty in this endeavor provides the seeker, in a secondary way, with the information basic to self-knowledge. To know oneself is to know both the good and the bad, the places transparent and the places opaque to God, and to be able to know the difference.

The emphasis on "knowing the difference" defines discernment. Discernment is the capacity to understand the good and the bad, the healthy and the destructive, and the godlike or godless within the seekers' realms of living. Seekers begin to learn and practice discernment in confession. By beginning with the impediments to the religious goal, as well as the places of achievement and progress in the individual's life, the believer becomes capable of seeing and understanding the same dynamics in society and in the world. Seekers look inward, then, not to define themselves better, but rather to discern better about their lives, their world, their relationships, and the ways of God in their midst. This capacity to see and perceive honestly is essential to the religious life.

But such self-knowledge is not easy in a postmodern environment. Advertisements that present unreality as reality bombard the postmodern person. "Political spin" presents lies as though they were truth, or at least positive interpretations that redefine reality. Ideology, whether religious or political, defines the way people relate to the outer world, so that seemingly without thinking, people hold views that are presented to them as a package. This list could be multiplied almost endlessly. The point is that each person must begin to explore the good and the bad, the healthy and the destructive, the progressive and the regressive around them honestly by first looking inwardly to the deepest needs, desires, temptations, and inclinations of each human life. Then, when honesty is achieved there, each must look out to the world of religion, politics, society, economics, and government to discern the same factors there.

So the ancient Greeks were correct in saying that self-knowledge is the beginning of all knowledge. In the postmodern context this truth extends the parameters to include the fact that self-knowledge leads to discernment, which in turn leads to a clear understanding of the good and evil in oneself, one's relationships, and the world.

24 / Holy Dying

THE INEVITABILITY OF death frames and concentrates living. The framing of life by death means that each person must live in the knowledge that this life is finite, limited, and subject to an end. Despite feelings in youth that life is forever, and that humans are invulnerable to the ravages of death, the reality stands that all will die. This frame challenges seekers to choose how they will live, to make choices about the valuable and important things of life, and to dedicate themselves to the good and the important. That is where the concentration that death provides enters the scene. Because humans are mortal and subject to death, death concentrates their efforts to live the life chosen intently, intensely, and deliberately. Death forces the seeker to think about concentrating on the important and valuable aspects of life. Because life is short, even if one lives a long time, seekers concentrate their efforts on the central things, not dithering away time on useless and worthless efforts and endeavors. Death both concentrates and frames living.

The Ash Wednesday service reminds mortals that they are dust and to dust they shall return. Human mortality need not be something morbid, but a reminder that the time allotted ought to be lived deliberately. Lenten practice encourages acts of mercy, reading of Scripture, meditation, special devotion, and special acts of self-denial. These central Lenten practices function primarily not to limit or to shrink the self, although that may be important to some, but to concentrate effort on important things, and to remember that humans have a short time to live and that they must, therefore, live it well. According to the faith, this means living in the continual remembrance of God, in the pursuit of the divine mandate for justice and peace, and in doing the good things that God has set before God's people. The practice of the remembrance of death focuses attention on that which is most good, most profitable, most holy, and most enriching to seekers and to the communities in which they live.

Part of the practice of holy dying includes living so that there are no regrets. There are two aspects of this. First, when seekers have erred and sinned and done things that do not conform to their own values, they need to confess them and to move on. The first aspect of a holy dying includes regular self-evaluation and confession, seeking the absolution of sins and offenses, and making a new beginning regularly in the life of faith. Second, each evening before retiring — for sleep has been metaphorized as a "small death" in religious literature — seekers should evaluate the day to concentrate on what is important, to make peace with those with whom they have been at war, and to reconcile the events, emotions, and thoughts of the day with the decision to live life in the presence of God. This form of regular self-evaluation actually prepares the way for seeing patterns that need to be brought to confession for absolution; it also is a means of recognizing, before the end of the day, the successes and failures, the joys and pains of that day, in order to resolve in the next day to live according to the patterns and beliefs that define holy living.

One way to become comfortable with one's own mortality involves attending to mourning those who have died within one's own circle. In earlier times, the communal attendance to mourning, and to the widow or widower and their children and families, constituted a sacred trust. Those in mourning were brought food, their houses cleaned and prepared for the display of the deceased, their clothing washed and prepared for the funeral and for the strict time of mourning to follow. The community of the living surrounded those in mourning in order precisely to minister to their needs. But this ministry is also reflective. Those attending to the mourners also find themselves thinking about their own mortality, their own fragile lives, and the close relationships that make their lives complete. By participating in the ceremonies of the dead, the immediate mourners and the communities in which they live both come to the point of understanding their own mortality — it frames and concentrates the lives of the living, while honoring the life and body of the deceased. Wakes, open caskets, services with the body brought to the church, grieving and crying, and eating meals in honor of the dead — all these rituals play an important part in the concentration of life for the living and the honoring of the deceased in their burial. Even though these realities, like the reality of death itself, are difficult and emotionally stressful, even threatening, they are important to the process of holy dying. The contemporary fear of such rituals shows how critical it is for postmodern people to retrieve the ancient practices in order to sanctify dying and to enrich living.

Ancient Western meditative practice, in fact, promoted a practice to image one's own death by contemplating the final days and hours of one's life in order precisely to understand the emotions and reactions, and by experiencing imaginatively the finality of one's own life. There are famous images of saints meditating, one hand on a skull, and the eyes focused on the cross. This may not be an instrument useful to many people, but it shows the way that contemplating death invigorated living. Perhaps postmodern people might consider an alternate practice to heighten the experience of living fully in the present: imaginatively putting themselves in the place of someone experiencing death, destruction, famine, or political and religious oppression. Or they may simply experience deeply and fully the grief of other people who are part of their communities. The important thing is to imagine and to experience beforehand the inevitability of death, so that it no longer acts as a deterrent or inhibitor of living, but as an enhancement.

Holy living and holy dying are thus deeply connected. To live well directs the person to die well, while death intensifies the richness of living. This is one of those ironies of the faith — that life and death are both holy and important aspects of living the godly life.

25 / Disappointment

THERE ARE TIMES in the course of life when profound disappointments occur. The world crushes in with the sense of deep gloom and profound loss of something for which there was deep yearning and yet incomplete satisfaction. The feelings project inward to the very center and core of the personality and the person's relationship to the world. The presence of the divine, and of a sense of a divine purpose, seem distant and forbidding.

The divine is met in disappointment precisely at the point where the interior sense of loss meets the reality of frustration. This may sound strange, but it is the sense of being directly connected to the interior life, to the very center and core of desire and yearning for the fullness of life, where disappointment brings knowledge of a fuller or more complete life, now seemingly lost and depleted. That connection with the real that is not yet, and the true that has been frustrated, brings the reality of the divine to the realm of experience. In that sense of loss and depletion, the disappointed person knows there is a reality more satisfying than the present experience. There is much more to living than has both met the eye and met the expectation of the person. Disappointment also points toward what the person really desires. It shows the way to the core issues and desires a person holds. It points the way to the direction and goals of the person, to a future that promises (even in fantasy) a fuller and more actualized life. It speaks to the inner yearning and inner desire that holds together human activity. These are positive things, even when they end in disappointment.

Ultimately that yearning, those dreams, those directions, point toward the presence of the divine, toward the sense of the fullness of life, and toward the plenitude of grace that speak of a divine force operative in the realm of everyday living, even if that divine force does not fulfill human desire and planning. The divine does not simply respond to human desire; nor, like a magician making things appear that were not there before, does the divine simply make things happen. Humans are enmeshed in a complex social web that influences significantly the human ability to act, to fulfill goals, and to live fully. It is not always that the divine presence will make all things possible and realize all things desired. Life is much more complicated than that. But the divine is still present in the disappointment — in that deep sense of the loss, the poignant grieving, the visceral emotion. The divine is fully there and present, even when the disappointments drag humans into darkness and despair.

Disappointment is like the refrain once heard in a parish: "So long as we pray, everything will be fine." Prayer was like a talisman that assured success in the way that the praying people wanted. This praying community was a search committee for a minister of the parish. They prayed. They were united. They were confident. And they were profoundly disappointed at the result. The person they called was not the person they thought they were calling. They thought their prayer would protect them from disappointment. But the disappointment began to push them into a new direction. They began to experience God differently and to examine their own desires and wishes more carefully, and (more importantly) to seek to understand how their disappointment was related to their own blind spots. The divine was present, but certainly not in the way that they understood at first. The divine was acting, but in ways that they were unable to see until they experienced their disappointment.

This is the reality of the divine in the midst of disappointment, disappointment that sets the stage for new avenues, for knowledge of self and the complexities of living, and the basis for an abiding trust in the presence of the divine, even when that presence is not fully known, experienced, or evident. In this way, disappointment is an important ascetical act — a time of conversion and renewal in the midst of deep emotion and frustration that forces a reevaluation of the understanding of divine presence.

26 / Striving ....

M OST AMERICANS THINK that the religious life is a process of ar- riving. The most important core of religion exists as a means to find the truth, once-and-for-all, to accept its trustworthiness, to live upon it, and to grieve deeply when a person or oneself falls away from what has been accepted as central and core. The long history of re- ligion, Christian religion especially, does not support such a concept of religion. Historical Christians metaphorized their religious energy as a striving toward God or toward holiness. These historical people understood the object of religion simply: to struggle to move, to set sights far above human capacity, and to soar to new heights and depths in creating a new self, a new society, a new world that current cate- gories could never even imagine. The striving revolved around always pressing forward and always moving toward what was not yet realized.

Inherent in the concept of striving stands the recognition that what currently is, does not satisfy. That does not mean that what currently exists remains outside of God, or divorced from the divine, but that what currently is presents only a shadow of what is to come. The sense that God continually unfolds visions and prospects far more glorious than what humans can know burdens the present good (or bad) with the sense of being inadequate, in process, merely a step along a very long road whose end can only be full union with the divine in its most concrete and glorious manifestation. What lies ahead becomes the draw, not to dismissal of what is, but to energize the movement into the future, into that which is not yet and yet is potentially present and active.

The striving ultimately relates to the desire to manifest and to make real the vision of God both in the life of the believer and in the world in which the believer lives. The vision draws, like light appearing over a mountaintop at dawn, making even the casual onlooker stop and notice the wonder that is unfolding. That sense of unfolding wonder and of manifest light, and even of the presence and glory of the divine, interrupts the cycle of daily living and of satisfaction or dissatisfaction with the current circumstances; it forces the eyes to look upward, outward, and forward to what is being displayed as a solid direction.

Most certainly striving remains a chronological metaphor. Striving talks about moving from the past, through the present, to a yet-to-be-realized future. And in this sense striving expresses metaphorically a passage through time. But there is another dimension that follows that metaphorizing. Striving also moves a believer inward, into the mind, into the emotions, into the deep reactions and responses to the self, the society, and the world. Striving instructs seekers not just to see what is outward, but also to experience deep within the self what is always present. Striving involves connecting with the interior divine, with the God who dwells within but whose presence seems submerged or dulled by the exigencies of daily living. Striving involves the believer in recognizing that the believer is a work in progress, an artistic creation still being refined, a person not yet fully emerged as complete. Striving, then, approximates the experience of becoming holy in the sense of becoming a person fully sanctified and harmoniously conjoined with the God who is present fully in the person as well as in the universe.

The conjunction of moving forward in time and moving inward toward the point where human effort meets the divine creates an anomalous situation that folds in on itself. The conjunction folds in on itself so that what may appear to be a movement forward actually may be a movement inward; what appears to be ahead actually exists within. And this anomaly has deep historical roots, because as the believer steps into the folds of the striving, the believer meets all those who have ever striven to manifest the presence of God, and those who have looked upon the dawn over the mountains, and those who have striven to be holy from the beginning of time. The community of strivers is not simply chronological. The companions on the way meet in this folding-in of time to the interior life and become the believer's companions in striving. They enter inward into human existence in the believer's striving and they stand at the end of the struggle in order to receive those who are working at their holiness and wholeness. The struggle of those who strove before merges with the struggle of the believers now, in order to create a reality far beyond the limits of time and space, a divinized universe caught in the folds of the striving that reaches at once forward and inward.

So striving remains the process of never arriving. It opposes what Americans value, because striving engages the sense of never being sure, of never being able to do anything once and for all times, of never being capable of resting on the sure knowledge of anything, including God. All these elements of living continually flow outward toward a divine presence, becoming more and more manifest in the universe, and fold inward on a divine presence, becoming ever more manifest in the actions, thoughts, and emotions of the person, and becoming more and more a part of the movement of all believing people to make the living God, of which they are a part, manifest fully in their lives and universes. Even the very holy never fully arrive, but strive, strive ever more diligently, toward the mystery that unfolds before their eyes.

27 / Oblation

ONE ASPECT OF human existence receives little attention in the postmodern situation: the necessity of oblation. Oblation is an offering of one's own well-being for the good of another or for the good of all others. Oblation presents an opportunity for giving of the self for others, in a context where giving itself is problematized by a normative Western culture that prefers receiving. The act of oblation locates the good of the other in the action of the one making the oblation, and hence it locates the well-being of all others within that same sphere. Oblation in this respect has a self-sacrificing dimension that recognizes the larger connection among all peoples and living beings and their mutual intercommunion.

The starting place for this experience of self-offering is found in the recognition of the interconnection of all people and all things in the universe. A person does not exist in isolation from all other people, nor do humans live apart from the rest of the ecosystem, nor do existent things on our planet live apart from all the elements of our universe and all other universes in the galaxy and beyond. All existent beings have a connection to all other existent beings to a degree beyond the level of comprehension of most people. It is a profound connection, deeply rooted in the similarity of all things existent, and the connection moves the aware person to experience the connection of the self to all others.

The interconnectedness and union of all existent beings in the universe leads to the question of responsibility one for another. What role does one existent being have in relationship to others, both in a limited and specific way, and to all others in a more general sense? How does the connection of all living beings lead to a morality of relationship that honors the interconnectedness of life? These are important questions, and the response to them results in an ethic or morality of relationship based on oblation.

The ascetical task of each human being revolves around articulating and acting in accordance with the recognition of this interconnection. One recognizes that there are other beings of which one's own life is a part, and one also recognizes that each being, although prone to think of itself as the center of its own universe, in reality is one being in an infinite connection of many beings constellated into a polymorphous complexity. In recognizing the existence of others, the ascetic offers the self to others for their benefit. The offering recognizes at once the interconnection of selves so that in working for the good of another, one is working for one's own good, not narcissistically, but out of the sense of the permeability of identity and the permeability of existence within the created order. But it is not the reflexive benefit to oneself that drives the desire to become an oblation to another, but the enjoyment of the deep communion of one with another that finds fulfillment in living for others.

Some people in Western society, however, continually live for others without the benefit of choosing so to do. Society expects self-offering from them either because of their social roles, their gender, or their race, for example. Oblation cannot be demanded of anyone. It cannot become merely a societal obligation imposed upon another for the benefit of the whole. This sort of imposed oblation distorts the nature of the interconnected state and moves toward social, political, or religious slavery. In such circumstances, the oblation of the person shifts from an orientation to another to an orientation toward articulating a defined and honored self in relationship to others. It is not the development of a self that destroys a theology of oblation, but the development of a self in isolation from others and a self insufficiently honored in relationship to others that destroys the asceticism of oblation. And this must be made very clear in the ascetical life, because great harm can come to those who are forced to offer their lives on behalf of others without choice or will.

When, however, the person is willing to embrace others freely and when the person chooses to offer his or her life to another, the mutual interconnection of all existent beings is honored. The person, stepping away from the egocentric and narcissistic orientation toward self alone, moves out toward others in an act of love and mutual affirmation. This extends beyond the human race: humans honor the earth by their refusal to pollute the waters and the air, and by living faithfully with the resources of the earth for the benefit of all its inhabitants (not just the wealthy ones). And the earth honors the galaxy by living faithfully within it, and the galaxy honors all other galaxies in an endless process of living such that the interconnection of all existent beings is acknowledged and honored.

The moral stance that emerges from this sort of oblation revolves around the response of one person, one society, one nation, one form of existent beings, to all others. Living within a world recognized as fully interconnected demands that ethics, morals, and modes of interaction speak to the larger benefit of the society. Ethics and morals cannot revolve simply around the benefit or harm to an isolated individual, or reflect the values or orientation of individuals who wish to act without reference to others. Rather, ethics and morals must also take into account the necessity of oblation, of self-offering, of living for others who also have a stake in the future of the universe of created beings. The benefit of the whole must have an important part in the formation of ethics and values of every being, precisely because existent beings are connected, and because whether humans like it or not, human existence is intimately linked to all other existent beings in the universe. There can be no benefit for the one person that does not at once benefit the whole.

This obligation of oblation has a deeply spiritual aspect. One way to articulate this spiritual connection is to say that when humans perform acts of oblation, the divine element within one person extends to meet the divine element in another. The interconnection between existent beings comes from their mutual participation in the divine, from their mutual recognition of divine honor and status, and from their understanding that the divine presence permeates all existent beings. So one human makes an offering of self to another, and the independent projections of the divinity connect with others in order to sanctify the whole of creation. The oblation of one to another becomes literally an act of worship of God, whose presence within and without the created universe implicates all relationships. The oblation and the ethics that develop from it also establish that there, at the heart of all relationship, stands the divine, whose presence activates and informs all actions between existent beings. In the end, every act of oblation is an offering to God-without from a person whose life is animated by the God-within.

28 / Perfection .... ༄

A T ONE TIME the language of perfection formed an important part of Western theological and ascetical tradition. Perfection articulated a goal that could never be achieved, and yet it organized and gave direction to human life. It resulted often in a debilitating sense of failure and inadequacy that emotionally crippled generations of people. The word connoted to many that they could become "perfect" and therefore never fail or sin. Even though the ancient literature purported to set perfection as a goal and not as a state to be achieved in human existence, the reality of sin and failure made that goal all that much more impossible to achieve. It created frustration and exhaustion without a sense of progress in devotion or virtue. Perfection was subsequently dropped from ascetical and theological language in the postmodern period.

Perfection, however, posits the question of progress in the religious life. It is not a question primarily oriented to arrival or achievement, but a question that continually places before the seeker the prospect of growing and developing ever more fully into a new being. The spiritual concept of perfection places a high bar on the possibility for human improvement and growth, and encourages the believer to pursue that which seemingly appears outside the possibility of achievement. Perfection goads the believer into moving, into weeding out failure and sin, into working through problems in order to experience a new dimension of living, into steadily and incrementally making gradual progress into living the religious life more articulately and authentically.

Perfection raises questions in postmodern minds because what constituted perfection in any given time revolved around a predetermined and a socially constructed given of a society. A community or era postulated only one perfection to be pursued, and only one set of criteria for evaluation of progress on the way to perfection. In the postmodern context this does not work. Religious people in the postmodern context realize that there are multiple agendas and different means of achieving them for each person and community of people. Measuring progress does not entail putting every person on the same yardstick, but of establishing the differences among people and measuring them according to their own stated purposes. Postmodernity must not abandon the concept of perfection, but rather it must abandon the singularity of perfection and the singular means of assessing the progress toward perfection. Plural perfections and plural forms of measurement replace the hegemonic singularity of past ages.

In the Greek of the New Testament period the word "perfection" could also mean "maturity." This may be the most helpful metaphorizing and rephrasing of the term. The ultimate aim for the seeker remains continually to mature and to grow toward a mature understanding of self and of the world. At some levels that maturity comes with simply reflecting actively on the process of living: there is a perfection that comes simply by living an authentic life without setting any goals at all. But there is also a maturity that comes through conscious and effortful reflection on the problems and issues that arise in one's life. Postmodern spirituality should retrieve this latter sense, which articulates the more proactive meaning of perfection. Life's problems and issues raise important concerns with which the seeker must deal, and the energy expended to deal with these concerns makes for progress, and progress moves the person toward maturity and perfection.

In the ancient language of perfection, there were always human models to follow, either in the person of a saint, or of a holy person, or of an elder. It is important to image that toward which the seeker moves. To imagine mentally the consummate image, what the seeker's life might look like and feel like, how the seeker might interact with others and value and honor the world and the universe — these images provide the end product, the image for perfection, and they aid the seeker in moving incrementally toward that wholeness and holiness. The image of the end product will be different for each seeker, because each has a different understanding of his or her own propensities and inclinations, but each unique image will call forth the best efforts of the seeker to make that image real, to create within the person the capacity to live according to the image; in short, to incarnate the image in daily living.

The various images of the final goal testify to the multiple ways of knowing and expressing the divine. It is not that only one image of God exists for all people, but that each seeker manifests a particular image of God in the daily events of living, relating, thinking, and emoting. The multiplicity of images creates a multiplicity of perfections and aims, and these variables express the presence of God incarnate in the lives of God's people and in the universe. The various images of God, and of perfection, point to the multiple expressions of a God who is ultimately beyond human categorization. The variable perfections concretize the infinitely variable images of God incarnate in human endeavor, and they provide the created universe with richness and depth. The beginning of the contemplation of this divine agency in the world and in the lives of seekers rests in the pursuit of perfection, in the incremental movement toward maturity, and in the ultimate presence of God imaged and made incarnate in the lives of the seekers, a presence that makes the world resplendent with divine glory.

29 / Ghostly Converse

THE PRACTICE OF RELIGION is not intended to be done in isolation. The entire Christian religious tradition encourages and even demands that the seeker enter what was called in the old English tradition, "ghostly converse," which means spiritual discourse with others. To avoid the narcissism and myopia of following a delusory or destructive path of religious practice, the ascetic masters advise each seeker to enter into conversation with another, preferably a more mature or seasoned seeker. This primary discursive relationship intends to assist each one in the discernment of what is appropriate and helpful, of whether one is acting out of an appropriate set of assumptions and understandings of the world, of whether one is responding to the divine impulse or out of a deep psychological need that may not originate in the divinity. Or it may simply aim to discern what the next steps or issues are that the seeker must address in the pursuit of the authentic practice of the religious life. This "ghostly converse" replicates in some degree the interior dialogue of a seeker with God; it also externalizes it in order to investigate one's deepest desires and impulses, and to submit them to corporate discernment. Since the Christian religious life is so communally based and so steeped in the theology of communal struggle, this discernment in the context of spiritual discourse plays a central role.

The conversation, however, between a mature and a younger seeker does not take place in isolation. Both partners in conversation must be part of a larger communal discourse in a local community. The discourse that wells up in individuals meets the discourse that wells up in the community and they mutually inform one another. The communal discourse primarily takes place around the weekly liturgy, by the community's delving into the Scriptures, seeking a word of life for itself; by the community's self-examination in light of the revelation provided in the Scriptures; by the community's intercession and prayer emerging from its corporate life; by the community's self-offering in the liturgy; and by its transformation into the living body of Christ through the sacraments. By locating the specific conversation within the context of a larger community conversation, the process of discernment and of seeking receives its grounding. The community conversation provides the context for more intense and individualized conversations regarding the authentic practice of the religious life.

But even communities need to be grounded in the larger discourse of the church and the discourses that take place in the wider society. Parishes and local communities do not function in isolation from the wider public and religious discourses of the day. Those discourses — as they express the needs and desires of the wider public and as they discern the presence or absence of the divine in the wider population — intrude into the life of the local parish and its members in their ascetical striving. And their intrusion is to be taken seriously as the context, the ground upon which the seeking after God takes place. It is not to be rejected, but integrated into the spiritual life either by affirmation; or after discernment, by rejection; or after prayer and more discernment, by transformation and reconstitution.

At each level of the constitution of the community, however, the godly conversation takes place. All of the discourses of the wider public and the church, of the local parish, and of the individuals seeking to live out their religious lives, constellate in order to produce a godly conversation that engages the person in the religious community and in the wider public as an instrument of the divine impulse. These conversations at once limit and expand the basis of conversation, ever spiraling outward from the myopic and the purely individual to the most public and corporate expression of the religious life. Discernment places limits on the practice, and discernment also expands the horizon; the conversation aims at discernment of what is proper and appropriate to each one living in religious community and living in the wider public arena. The discernment itself both liberates and restricts, while also adapting the larger spiritual discourse to the specific needs and personal makeup of the seeker.

30 / Ennui and Steps ....

THERE IS NO DOUBT that the project of divinization in its various arenas (personal, communal, and cosmic) seems overwhelming. The enormity of the divinization only seems greater as the ascetic begins to make progress, for the extent of the project seems always to loom larger than any one person or group can accomplish in one lifetime. That is not a mistaken perception. Divinization even at the personal level cannot be achieved easily, and in the communal and cosmic dimensions it is even more difficult to achieve.

Ancient ascetics warn against a kind of ennui that saps the energy and makes the project so large that it thwarts effort. Their sense was that given the difficulties, the ascetic could fall into a kind of stupor that prevented any activity at all, let alone active pursuit of the as-cetical goals. Ennui in the face of the enormity of the project is an understandable response.

The antidote to ennui is the process of setting more limited in-termediate goals, and striving to achieve them in small incremental steps of improvement. Rather than envision the large project at its most universal and cosmic, the ascetic sets more local goals. These goals might include very achievable things: the repetition of a prayer a number of times, the strenuous effort not to be debilitated by anger, the withdrawal into prayer for a longer period of time, the concentration on service to the poor for a particular period of time or for a limited project. These intermediate goals relate to the larger, more universal goal by being stages or steps along the way that may be more easily assessed; they provide a sense of making progress along a very long and difficult road to divinization.

In a postmodern context the concept could simply be described as making and marking incremental steps of progress each day. The in-cremental steps gently and perceptively set the ascetic on the right path and give the sense of a just-noticeable difference in progress. The incremental steps may relate to attitudes toward others, dealing with an internal habitual situation that is debilitating, or simply engaging in the habitual forms of prayer during a difficult time. The goal is making just-perceptible progress.

The same applies to communities. The desire to alleviate world hunger may cause ennui by the sheer enormity and complexity of the problem. But a community may begin working at various levels, in manageable ways, to achieve the goal. This might include a program of feeding the local poor with a hot meal and a food pantry, while at the same time sending members of the community to work with third-world farmers, while at the same time raising funds to buy food for those suffering the effects of a famine. Each of these in its own way relates to the larger goal, but in smaller, more measurably achievable goals that keep the energy and enthusiasm of the community high. Again, the criterion is a just-noticeable contribution to the issue or problem the community wishes to address.

And, of course, the small and incremental steps toward the repair of the environment also takes on enormous importance. These smaller steps — picking up trash on the street, or recycling aluminum cans and plastic containers, or properly disposing of hazardous materials like household paints or motor oil, or the governmental cleanup of biochemical waste sites — set the stage for the eventual transformation of the universe. The small steps move the seeker incrementally closer to the ultimate purpose to display the divinized nature of the universe.

Ennui does indeed set in. The tasks are indeed far beyond a person's or a community's capacity to achieve. By setting smaller steps, seekers value the larger task, hone the work of the divine in small things, and simultaneously make sure and steady progress toward the point when God will be all in all (1 Corinthians 15:28).

31 / Virtues

Historically the Western asceticism originated with the pursuit of virtues. The classical Western tradition of religious and philosophical discourse understood the virtues as universal and intrinsically related to one another. The tradition held that there were a fixed number of virtues that every human interested in pursuing excellence would strive to achieve. The virtues (in their Latin Christian form) were divided into the theological virtues of faith, hope, and charity (generally not found in the pre-Christian philosophical system), and the cardinal or moral virtues of prudence, justice, fortitude, and temperance (generally found throughout the classical Greek and Roman philosophical systems). Most philosophical and religious seekers would have found themselves striving for the perfection encapsulated in these virtues, and the effort toward them constructed what would have been a universally (Western, male) understood "perfectly moral" person.

Obviously such a universalizing theory of virtues does not meet the needs of a postmodern world. Postmodernity questions the universally applied categories and pushes toward categories reflective of racial, gender, ethnic, social, linguistic, political, religious, and philosophical difference. In such a context, universal categories cannot stand; no one universal standard exists by which to evaluate and judge all diverse persons, societies, ethnicities, and the wide spectrum of sexual orientations. This shifting ground under the question of the virtues, however, does not mean that the pursuit of virtues must be abandoned, but that it must be both decentered and deuniversalized.

The virtues may be understood as proximate excellences intermediary to the achievement of the ultimate state, deification. Virtue (Greek, *aretai*) means "excellences." The excellences articulated, concretized, and enacted culturally recognized moral and religious behaviors that were part of a program of self-construction and social reconstruction that had the city or republic as its beneficiary. They were goods enacted by the person for the benefit of the community, described as the "excellences" to be pursued by those seeking virtue.

In the postmodern and ascetical context-seekers understand the virtues as proximate and intermediary because they stand as temporary and shifting platforms toward which the seeker aims in the short term in order to achieve the ultimate state of deification. Seekers name them proximate because they stand closer to the unfinished deified product in a person, society, and cosmos. They stand closer to the immediate work in progress. They consider them intermediary because the virtues represent not the ultimate state, but smaller objectives on the way toward deification. As such, these proximate excellences must be projected by each seeker as the seeker discerns particular needs on the path toward deification of self, society, and cosmos. The virtues in a postmodern ascetical context shift according to the various contexts in which they are projected by the person, the society, and the corporate body of the whole cosmos.

The virtues work in this manner. A seeker projects an image of the final state of deification and develops a sense of the concrete appearance of individuals, societies, and the whole cosmos in its deified state. That projected image shifts according to the seeker's unfolding understanding and perceptions, and successes and failures; it is not a permanent image of deification, but a transitory one based on the best imaging possible for the seeking person or community at a moment in time. The envisioned and articulated characteristics of this ultimate vision of the deified world break down into specific imaged elements that constitute the full vision. In a society, for example, it may be that the image involves justice and equality for all as the final deified state, but the more proximate excellence to be pursued is the establishment of equal medical insurance and unimpaired access to medical services for everyone in a given region, then country, then continent, then world. These proximate virtues will become more accessible states on the way to the ultimate state, deification.

On a personal level, the image of deification may revolve around the peace and harmony of a person in relationship to other persons and societies. The more proximate excellence, then, might simply be reconciliation with adherents of other religions; striving for equilibrium in the face of heated opposition from others; standing unperturbed in the face of social, political, or religious attack; or responding to those attacking with equanimity and grace. The proximate state enables the seeker to build habits of reaction that will move the seeker closer to the ultimate state. Those proximate excellences, however, will shift and change as the person grows and develops, and as the seeker advances more articulately toward deification.

Virtues, then, continue to play an important role in ascetical effort and striving. They do not, however, stand as universals, but as temporary and proximate excellences that incrementally advance the seeker toward an ever-shifting image of deification.

32 / Union with God ....

M OST CHRISTIAN LITERATURE fears the implications of the concept of union with God. To accommodate the fact that throughout the history of Christianity various venerated people have claimed to have experienced such a profound union, Christian theologians have created the concept of mystical union. Theologians describe mystical union as a state so far removed from human effort that it requires an infused grace, a grace given to particular individuals found worthy of God's immediate and unimpeded union. The mystical union remains an exceptional, God-given, and temporary state for a particularly worthy person. It remains outside the realm of universal possibility and achievability precisely in order to protect the sovereignty and transcendence of God and the mutability and limitations of human beings.

But the concept of union with God plays an important part in the ascetical frame of mind. The distance between humans and the divine, so protected by the conceptualizing of union as an extraordinary phenomenon, replicates a worldview that strictly bifurcates the heavens where God dwells from the earth where humans dwell; it replicates the hierarchical geography of a God in a transcendent world and humans in a material world. Such conceptions do not assist the ascetic in transforming the self, society, or the cosmos. Asceticism must take the concept of union with God seriously at two important levels: it presents an ultimate state metaphorized as divinization, and it simultaneously describes the means toward that divinization. Those seeking the divine manifest an energy and a dynamic at once interior and exterior to themselves.

Although shocking to Western sensibilities even though sacramentally the Eucharist affirms such a union, union with God defines the ultimate state of human existence. Union with God sacramentally and ascetically metaphorizes the eschatological end of human existence. That union, however, precisely as an end, does not restrict itself to humans alone. Societies, indeed the whole universe, must be fully united with God. The aim embraces the restoration and reconstitution of all things as part of the divinity so that the divine appears resplendent and people perceive the divine in every aspect of the universe of humans and existent things. This constitutes a true mystical union, to use the old language, not just of humans with God, but of societies, cultures, the world, the various galaxies, and the entire universe, with God. Union with God becomes a metaphor that gathers and organizes energy for divinization and transformation.

But union with God also mediates that end. Individuals and societies can only work toward divinization to the extent that the divine already indwells the human person and creates the fabric of human existence. Humans do not pursue something completely exterior to themselves; rather they pursue something they experience from within as part of the greater manifestation of the divine. This part of themselves draws them toward itself precisely because it already functions within them. The interior divine presence moves the person toward the ultimate divinization. Seekers know God both as within themselves and as something without, as both energy and end product, as both means and end. God activates the interior divine impulse seeking to be united with the transcendent divine that holds together all existent beings and phenomena.

The historical impulse of the church to identify the experience of union with God as a mystical one is correct. Union with God, in whatever way it is described, enters the realm of mystical understanding, apprehending, and existence in the world. The early church failed by defining this experience and way of living as unusual, rather than the norm. Everyone who has been baptized into Christ, who has died with Christ in order to rise with Christ (Romans 6:8), has been inducted into a mystical body of Christ that stands at once divinized and divinizing. Baptism both divinizes and begins the process of divinization. The union effected through baptism both sanctifies and sets forth a yearning for the sanctification of all. This is mysticism at its very best.

Obviously not all who have been baptized experience or understand themselves as in this mystical state. Nor do they act according to their divinized status and yearn for the divinization of all things. This means not that the person is evil or that baptism has not effected change, but that the person chooses not to operate from the resources given in baptism. Union with God only functions when activated in the ascetic efforts of those wishing to live according to what has been given them and to strive for what divinization lies ahead. Each person must decide to become a seeker who actualizes the divinization of baptism in a life of transformation of self, society, and cosmos.

33 / Ascetical Eschatology

T HE PURSUIT OF an authentic practice of the religious life finds its fullest expression not in the past, but in the future. One does not act simply to conform to patterns of the past, but rather to become a new person, a different person in the future. It is the future state that calls forth the specific practices of the moment.

Eschatology ponders the understanding of the last things, the final cause(s) that focuses attention and organizes a way of living so that in the end, at death or at the final consummation of history, the seeker will have arrived at the state to which the seeker has been called. Imagining the end product of a life has important consequences and effects. Locating the look, the feel, the quality, the expression of the person one wants to become and then finding ways to bring that person into existence in the present time defines the eschatological orientation of asceticism. The image of the final product in all its complexity and beauty calls forth the actions and practices of the moment, so that incrementally that final product, that eschatological picture, becomes real and active in the present.

Religion, especially Christian religion, tends to be oriented toward the past. It looks to history, to the historical development of doctrine and practices, and seeks to replicate those historical patterns in the present. Theology and historical theology orient themselves toward reconceptualizing in the present what was known in the past. Certainly liturgy performs this function by connecting the past to the present by conveying liturgical forms and prayers into the modern period. These orientations to the past have their function and importance, but they do not necessarily advance the ascetical program. Asceticism looks to the future: to the development of the person unfolding through current practice, to the growth and maturity of the community of faith as it makes its way forward into ever more authentic living, and to the final consummation of human and cosmic effort in the evolution of the cosmos toward its infinitely complex final moments.

The past, however, does not completely disappear in the ascetical struggle toward the future. The historical past constitutes one element of the present moment. History stands in the present as an instantiation of human effort and achievements. It represents the road that has already been traversed as it leads toward the eschatological future that is unfolding in the present. It is not that the past is not relevant, but that the past does not determine the future. The orientation toward the future calls forth the effort.

The question of desire impinges here. What draws a seeker, or what commands a seeker's attention and energy, is the desire to become what has been envisioned as possible. Some articulate this possibility as holiness, or sanctity, or as a state of calm and equilibrium, or as energetically forceful. Whatever the final image that the seeker projects as the eschatological image for the self creates the desire to pursue that image even when the odds of success are slim. The desire arises in the imaginary of the future. When one projects the image of a new person as a final product, however one defines that newness, then the desire to see it unfold and become a reality in the present occasions the effort and the practices to make it real now.

The same desire implicit in the positing of a final image accrues to a community. When people band together to envision a better social world — for example, a fully just society where society treats each of its members with respect and where society meets fully the physical, social, and psychological needs of each person and group — the desire for such a society draws forth their effort. They begin to do the very things that will make that future world incrementally real in the present time. The eschatological future calls forth the effort and energy to recreate the world in the image projected by the community.

And again, the same may be said of the cosmos and the universe. No one knows comprehensively the ultimate end of the universe, but one's concrete image of a desired cosmic reality still stands as an important conceptual tool for envisioning it. The image assists and organizes the energy for evolution and development not because it is possible, but because human effort needs such images to grow and to assist the universe to unfold toward its natural and supernatural final state.

Asceticism, then, in every way orients not toward the past, but toward the future. It plots the plan of gradual development that makes the future real in the present moment. This gradual development becomes an incremental progress toward the future that gives depth and meaning to present activity and thought.

34 / Mary, the Mother of God

THROUGHOUT CHRISTIAN HISTORY Mary, the Mother of God, has formed a central locus to Christian devotion. Her historical significance, however, differs according to various traditions. The Eastern Christian church portrays Mary, the Theotokos (the "God-bearer"), as a strong warrior who protects the church from attack and who stands ready to defend the needs of the people over whom she acts as an emperor or empress. The Eastern Mary embodies a fierce protectress of the faithful. The Western church portrays Mary as the obedient and pure Mother who mediates between her all-powerful son and the human family whom she has adopted as her children. The Western church understands her purity and obedience to have given her special access to God for the benefit of those who express devotion to her. The Protestant Reformation mostly displaced the devotion to Mary, although some Reformation churches retained a devotion to her using the model of the earlier Western church.

In historical perspective Mary filled the distance between the human and the divine realms by bridging the increasing sense of disparity between sinful and rebellious Christian people and an all-powerful and stern sovereign. Mary remained accessible as God became less accessible and more distant from human existence.

The postmodern context, however, does not metaphorize God as a distant and unconnected divine agent outside the realm of human existence, but as a divine agent and energy deeply involved in human life and agency. Without distance between the human and heavenly realms, no gap exists to be filled, no need exists for a bridge.

Why do people venerate Mary? How can her place be retrieved in a postmodern ascetical theology? In the postmodern context Mary represents the sheer power of the potential fusion of a monadic universe in which the human and the divine realms can neither be differentiated nor distinguished. In the Theotokos all things become fused into one plane of reality that at once manifests the depth of an inconceivably vast universe (consider the human attempt to explore various universes in our own and other galaxies) and at the same time the specificity of the minutest act of will or expression of thought. The fusion of the two dynamics of the universe — the infinitely small and the infinitely large — marks the place where Mary, the Mother of God stands. She is the nodal point directing human consciousness toward that which stands beyond all possible conception and that which is most concretely enacted in the world.

As that nodal point, however, Mary, the Mother of God, signifies the power of the fusion of human and divine energies in one cohesive world. Mary represents not just a passive engagement of the human and divine, but an active, energetic, willing, and eager collusion between human action and divine mandate. Her willing collusion changed the nature of reality for the people of God. She forges a new reality no longer enslaved to a duality of separate human and divine realms, but now fused — as the mystics of old said and as modern physicists insist — into one powerful and complex interactive system without limits, unbounded, and continually flowing into new patterns of life.

Mary, the Theotokos, then, stands as the ensign of a unified world and of a world existing in a complex manner on a single plane. She brings together what appeared at other times to be separate realms, divided worlds, contrary impulses. She fuses them into one cohesive, yet always complex, potential for living fully and richly in the world and for transforming the world into a place resounding with the presence of God. The Theotokos makes it possible to destroy the bifurcations and dualities that have distanced human and divine and to unite them into one rich dynamic of living faithful to the understanding of a God fully engaged and active in the human and cosmic realm. In a delightful way Mary, the Theotokos, energetically provides witness to the postmodern sensibility and she makes possible a transition in the religious life from a dualistic to a monistic perspective and understanding. Mary makes possible the shift from modernity to postmodernity, because she fuses the perceived dualities of existence into one plane of activity and engagement.

35 / Progress

THE NOTION OF PROGRESS is among the oldest and most consistent elements of asceticism, beginning in Greco-Roman philosophy and continuing in Christian asceticism. Progress, the structured and measured advancement toward an end, has historically been understood as linear: a seeker advances directly toward a goal and progress measures the incremental intermediary stages of development in attaining it. Such a linear view actually remains much too simple to explain the concept of progress even in its historical contexts; in a postmodern context such linearity does not do justice to the complexity of progress. Postmodern asceticism recognizes both the shifting nature of the desired end result and the continual adjustment of the means to advancement toward it. Measurement and evaluation — that is, progress — must also be conceptualized as fluid and adjustable.

The ascetical project may be described in the following manner. A seeker forms an image of a state to be pursued, based on a schema constructed from current knowledge, understanding, desire, and experience. The seeker employs these three elements (image, final state, and schema) to construct an ascetical program: pursuing the final state as imaged in the seeker's imagination and as based on the schema of the seeker's current understanding. As the seeker advances, however, the schema itself changes to reflect the newer and emerging understanding. The schema itself shifts in response to the unfolding of new experiences, different desires, new circumstances, and a more advanced level of divinization. As the schema shifts in advancement, so also does the final state being pursued. The imagination, working on different data, projects a more refined image and alters the end to account for the refinement. The ascetical project consequently shifts to accommodate the new end by creating different practices to instantiate it. And this cycle continues throughout the life of the seeker. The same processes apply to communities of people who are engaged in ascetical seeking.

In such a context the notion of progress must be able to accommodate the shifts and movement in the ascetical practice. Seekers must no longer imagine progress as linear, except in the smallest of chronological sequences of evaluation, but they must rather imagine progress more as a spiral. As the schemas, images, and aims shift, and as the seeker sets forth a different set of practices to achieve the end, progress continually measures and documents the incremental advancement as well as the shifts in understanding accompanying the advancement. Progress becomes the measurement of incremental advancement along a shifting path. Progress is measured not according to a fixed pattern of a fixed goal, but rather according to a fluid and constantly shifting process.

In fact, the evaluative function of progress enters into the process by providing information in the adjustment of the schema. The schema shifts and changes according to the internal measurement and evaluation provided in the process of assessing progress. While making progress, the seeker enters a different imaginary and begins to conceive the objectives and practices from a different point in the process of advancing. The functional import of progress, then, does not relate to the static information about achievement, but to the continually self-reflective responses to the activity and practices instantiating the imagined final state. This means that progress functions not so much as a measure, but as a resource gathering a steady stream of information along a constantly shifting process of advancement toward divinization.

36 / Empowerment .... ॐ

ONE OF THE BENEFICIAL by-products of incarnational theology is the ennobling of human existence. Humanity, precisely because the divine chose to dwell in human form, receives the honor, the glory, and the power of the divine. Human beings live nobly as the site of divine habitation. In fact, the human condition cannot properly be differentiated from the divine, because the union of human and divine is so complete, so transformative, so incredible that all categories of differentiation fail and dissolve. Ascetical theology demands such a high anthropology.

The divine ennobles the human state: the divine power dwells in humans, animating and transforming human agency. This empowerment has two aspects. First, the divine indwelling empowers human activity and this empowerment of human activity sanctifies human effort. Since there can be no clear distinction between humanity and the divine, at least no functional differentiation since the union remains so complete, then human effort must bear the marks of divine presence. Human effort, even when it falls short of complete transparency to the interior divine impulse, manifests the presence of the divine in every action, thought, and emotion of human beings. If one wishes to see the divine in the world, look to the people who present the divine energy in the world: those so empowered to be able to present (perhaps, re-present) the divine to others, who in turn also bear the marks of the divine.

The second aspect relates closely to the first. In addition to the divine empowerment of human agency, the divine empowers humans to be agents of the divine in the functioning universe. This means that the divine has not ennobled humans simply to empower them as an honor, but that the divine empowers humans to function as divine agents in the universe. The divine relies upon human agency manifesting the divine impulse to effect the transformation of the world. The ennoblement of humanity has, therefore, a condition and a purpose: the divinization of all existent life, the manifestation of the divine in every realm of existence throughout the universe. The divine dependence upon human effort reflects the quality of the ennoblement bestowed upon human beings, a dignity of both substance and effort that enables humans to instantiate the divine presence.

Such empowerment, however, also carries great responsibility. Human dignity must first be corrected through discourse with other persons and communities throughout the world; then, manifesting the divine impulse, it has as its good purpose the transformation of the world. Activity that destroys the world, or that harms other people, or kills, or maims, or abuses does not manifest the divine impulse and must be dishabituated and transformed. Activity that benefits only one person, or one group of people, similarly must be closely evaluated. Activity that seeks to denigrate others as unworthy of the divine presence must also be examined closely. The responsibility is great, but so also are the dangers of misuse of the divine impulse. So, the empowerment of human beings in its dual aspects requires significant effort both to manifest the divine and to protect the integrity of divine agency in the existent universe.

But the dangers and the responsibility should not be used as excuses to denigrate human nobility. The ascetical task depends upon a sense of cooperation with the divine in divinizing the existent universe and everything contained therein, and such human effort should never be squelched or inhibited out of fear. The fear should rather empower the person to live out of the implanted divinity; it should empower the community to instantiate the divine in the world and the universe to reflect the divine presence within it.

37 / Thorns and Impediments ....

T HE ASCETICAL STRUGGLE has often been metaphorized as a difficult hike up a high mountain. The metaphor includes the strenuous effort required, the difficulties of climbing, and the occasional encounter of impediments on the road, especially a thorny path. Macarius the Egyptian, a fourth-century ascetic monk, writes in particular of the encounter with thorns on the way of progress, and his vivid descriptions give important instruction about the attitude and effort in the face of thorns and other impediments. This theory of thorns provides important information for the postmodern ascetic.

The thorns, theorizes Macarius, demand that the ascetic pay attention. Thorns cannot be ignored, because if one tries to do so, the thorns cause damage not only to the body by wounding it, but also to the clothing by tearing it. The damage, that is, occurs to both the outer and the inner person. Thus he says the thorns demand the ascetic's attention. This is the first point.

The seeker must contemplate the thorns and take stock of the potential damage to body and clothing. Thoughts of continued progress must take second place to the immediate consideration of the thorns. The ascetic, in understanding the thorns as impediments, comes to understand precisely what stands in the way of progress, and how to traverse that section of the path in order to safely move beyond it.

The second aspect involves a plan to pass through the thorny patch without significant damage. The thorns cannot be ignored, so seekers must consider their damaging effect to be the basis of a plan to pass through them. The ascetic gathers clothing close to the body so that it will not be caught in the thicket; the ascetic walks steadily and firmly, not expanding the body, but trying as best as possible to contract it by placing one foot directly in front of another. The plan for passing through the thorns provides important information on the capacity of the person to adjust to difficulty, and it is vital to the ultimate success of the ascetic.

The third aspect is joy. Once the ascetic has maneuvered the thorny patch, and taken note of the damage to the body and the clothing, the ascetic experiences joy that progress has been made despite the impediments. The joy comes because the thorns did not succeed in stopping progress, nor did the thorns damage the seeker's progress. Even the slowing down of the trip, the slow movement through the thorns, and the seeming impossibility of progress yields to joy; looking back, the ascetic sees that even though the distance covered was only a few feet, many miles were traversed in interior progress. The reflective joy acknowledges a maneuver well accomplished.

This little allegory of the thorny path encourages postmodern seekers, especially as the progress often seems so little and the impediments to divinization so great. Looking around at the state of the person, the various societies, governments, and the environment, the seeker could conclude that the effort is worthless, lacking in success, futile, and ultimately hopeless. That is the work of the thorns on the path. The ascetic must look closely at those impediments to progress toward divinization of self, society, and universe and begin to form a strategy for passing through them without ignoring the difficulties, but also without being overwhelmed by them. Studying the impediments and their effects provides important information to those who persist in the ascetic struggle. The analysis does not intend to undergird the level of difficulty, but to open a way to progress and advancement. Certainly, the ascetic will experience the pain of travel through the thorns — the pain to both the mind and the body, the psyche and the person. But such pain will not ultimately triumph, because of the attention given the thorns, the plan to traverse them, and the joy that follows the successful advancement. Such is the work of thorns and other impediments.

38 / Anticipated Joy

OFTEN ASCETICAL PRACTICE sounds like sheer drudgery. The emphasis on struggle, attainment, progress, impediments, and disappointments tends to characterize ascetical practice negatively. That characterization has some validity, but another side deserves to receive serious attention. That correlative stance may be described as the reality of living in anticipated joy. The joy that the ascetic feels reflects not only the progress that the ascetic makes along the way, but also living out in the present a joy that is yet to be fully realized. Now, in the present moment, the ascetic lives out the eschatological and future divinization — the joy beyond all joys.

The anticipation of a fuller joy animates the experience of making progress. In incremental ways, what will be more fully realized and instantiated in the future comes to have an effect on the moment. The present life lives into that final joy, bringing a deep sense of fulfillment and accomplishment into the present moment, even if that moment only partially realizes what will ultimately follow.

Corporate bodies also experience this joy. It is a joy of seeing one or two small instances that portend the coming of greater things: the building of a house for a homeless family presages the coming of justice for all the poor; the distribution of food to the hungry poor anticipates the eschatological banquet where every need is fulfilled for all existent beings; the repair and restoration of a chemical dump-site inaugurates a time when all the world's physical resources will be honored. These communal experiences anticipate a joy that the ascetic experiences incrementally in the present moment, but which will be more fully lived out in the future, when the advancement toward divinization is more complete.

This joy cannot be forced, however. It is not a joy that can be manipulated, or become a reason for living the ascetic life. One lives the ascetic life in order to accomplish personal, social, and universal divinization. The joy springs up naturally as one begins to make the correlations between present activity and the anticipated state. The joy results from seeing the connection between small present actions and the instantiating of the eschatological vision that animates the ascetic's work. Groups of people who force that joy, who bring the eschatological too much into the present moment before its time, use the joy as a means of motivating others to endure. That is a dangerous situation, often created by various eschatological religious groups. But true joy erupts as an offshoot of the ascetic labor, not as a cause of it. The struggle brings joy, as water to a thirsty traveler, precisely in order to refresh and strengthen for the journey.

Living in anticipated joy enables the seeker to continue, expands the vision of the eschatological final state, animates the effort to instantiate the divine and to effect the more complete divinization of the universe. The emphasis rests on the fact of living it out, not on the joy, for in the living out of the ascetical life, the seeker begins to glimpse realities and possibilities not immediately evident or available to the human imagination. By living in anticipated joy — that is, by connecting current action with eschatological goals — the seeker begins to participate in the establishment of the new person, the new society, and the restoration of the universe in the divine.

39 / Self-examination ....

A N IMPORTANT ASPECT of the religious life is self-examination. The process of assessing the status, effectiveness, and direction of one's own life is a fundamental dimension of the ascetic life. The masters of the religious life suggest daily examination of the self before retiring to sleep, with a more vigorous self-examination in preparation for the sacrament of confession. In each case the goal remains the same: to evaluate the successes in advancing toward divinization and to acknowledge the impediments that inhibit that advancement.

Self-examination ought not create guilt, because it does not intend to force the self into divinization, but simply to evaluate honestly and directly both the positive advancement and the negative elements that stand in the way of that advancement. Honesty about the status of a person's life forms the foundation for real advancement. Without honest self-examination and self-evaluation, progress is difficult, because no basis exists to function as the starting point toward achieving the eschatological goal. Fantasies about one's real self, noble as they might be, do not assist the person in real growth. In fact they become a major hindrance.

So the examination process ought to be simple and honest. What has brought deep and abiding joy today, and how does that joy relate to divinization? What has caused pain and hurt, and how does that pain or hurt relate to the immediate and the long-range images that have been proposed for advancement? Have the aims of the day been achieved, and if so, how successfully; if not, what prevented their achievement? Has there been a clear focus on the memory of God or have the immediate tasks of the day diverted attention in other directions? Were there any pangs of conscience invoked today, and how should they be understood and interpreted? These and many other such questions take the seeker to a place to evaluate and assess progress.

Sifting through the experiences of a day brings both joy and sadness. It is not entirely a positive process: it would be easier to suppress and ignore direct confrontation of one's own failures and hurts. But in the end such suppression harms the person because it creates a surface illusion that nothing is wrong, nothing amiss. The acknowledgment of failure and hurt in relationship to the divine presence within the person brings an increment of healing. Each individual does not strive alone; the divine energy remains active all through the day, even in failures, even in hurt. Nothing occurs in the absence of the divine; self-evaluation connects the seeker with the divine impulse and reorients efforts. Then the divine presence may begin to work with the seeker to overcome hindrances and to work actively with factors that aim toward divinization. The movement toward ultimate divinization, that is, does not cease even in failure, and self-examination honestly acknowledges that even a person's failures ultimately will lead toward divinization. So self-examination ought not to be avoided.

Similarly on the corporate level, communities must examine their progress, failures, and impediments. This is the function of the general confession in the context of the Eucharist: to provide time for the community to reflect on its successes and failures in light of the Scripture of the day. This theological evaluation aims to assess the progress toward divinization: it does not simply function as a programmatic evaluation to assess the success or failure of specific communal projects. The community must ask itself how it advances toward the eschatological divinization of all individuals and every society, and toward the sanctification of the existent universe. These evaluations by a community do not refer only to religious community, but to every community both social and political that has the responsibility for the transformation of people's lives and the enhancement of the quality of life with justice and equity. Regular evaluation assists in the progress, and offers a solid basis for subsequent action.

In the end the honesty about one's life-situation counts the most. The specifics of successes or failures, progress or debilitations, do not matter as much as the honest assessment of the day's activities. Honesty allows the person to bring both good and bad, successful and unsuccessful, actions and thoughts into the divine presence. This engagement with the divine presence sanctifies even the failures as part of the overall advancement toward divinization.

40 / Mystic Communion

CHRISTIANITY'S DEEPEST MYSTERY is the one that describes human beings as the body of their God, the body of Christ. For Christians the term "body of Christ" (1 Corinthians 12:14) presents a wonderful ambiguity because it may refer to so many things at once. The body of Christ may refer to the historical person of Jesus; or it may relate to the sacramental body and blood of Christ given to the believer in the Eucharist; or it may signify the corporate body of all baptized Christians who have died with Christ in order to be raised with him (see Galatians 3:27); or it could mean the final and eschatological restoration of all things into Christ so that "Christ will be all in all" (1 Corinthians 15:28). This profound ambiguity of signification makes the concept of the body of Christ a sweet, mystic communion.

Each baptized person becomes a part of God's body ("our bodies are Christ's parts" 1 Corinthians 5:15). The very meaning of the sacrament revolves around the grafting of new members onto a corporate and divine body that has existed through the ages and that moves toward the divinization of the universe. The union between human and God inaugurated in baptism cannot ever be severed; it is indelible, permanent, and fully effective always, even when the person does not acknowledge it.

That union with God drives the believer into community with the many others who have been baptized. The groupings almost boggle the imagination: from a local religious family, to a parish, to a regional ecclesiastical unit, to a denomination, to the conglomerate of denominations, to the religious practitioners outside denominational lines, to the reality of the connectedness of all human beings to God through the incarnation, to all those throughout history who have yearned for God and sought to fulfill their yearning, and finally to the connection of the person even with nonhuman existent animals and things. The union with God effected in baptism creates a widely diverse set of communities, of bodies, all of which ultimately (from a Christian point of view at least) constitute the body of God. The ritual enactment of this divine body in the Eucharist becomes a central tenet of Christian faith.

To see the interconnectedness of self to other selves and to community provides an important context for the ascetical life. So much of the description of practices focuses on the individual person, as though each person could be isolated from others. In fact, each person lives in a wide assortment of communities, and the self in most respects cannot be excised from them. To struggle then toward divinization means that the seeker must struggle not only within the self, but also in the various communities in which the seeker lives. The believer implicates these communities in the process of divinization, precisely because they are a vital part of the person's identity and the context for the struggle toward divinization. The communities, then, must be an explicit part of the seeker's world in prayer, self-examination, and the realm of action. To be a part of the body of Christ means being a part of every such community wherever it exists in the world, and with every being who has ever been part of the body of Christ throughout time.

This wider communion infiltrates the conscious life and prayer of the seeker. By visualizing the connections among so many people living and dead, seekers recognize the mystical expansion of the self far beyond the confines of the individual body; they recognize the basic connectedness of all things in God and the unity of all existent beings to the source of their life and being.

The sense of mystic communion also provides a corrective to myopic efforts. Individuals and communities cannot pretend that their good comprises everyone else's good, because they acknowledge the full extent of the interconnectedness of all beings and things. The connections make such limited and self-serving projections difficult. On the other hand, the recognition of the communion of all people and things widens the horizons and opens the possibility of seeing and living a far more expansive life. And it brings to mind the vastness of the process of divinization that is to take place. This wider and expansive vision of the fullness of God, the divinization of the universe, becomes palpably real in the gradual expansion of the mind to recognize the sweet, mystic communion of which the seeker is an important part.

41 / Habitual Prayer

T HE ASCETIC LIVES in two worlds simultaneously: the current real world of daily existence; and the even more real, emergent, eschatological, and divinized world toward which the ascetic works. The bridging of these two worlds defines both the problem and the glory of daily existence: to live fully in the world that currently exists while keeping the eye and the heart on an emergent divinized world that is yet to be fully instantiated and realized. Certain habits anchor the ascetic in the emergent world and provide the ascetic with a sure sense of its reality, even though the emergent world has not yet become fully instantiated. One of these habits is prayer.

Prayer may be understood in this context as the discourse and conversation of the divinized world in the present. Prayer engages as real and present that which will ultimately be actualized, when the eschatological reality of the divinized selves, societies, and universes will no longer need prayer because the divinization will be so complete. The ascetic enters into that eschatological discourse in the present by setting aside times for prayer and meditation.

In a sense, what the ascetic accomplishes through prayer is simple. The ascetic at prayer has already entered into the full reality of the divinized world and stands there as one in deep conversation in it. Prayer for the ascetic consists of a fleeting moment of living in the future, a time of instantiating in the present the reality yet to come. Prayer works as an anchor, because it trains the ascetic to experience now something that will be more fully realized at the end, when the process of divinization and sanctification is complete.

The cycles of prayer for each ascetic will be different according to life patterns, but the tradition transmits some regular patterns that assist the ascetic in organizing a proper cycle. Two poles define the tradition: the one of the individual and the corporate, and the other of daily and weekly cycles. In individual prayer the ascetic enters and explores the future divinized world for the benefit and enhancement of oneself. This prayer creates a time for personal satisfaction and growth, and the tradition locates that on the one pole of daily prayer. Each day, in order to allow the person to experience the future state in the present, the ascetic sets time apart to pray and to live in that future world the ascetic works to instantiate in the present.

Corporate times of prayer, called worship, happen less frequently than the individual times. This is the other pole of habitual prayer. When the community of ascetics gather, once or twice a week to pray together, they enact the emergent divinized world in the present. They live in the world that is to come. Their discourse and interaction reflect the patterns that will exist in the future divinized world. The vision of God explored in the corporate gatherings influence the understanding of individual and society alike; they begin to envision the possibilities of living in the divinized world by practicing in their corporate assemblies. From the perspective of the gathered community at prayer, new visions, new images, adjusted desires and hopes, and ever more deep understandings of justice and peace emerge. This corporate time also sets the agenda for the times of individual prayer. Corporate prayer points to new arenas in need of divinization, new issues that need to be explored and studied in order for seekers to work more effectively toward divinization. And corporate prayer reveals persistent and perturbing hindrances that stand in the way of divinization for individuals and communities.

The habit of prayer — that is, the habitual and regular practice of entering the emergent world and discoursing there — strengthens the ascetic's resolve, especially in times of turmoil and dryness. If the ascetic adheres to habitual cycles of prayer, individual and corporate, daily and weekly, then a habitual anchor already exists, when difficult times arise, to provide solace and strength. Prayer anchors the person in what is to come and thereby supports the ascetic on the way, especially when that support is most needed in times of trial and frustration. Prayer, then, must not be occasional, but habitual, on a regular cycle so that the anchor is strong and the strength is certain.

42 / Assembling the Social Body .... ⌇

THE SELF IS NOT ALONE. Although Western people think of themselves primarily as isolated individuals, formed into societies and nations by the collection of individual people into groups, the ascetic person understands the social nature of the self itself. The ascetic understands the individual, isolated persona of the West to be at best an illusion and at worst a delusion, for the ascetic understands that there are many people who have become a vital part of the ascetic self. To assemble this company of people who have become a part of the self is an ascetic practice that undercuts illusion and delusion and establishes the corporate self, which includes the presence and activity of the divine itself.

In the tradition, historical Christians considered these corporate elements that inhabit the self primarily as other divinely inspired beings: one's guardian angel, or one's patron saint, or Mary the Mother of God who is refuge to sinners, and always the beloved Jesus into whose body the ascetic has been grafted by baptism. When the ascetic thought, or considered action, or contemplated, or prayed, these agents living within and operating through the ascetic would assemble, so that the ascetic never thought, acted, contemplated, or prayed alone. These divine beings always accompanied and guided the ascetic from within.

In a postmodern world this list of inwardly dwelling assistants and parts of the social body may be expanded to include many people both living and dead, both known to one personally and known at a distance or from public accounts, both good and bad influences. The bad particularly need to be acknowledged as part of the social body, because their influence frequently manifests itself indirectly and unconsciously. Here might be an abusive man or woman in the family, perhaps a parent, or sibling, or relative whose abuse is hidden deep within the person, but whose effect is felt in the daily activities of living. Similarly, there are good influences, those teachers, clergy, politicians, and neighbors who have become a part of the ascetic by virtue of their positive influence. This community might embrace a member of a religious community, or childhood friends, or close colleagues at work who have become an important part of the ascetic's life. All these people, both while they are living and when they have died, exert an influence on the ascetic and by virtue of that influence have become incorporated into the social body of the ascetic. They present themselves frequently in the ascetic person's mind (whether consciously or not), social formation, and prayer.

The practice of assembling the social body is simple: making a list of those people living and dead who have had a significant influence in the person's life. Digging deeper for memories of these people and influences becomes a means for the ascetic to understand the expansive and social contours of the ascetic's life, and a means of forming an interior community of familiars. Making these people an articulated and intentional part of the self both reveals the self to the ascetic and at the same time connects the current self to its past and its environment. The practice makes connections interior to the self that form the basis of ascetic growth.

The inwardly dwelling and acting divine presence constitutes the most important influence in the construction of the social body. The experience of oneself as divinely loved, divinely inspired, divinely appreciated, and divinely directed empowers the person to live fully and boldly. That the divine would dwell in the self, and that the self is worthy of such divine presence, creates the proper environment for action, thought, and prayer. But the experience of the inner divine impulse comes only as the ascetic assembles the various elements of the social body. Here in this assembling, the ascetic builds the basis of the self solidly not only in the divine, but also in the community from which the self arises. The human person is never completely divorced from the divine or from other people — they are always knit together in a mystic sweet communion.

43 / Cultivation and Avoidance ....

A SCETICISM TRADITIONALLY revolves around the cultivation of the virtues and the weaning of a person from the vices. The Western philosophical and religious tradition employs singular language to describe the virtues and vices, because both philosophy and theology promulgated one comprehensive system of virtues and vices generally accepted as universal. Of course, such a Western hegemonic orientation toward the virtues and vices can no longer stand, nor can one speak of universal systems of virtues and universal understandings of vices. The ascetical question, however, of the cultivation of certain attributes and the avoidance of, or weaning away from, certain others still holds great interest.

In a postmodern context virtues might be described as the desired attributes or elements that describe the final product, or end, of a way of living. The seeker projects an image of the desired personality or subjectivity and that image may be broken down into smaller malleable bits of human action and reaction that become incremental steps to the attainment of the full image. Those incremental bits of behavior, deeply desired and imaged in their totality as the object toward which the seeker moves, constitute virtuous behavior. By pursuing those elements vigorously, the seeker eventually begins to make progress toward the attainment of the final state, or the instantiation of the image that was projected as the final product of the seeker's work.

Likewise postmodern people understand the vices as the impediments or obstacles to the instantiation of the projected and desired image of the subject. Vices represent any pattern of behavior, instinct, or thought that interrupts the progress toward the instantiation of the image. Vices obstruct that progress and create a detrimental pattern of behavior or create a situation that inhibits the desired progress and advancement toward the goal. Even situations and characterizations commonly considered good, or that function as virtues to other people, may be vices to another, precisely because a universal system does not exist. Only a system completely oriented toward the attainment and instantiation of an image of a person in the making exists.

Although this sounds as though the entire system of virtues and vices orients itself only to the individual, that is not entirely the case. Groups of people living in community, who set goals and forge a common understanding of the eschatological society toward which they orient themselves, also identify common vices and develop common virtues that assist them in their progress toward the desired commonwealth. There may at times be conflict as a community grows between the individual virtues and vices and those of a group, but still the process of identification of incremental stages of growth leading to progress in the instantiation of the commonwealth still stands as a site for negotiating the vision and its achievement.

It is not an easy matter to project an image of a desired individual goal, nor is it simple to forge a common vision for the evolution and development of a commonwealth. The effort, however, is necessary. One does not make progress without direction. This does not mean that all indirection, and every circuitous route to the goal represents error, but that even the seemingly aimless meanderings of a seeker or a community must be integrated into the incremental movement toward the articulated end. Indirection only becomes a vice when it prevents, or inhibits, movement toward that end. It is not wrong in itself. Often such side roads result in a reevaluation or reimaging of the final end so that flexibility actually functions as a means of adjusting the image according to new information and new impulses. This means that the end does not exist as an absolute, even when it is forcefully projected. All ends are contingent, and, therefore, the manner in which they are instantiated remains a flexible process.

Virtues and vices, then, are never set in stone. So many factors impinge — gender, race, class, age, ethnicity, maturity, levels of energy, and many others. At each point the characteristics of the final purpose, the eschatological image, shifts and so does the understanding of the virtues and the vices as they accommodate themselves to the revised and shifting image. Seekers greatly enhance their progress, however, by the cultivation of the specific virtues and the consequent avoidance of stated vices. Even without a universal system, the methods still enhance the ascetic road.

44 / Baptism ....

R ELIGIOUS RITUALS hold an important place in human existence. They confirm that which comes from religious tradition that still holds value, they solidify religious identity and religious communal relationships, and they bring the sacred to bear in circumstances in which the sacred is not seen. For the Christian ascetic, however, there is one ritual that bears primary and foundational importance, the rite of baptism. Because of their connection, the supplementary rite of chrismation (confirmation in Western Christianity) must be considered together with the rite of baptism.

In baptism the believer participates in the death and resurrection of Jesus Christ in order to be fully grafted onto Jesus' mystical body (see Galatians 3:27; Romans 6:4; and Colossians 2:12), the embodiment of God in the world, the church. The fact of dying and rising marks the death of an old person, one who seemingly lived outside the realm of divine presence, and the birth of a new person, one in whom the divine presence is indelibly marked. The constellation of an old identity or person that has died and the emergence of a new person or identity that is inaugurated in the sacramental rite provides ascetics with the pattern that molds their experience and gives direction to their efforts. The tension between relating to the old identity and allowing the new identity to emerge replicates the tension between remaining in the current situation and growing into deeper and more profound divinization through regular and habitual practices geared toward divinization. The ascetic stands with this dual identity, yearning for the manifestation and development of the emerging and more divinized self while yet faithfully living in the present moment. For the ascetic, although the old self has died, the effects of that self remain a continual influence to be battled as the new, more divinized self struggles to be firmly established.

Baptism also inaugurates the eschatological community of divinized people. The sacramental rite produces in the present life of people the very divinization that will ultimately become the norm for all existent beings. The divinization exists in potential form in baptism, or more accurately, baptism plants the reality of the future divinization in the person and allows the person to live and to create that alternatively divinized self, society, and cosmos. What baptism firmly plants in the present will be fully manifest in the future. For the ascetic, this means that the end toward which the ascetic struggles already exists and has reality. Baptism guarantees the success of the effort so that every conforming of the self to the divinized reality given in baptism moves the self incrementally toward complete divinization.

Finally, baptism empowers the person and the community to be the divine agency in the human realm. This empowerment enables the divine impulse to be activated in every human individual and social action and thought. For the ascetic, to live the baptismal life consists of being empowered to soar to the heights of human potential for divinization. Baptism empowers the ascetic to do what seems impossible, to think what seems unthinkable, to live a divinized life in a context that seems antipathetic to divinity, to experience divine sociality in every social context, and to transform the world from the deadening place of degradation and human exploitation to a place resplendent of the divine. In short, baptism empowers the ascetic to pursue divinization vigorously.

What enables the ascetic to visualize and understand the activation of this divine potential? The correlative sacrament of chrismation (confirmation in the West) accomplishes this. The pouring of the oil

of the Holy Spirit over the body after baptism signifies the consecration of the senses. Chrism transforms the senses, and enables them to
experience divinization completely. For example, chrismation enables
the believer through bodily eyes and sight to see the divinized self,
society, and universe in the present. Through the heart, chrismation
opens the believer to living emotionally as a divinized person. All the
senses receive chrismation in order to allow them to see in the present
that which will only come in the future. The ascetic relies upon this
chrismal sanctification as the means constantly to focus attention on
the reality of the divinization that is to come as it is instantiated in the
present moment. These sanctified senses enable the ascetic to see in
the present that which will only be seen and known fully in the future,
and this process encourages the ascetic during the struggle.

In an important way, the ascetic takes on the reality of baptism
and chrismation as the central focus of life. Ascetics are not more
perfect, they are simply more focused, or more intentional, and perhaps
more visionary about the ultimate divinization of the self, society, and
the universe. Chrismation allows the ascetic to experience that joy
now, while baptism assures the ascetic of the ultimate success of the
venture.

45 / Concupiscence

CONCUPISCENCE, or inordinate desire, holds a primary place in the
tradition as the central enemy of the ascetic. These inordinate desires for pleasure revolved around the pleasure of sexual expression and
the pleasure for wealth and riches. The tradition formulated systems to
counteract both sexual and economic desire by vigorous suppression
and careful submission of these desires to the ultimate goals. Such
systems do not work well in the postmodern situation.

The problem with concupiscence revolves around the question of
the desires being "inordinate," not oriented toward a particular end,
nor "ordered" in relationship to some worthy purpose. A by-product
of this "inordinate" status was the problematizing of all desire and
pleasure so that the human condition was left bereft and joyless. But
the question of the ordering of desires holds some potential for good
use in a postmodern asceticism.

Desire and yearning play an important role in ascetical effort. When the ascetic projects the image of the eschatological end that encapsulates the vision of divinization of self, society, and the cosmos, that vision draws the ascetic to itself. The ascetic also begins to yearn for the vision that draws and to desire that image to become instantiated in the present, that is, to become real. The pursuit of that image, even as it shifts and changes, produces pleasure and delight. The yearning and the desire lead directly to pleasure, and therefore cannot be rejected nor problematized.

The difficulty does not revolve around the experience of these desires and pleasures. Nor does the difficulty reside in the necessity that these desires and yearnings must be oriented toward divinization alone, either in an ultimate or a more proximate way. Rather the problem relates to the person's desire and yearning for things that actually inhibit or prevent divinization, that is, for things that are not beneficial to the person. Postmodern society manifests many such "inordinate" desires: for drugs, success, money, sexual relationships, and fame. These desires tend to inhibit the progress of the ascetic toward divinization, and, therefore, the focusing of attention on them becomes a detriment to and not an enhancement of divinization in whatever form being imaged and pursued at the moment. Desire and yearning, even for sexual relationships, money, power, and success do not of themselves inhibit the divinization of self, society, and the cosmos. Money, sexual pleasure, power, success may actually manifest the divine in the existent order, and hence present the true ascetic's work toward universal divinization. Pleasure in this way is not problematized, but rather destructive pleasure is the problem; the same applies to desire and yearning. Constructive, healthy, enhancing desire and pleasure further the program of divinization for the person, society, and world.

There are two underlying issues that must be addressed. First, the old ascetical systems that problematized all pleasure and inordinate desire did not function with a sufficiently incarnate divinity. They problematized the physical, the flesh, as in itself unwilling or unable to participate in the divine. Therefore the spiritual realm ruled over the physical. This denigration of the physical led to excesses for individual people, for societies, and for the ecological preservation of the world. Such attitudes may be metaphorized as the dominance of human over animal, of spiritual over physical, and in many other perceived polar opposites, any situation where one member takes precedence over the other. Such metaphors damage seekers and should be rejected. It is not a question of dominance, but of manifestation: the divine compels the ascetic, indeed the believer, to manifest to the outer world the inner divine impulse and presence.

The second issue relates to the process of taking joy in existent things precisely because the divine energy and presence makes them enjoyable. The old ascetic system bifurcated the world of the divine from the human realm — they were separate and antagonistic. In an incarnate theological view, and from a postmodern perspective, the divine dwells, infuses, inhabits, energizes, and functions in all existent beings and things. Nothing may be understood as outside the realm of the divine, either actually in the present time or potentially in the pursuit of the eschatological end. The divine is ever-present, ever-active, ever-available to human interaction; thus humans may safely enjoy and rejoice in existent things precisely because the divine is present in them. The ascetic, then, takes pleasure in the presence of the divine wherever and whenever the divine might be found. The ascetic delights in the manifestation of the divine in other people, in the self, and in the existent world. It is a delight to be savored and cherished, because it witnesses to the reality of the incarnate divinity permeating the world.

Although in the postmodern situation, the old concept of concupiscence must be rejected, the concept of concupiscence actually leads to a more profound understanding of the nature of pleasure, desire, and yearning. In the end, the new understanding of concupiscence enhances the ascetic's life and connects the inner desires with the reality of the divine in the present and in the ultimate divinization of all things in the future.

46 / Pride and Humility ....

P RIDE HINDERS the ascetical effort by drawing attention and energy away from the focus on divinization and attracting it to the person. The ancient tradition treats pride in this way in order to reorient the seeker toward a focus on God alone and to diminish the seeker's orientation toward the self. This orientation was often named egotism. The postmodern world, however, understands the self as a fragile construction and attention to it has very positive consequences: in that focus the person comes to understand the impulses and desires that operate within and then may begin to form and reform them. So, in the postmodern situation, pride in oneself and one's accomplishments cannot be rejected; the accomplishments (and the hindrances to such accomplishments) must be understood in order to make progress. In postmodernity, pride cannot categorically be rejected.

The larger issue that pride raises is that of humility. It is not that seekers should not take pride in the progress toward divinization, or that a community should not be proud of its efforts to establish divinized societies and organizations throughout the world. The issue rather is one of connectedness. Seekers must understand that their success and their failures are linked to every other success and failure in the universe. Each seeker's effort conjoins those efforts of every other seeker, and each community's efforts conjoin those of every other community seeking divinization, and all the universes of the known worlds conjoin all the others, even ones we do not yet know. This connection of one thing to the other and the recognition of the intercommunion of all existent things is known as humility.

In its original linguistic meaning, humility refers to being close to the earth, the Latin *humus*. The word often referred to the process of knowing that one comes from the earth and passes into the earth in death, from dust to dust, from earth to earth. This awareness provides a context for human effort. At once it provides pressure to achieve, because time is short for each person and the efforts limited. It provides another context: all the efforts and accomplishments of a person will eventually turn to dust, because the person will die and return to earth. Humility was the virtue that held these things in tension, and it was an antidote to pride in the ancient system of asceticism. One could not take pride in one's efforts because one knew one's place: all would return to dust and dirt, the appearance of success was only an illusion that deluded.

In the postmodern situation, humility's insistence upon the interconnectedness of all things becomes critically important. Visualizing, and thus experiencing, that interconnection provides a profound vision of the expansiveness of the divinization project and the minuteness of one's own effort. The ascetic experiences in this vision the fact that all existent beings, as science tells us, consist of the same atoms; even at the subatomic level, the basic elements of the universe are consistent and constant in plant, animal, human, air, water, solid substances, stars, galaxies, and all other elements that exist. The ascetic's recognition of that interconnectedness, and the placement of oneself into the context of such cosmic interconnectedness, constitutes humility, the recognition of one's proper place in the universe.

But humility goes much further: seekers unite their individual efforts to others' in the acknowledgment that no one lives isolated from another. One person's recycling of used bottles and plastics does not conserve the world, but one person's effort joined with many others has an enormous impact on the environment. This context of conjoined effort constitutes humility, because each seeker recognizes the necessity of relationship with other seekers in order to accomplish common aims. Likewise a community's effort to alleviate hunger in the world will not ultimately be successful without combining the efforts of many such communities working on multiple fronts to alleviate hunger locally, regionally, and globally. The combined effort provides a context for understanding the individual and local effort, and that context produces humility.

This understanding of humility, the recognition of one's proper place in the cosmos and one's interdependence with others, has a very positive outlook. Such a concept strengthens human effort rather than denigrating it and generates positive and constructive energy for divinization by individuals and groups of people.

47 / Embracing Difference

MOST RELIGIOUS COMMUNITIES prefer homogeneity, a singularity of class, values, economic status, race, politics, or religious identity. Communities tend to prefer such sameness because it creates and undergirds solidarity. Members of the community understand one another not through discourse and discovery, but by often unexpressed similarities of values and perspectives. The homogeneity of a community supports or expresses various perspectival preferences and values across a wide spectrum of subjects. The similarity of perspective creates a sense of safety, a bulwark against disagreement and confrontation among people who might differ in various ways from the norm established in a homogenous community. Such solidarity and homogeneity is not wrong or bad, but something that simply must be acknowledged.

Difference disrupts such solidarity. When divergent views, or practices, or races, or finances are introduced into a community, or when a community encounters such difference elsewhere, the solidarity and homogeneity are ruptured and a fissure is created. That fissure, that break in the facade, provides the ascetic with an opportunity for growth and transformation. The embracing of difference becomes an ascetical discipline, for the ascetic continually breaks old patterns of habitual living in order to enable and permit a new pattern to emerge, a new pattern more oriented toward the project of divinization. So the ascetic uses the encounter of difference as an opportunity to break the old identity and to inaugurate new dimensions of the emergent divinized person.

The encounter with difference demands discriminating attention. The discrimination involves establishing precisely how one person or situation differs from others. This discrimination requires careful analysis and attention to details in order not to skim the surface of difference, but to understand its depth and complexity. Underlying this attention to the details and specificity of difference is an important theological principle: all difference reflects the divinely inspired variety in the universe. If the divine impulse has been planted in all people, in every social grouping, and in the universe itself, then everyone and everything must be approached as the bearer of the divine in its infinite variety. The divine presents itself in every creature, event, person, and circumstance within the universe; therefore the encounter with difference becomes an encounter with the various manifestations of the divine.

To put this in another way, the encounter with difference presents an opportunity for new revelations of the divine. By comparing the way in which the divine manifests itself in various forms and manners in a wide variety of contexts, the ascetic begins to understand how the divine operates not only in the other, but also within the ascetic's own self. The revelation reflects backward on the ascetic, to reveal the inner workings of the ascetic's own alterity, while at the same time stretching forth to reveal the difference in that which the ascetic sees as different. Treating the encounter with difference as a revelatory process, the ascetic comes to value not only the ascetic's own values and perspectives, but also those of the other with which one's own perspective is being compared. The comparison creates a new solidarity, now not in homogeneity, but now in the communion of all things in the divine. The new solidarity underscores the commonality of all things in the infinite variety with which the divine is understood, expressed, manifested, and operative.

The embrace of difference, then, as an ascetical discipline, is a means of embracing the yet unknown and the yet unencountered reality of the divine in others. The embrace not only reveals but also expands, because the ascetic who embraces difference finds the old categories binding and restrictive and the new categories confrontational and challenging. The embrace of difference opens the ascetic to ever-divergent and new ways of seeing and knowing the divine. The embrace of alterity becomes a time to search out new ways of experiencing and instantiating the divine.

48 / Demons and Ascetic Evil .... ᒧꙿ

CHRISTIAN ASCETICAL TEXTS all refer to the battle of the ascetic with demons and the devil. In many respects this mythical and archetypal figure (the devil, with the army of demons attending) became the prime enemy to be combated by the struggling ascetic. Ascetics metaphorized this struggle as a war between the ascetic and the devil and demons. In fact, the ancient ascetical literature spends a disproportionate amount of space describing the demonic attacks, strategies, effects upon the ascetic, and changeable appearance of devil and demon. Ancient ascetics clearly engaged in a discourse and a study of demonic engagements. In desert monasticism the monk withdrew from the companionship of other monks to enter the desert alone in order to do battle solely with the demons, who became the monk's only and constant companions. The demons played an important role for the monk, and for ancient ascetics in general, because they taught the monk where the most growth and transformation were necessary. The demons pointed to lust, gluttony, pride, envy, anger, illusions of grandeur; and the monk immediately understood that this constituted the next arena to conquer in ascetical practice. The demonic, that is, played an important and positive role in the perfection of the monk.

Clearly this concept of the demonic must be differentiated from the general problem of evil, at least for the individual ascetic. In the postmodern world, where demons are no longer recognized as a part of the worldview, demons might more properly represent the tendency toward destructive patterns of behavior and thought that hinder one's progress toward divinization. The ascetic must confront these persistent debilitating patterns not as something exterior to the self, but as something arising within the self that prevents advancement toward divinization. Some of these demons, however, may also be exterior, that is, they may be persistent debilitating patterns of social relationships or social structures and institutions that impose themselves on the ascetic and prevent the ascetic from being able to progress and to advance. These social structures and institutions must also be confronted and mastered before the ascetic can make progress. In the case of individual and social debilitating patterns and structures, the ability to stop progress and to destroy the energy or ability of the ascetic to advance is enormous. Experientially, it is as though the ascetic has confronted a stronger and more powerful agency — but that is only the appearance, because through incremental and particular effort the ascetic will indeed overcome the obstacles and begin to advance again in the way toward divinization.

There is another nonascetic way of understanding evil, which does not relate to this ascetic system, but which refers to the general problem of evil in society. This evil shares characteristics with ascetical evil in that it revolves around persistent patterns of a person, a social group, or an institution that stand in the way toward divinization. This evil, however, exercises great power over individuals, societies, governments, and geographical spaces. The exercise of that power opposes the impulse toward divinization and thwarts efforts to image and to live in ways that bring about the divinization of individuals, societies, and the world at large. The combat with this evil ought not be treated as metaphorical, and the very positive role that the demons play in ascetic theology ought not to be projected on evil powers. As with the ascetic, evil persons or institutions may be known through their effect upon others. Such destructive and powerful forces are to be vigorously opposed with serious and intentional discernment of both motives and effects.

In the end, however, the true ascetic cannot yield ultimate authority to any kind of evil person, being, or institution. The usefulness of every encounter to the ascetical divinization seems to take precedence over all other issues of evil. The ascetic learns from successes as well as failures, from the divine impulse as well as from the forces that oppose the divine. All things ultimately will be incorporated into the divinized self, society, and cosmos.

49 / Praying the Bodies .... ⟳

PRAYER INVOLVES turning toward the divine. The divine is present
both within the person, in the community of believers, and in the
universe; yet the divine is simultaneously transcendent to all existent
beings. Prayer simply involves entering discursively into the mystery
of the divine presence. The discursive nature of this encounter with
the divine mystery involves not just words, but actions and reactions,
images, music, motion, smell, and all the other means by which humans commune with one another and with the divine. Prayers may
be spontaneously enacted by an individual, or they may be set prayers
(words, rituals, actions) that connect the person to a wider community, or they may simply be the intellectual and emotional sense of the
union of all things in the divine. The variety of prayer is infinite.

Each of the bodies must learn to pray. The individual body turns attention to the interior presence of the divine, and engages that presence
through words, or gestures, or images. The interior divine presence
does not stand apart from that presence in other people, in societies,
in nature, and in the cosmos, but functions as a localized presence
available to the individual at any time.

That conversation with the interior divine presence begins the process of connecting the individual to wider communities, a process that
leads to praying through the social body. Beginning with the assembly
of those who form the social body, the seeker begins to pray in the
assembly as it is present in the imagination. Here all the influences,
the various parts of the individual's social body, enter the discourse
with the divine. The seeker, then, prays not only through the discourse emergent from the seeker's own prayer, but also through the
prayers refracted through the prayerful encounters of all those in the
social body. Reaching back into the past, the seeker may pray in the
manner of a beloved relative, or a familiar saint who has influenced
the seeker's life, or a traditional method of prayer that has had an
important impact on the seeker. Reaching out to those still living and
present, the seeker prays through the personalities of family members,
friends, colleagues, and others whose distinct personalities both inhabit the individual body and whose presence and influence continue
to be felt.

Both the individual and the social body seek out the prayer of
the corporate body. For the Christian, this corporate body includes
not simply the local congregation of which the seeker is a part, but

also the regional and denominational connections of that congregation. The corporate body extends from that specific tradition to the whole body of Christ throughout the world and throughout history. The discourse that emerges from the entry of individual-body prayer and social-body prayer into the corporate environment enlivens and energizes the conversation and communion with the divine. The identities and personalities of all the bodies are mutually transformed and reformed by the interaction that shifts boundaries of identity under the influence of union with the divine.

Perhaps the most important facet of praying with the various bodies revolves around the shift and transposition of perspectives that takes place. In the discourse with the divine, the individual body, the social body, and the corporate body continually shift in perspective both on the divine and on the process of divinization. What appears sure in one environment shifts and changes in another, and what seems weak in one environment becomes strong and central by association with the others.

Praying the bodies is not a static phenomenon, but rather changes and transforms itself as the goal of divinization itself undergoes the constant changes in proximate goals. As the understanding of the divine increases in complexity over time, so will the manner, expression, and understanding of prayer; and prayer itself will continually adjust to the shifting images of divinization that emerge from the conversation. Praying the bodies is central to the ascetic project of divinization.

50 / Sacraments and Life

A SCETICS BECAME SACRAMENTS. Ancient ascetics of the desert tradition withdrew from the church and its sacraments, believing that a strong identification with an organized church made the advancement toward divinization too complex and too complicated. Many monks avoided the sacraments as implicating them too much in the way of the world from which they had withdrawn. Western monasticism, in its primarily communal (coenobitic) form, incorporated the appropriate sacraments into its communal life, regularly celebrating the Eucharist and requiring the sacrament of penance or confession. In either system, the ascetic became a sacrament: an outward and visible sign of an inward and spiritual grace, as the tradition defines it. The ascetic attended to the interior presence of the divine and strove to manifest that presence in body and life.

The tradition defines seven sacraments. The two chief sacraments are baptism, the rite of regeneration (West) and illumination (East), and the Eucharist, the celebration of the transformation of the bread and wine into the body and blood of Jesus Christ and the sanctification of the local congregation as the body of Christ in the world. The five secondary sacraments are: confirmation (West) or chrismation (East), the sanctification and empowerment of the person to live the Christian life; confession or penance, the restoration to baptismal glory after sinning and repenting; holy orders, the setting apart of clerics for the offices of the church; holy matrimony, the sanctification of marriage and the family; and holy unction, an anointing for death (West), or the sacrament of healing (East). These seven sacraments laid out an organized system for the consecration of stages of life for any believer.

In a more general and theological sense, sacraments are rites and practices that acknowledge and solidify the union of the divine and the human in concrete existence. Sacraments make instrumental and visible the reality of the divine union with existent beings, and they order and structure the religious life around that reality. The ordering of the sacraments, and the continual repetition of those that could be repeated (Eucharist, confession, unction) provided the structure for the common believer to advance toward sanctification and renewal by incremental stages. That is, the sacraments constituted an ascetical system imposed by the church on the daily life of common believers, and in that sense the sacraments made ascetics of all believers.

Monastic ascetics fled the sacraments because that order and ascetic discipline did not align with the path toward sanctification and divinization they had chosen. The two paths conflicted in their organization and structure, so the ascetics by necessity chose other sacramental rites to order and structure their lives. These early monks sacramentalized the clothing of a new monk, when the novice monk started on the road toward divinization; the taking of the greater schema (an article of clothing worn by monks under their habit and given to them at their clothing); and the monk's profession of lifelong and total commitment to divinization above all else. They also sacramentalized the relationship of the elder to the less experienced monk and the weekly community meeting (*synaxis*), when the monks came together for prayer, vigil, instruction, and the weekly celebration of the Eucharist. Confession was not necessarily to a priest, but to an elder ascetic further along the path of personal divinization; it played an important part of the desert monastic experience.

In the postmodern context, there still stands a need for sacramentalizing life, but not necessarily a need to tie all such sacraments to the traditional seven. As the ascetic image and instantiation of the eschatological vision of divinization shifts and changes through the ascetic's efforts and over time, there will be occasions when temporary and interim acts will be needed to demarcate one stage, or one time, or one event from all others as a turning point in divinization of self, society, and cosmos. Postmodern sacraments might include such acts as having regular family dinners together or going to a film and spending an evening discussing it or climbing mountains with intentional friends so as to participate in the natural environment in a special way.

Sacraments, in other words, will continue to acknowledge and witness to the union of human and divine, existent beings with the divine, but will do so in ways more responsive to the shifting and changing interim goals toward divinization. The order, arising from within the chaos of enormous numbers of efforts both personal and corporate toward divinization, gathers a space as a platform, or an event as a boundary, to provide sure footing in the midst of a constantly moving stream of efforts toward divinization. The sacraments provide the stability in the midst of the innumerable images of divinization to evaluate and project new images and new visions of the divine. These sacraments will reflect things that the tradition could never have envisioned, and like the monks of the desert, will reflect the need to define and redefine for the immediate context new ways of sacramentalizing life.

51 / Ascetic Confession

A T THE HEART of the monastic desert tradition of asceticism stood confession. Perhaps the heart of all communal monastic asceticism revolves around the revelation of one's thoughts and sins to a spiritual master. In an ascetic environment, this confession, the acknowledgment of oneself to another and the disclosure of one's most intimate and (often) frightening thoughts to another, grounded the personal struggle and personal self-understanding in a sacramentalized

relationship with an elder ascetic. The stated purpose of monastic ascetic confession was manifold: to release the novice from the burden
of the interior thoughts that would compulsively inhibit progress toward divinization; to comfort a younger ascetic when difficulties and
temptations arose that were too embarrassing to acknowledge and were
humiliating to the self; to cleanse the way of past patterns of behavior
in order to clear the way for new; and to socialize the personal effort
of the novice ascetic by linking the novice's struggle to that of another,
one more experienced and more seasoned in the ways of divinization.

In the postmodern situation the linking of the personal ascetical
discourse to that of another, to a seasoned and experienced ascetic,
provides the basis for important discernment about self and progress.
Ascetical confession establishes the link of one to another so that a
person may recognize delusion and begin to redress it. The socializing
of the interior processes, understood as confession, protects the ascetic
from proceeding along paths that ultimately will not lead to divinization. Self-examination in this sense, before another person, guards the
ascetic and secures the means of intervention in case of difficulty.

But the postmodern ascetic confession also bears a corporate responsibility. Communities need to examine themselves in relationship to
their delusions and sins whenever they gather. In other words, just as
individuals need to be responsible to another, to socialize their interior
struggle, so must communities who are pursuing divinization. Communities must examine themselves to reveal the elements and factors
detrimental to their progress, and to see impediments and hindrances
to the achievement of their articulated purposes. The community
must continually examine its interior organization, its effectiveness
in pursuing its aims, the appropriateness of the interim steps toward
divinization, and all other aspects of its corporate life. Corporate confession and self-examination becomes an important instrument for the
continued sanity and safety of the community.

In the postmodern context ascetic persons or communities ought
also to examine their relationship to the natural world. It is no longer
sufficient to look at human lives individually or socially as the only
concern for the process of divinization; ascetics individually and cor-
porately must examine their relationship to the natural world. The
environment, including all the natural resources of water, air, and earth
also manifest the presence of the divine. Ascetics, therefore, must examine themselves in relationship to the way in which they have either
abused or enhanced the environment. Abuse of the environment, like

a devastating thought or action needing confession, signals a pattern of behavior inimical to sanctification. The natural world may no longer be separated from the realm of the divine; individual and corporate ascetics must consider it part of their responsibility and therefore subject to their confession.

Finally, in the postmodern situation individual and corporate ascetics must also examine themselves as they relate to societies different from their own and to religions different from, and perhaps inimical to, their own. Like the natural environment, other societies, cultures, and religions are a part of the universe humans inhabit. The treatment of the other, regardless of what that "other" is, reveals the inner development of the ascetic. Hatred, mistrust, or demonization of the other indicates the presence of serious hindrances to divinization. Respect, understanding, and acknowledgment of the legitimate status of the other point toward the incorporation of all things into the way of divinization. They indicate a degree of ascetical success.

Ascetic confession, then, represents an important tool for assessing the impediments toward divinization and imagining new ways of moving forward. By socializing the interior life in relationship to more experienced ascetics, the individual protects against delusion. By insisting upon ascetic confession for the community, not only is delusion avoided, but also the community has a vital and honest means of assessing progress and effectiveness on its way toward divinization. By expanding the horizons of ascetical responsibility to include both the natural environment and people of other cultures and religions, the postmodern ascetic acknowledges and witnesses to the divine presence in all existent beings, and unites self to the divine presence working mysteriously in every person, society, and universe.

52 / Utopia

N ON-ASCETICS HAVE OFTEN accused ascetics of pursuing utopia. They say ascetics promulgate futile efforts to create what ultimately can never be attained or real. This is a legitimate accusation, and it is true: ascetics pursue a utopia, the divinization of the self, of all societies, and of the universe itself. Divinization indeed constitutes a utopia: it is idealized, fictionalized, perfectionist, demanding the best efforts of all people, and ultimately remains unattainable. The

patterns of divinized living and relating, thinking and feeling, and functioning in the universe will never be fully instantiated. And the ascetic
embraces this utopian drive with joy and energy.

The pursuit of utopia creates a holy chaos, which energizes and
vivifies the ascetic. The very fact that utopias are idealized and
perfectionist, and thus unattainable and impractical, makes them dramatically attractive. Ascetics yearn deeply and passionately for things
that, from most perspectives, simply never will be real; they will always remain beyond the ability and capacity of any person, any social
group, or even the universe itself. And this captivates the ascetics'
imagination.

A utopia stimulates the imagination precisely because it contrasts
what is present and functioning with what might be. In a utopia,
present reality meets eschatological vision, and the imagination of the
ascetic immediately begins to ruminate on the manner of getting from
the present to that eschatological end. The fissure created by the contrast of what is with what might be actually overthrows the dominance
and hegemony of present patterns of living. Utopias unseat and dises-
tablish current identities, social organizations, religious movements,
governmental agencies — life in its most complete description. Current realities tend to appear ineffective and unsavory in the presence of
the utopian vision. And the ascetic begins to envision ways of moving
toward the utopia. The ascetic, relying on an interior divine impulse
and the experience of knowing the potentialities of self, society, and
universe, begins to envision the incremental steps that will lead from
this to that, from the present to the eschatological, from the possible
to the impossible. Step by small step, the ascetic advances toward the
utopian vision, incrementally instantiating small, negligible elements
of that vision in the present. As progress is made, the ascetic adjusts
the utopian vision to accommodate the new learning and experience
encountered in the pursuit. The incremental steps constitute a creative
overthrow of current and existent identities and structures in order to
instantiate almost subversively a utopian vision.

Utopias create holy chaos. The fissure creates an energy, a force,
a drive for re-visioning the nature of individual life, for rethinking
and reordering social relations, and for reimagining the nature and
meaning of the universe. This rupture in hegemonic and established
systems of identity, social relations, and understanding of the universe dismantles the structures from which the ascetic withdraws and

simultaneously posits an image for the ascetic to pursue. This creative withdrawal may only occur in the presence of a utopia that draws the ascetic into new and different ways of living, ways that often are in conflict with current identities and structures. In this way, a utopia concentrates the ascetic's energies and efforts in the process of struggling. The pursuit of the utopia draws out the best of the ascetic, because both the utopian and the ascetical life demand vigorous effort. The process of gradually instantiating a utopia of divinization defines exactly the heart of the ascetical process, namely, to struggle as individuals or as social groups to divinize the self, society, and the universe. The holy chaos of a utopia begins the road toward divinization, and the ascetic looks into the eschatological and impossible future and rejoices.

53 / Withdrawal

T HE FIRST STEP is withdrawal. In many ascetical religious systems, the first step toward pursuing holiness or divinization requires a withdrawal or retirement from the world of daily activity, including family and other social relationships, business, and engagement with affairs in the public realm. Such a "retirement from the world" as it is known, created a psychological and religious space for a new person to emerge. Withdrawal intended to disengage energy and effort from common responsibilities, which constructed a particular identity and came with specific entanglements and responsibilities, and to begin immediately with all the resources and energy available to construct the new identity, that of the ascetic pursuing holiness or divinization. The traditional metaphor, deep in the psyche of Western asceticism, describes a withdrawal from the city to the desert in order to pursue the ascetic life.

This traditional concept of withdrawal, however, came at a price. Ascetics were encouraged to reject "the world" and its entanglements as a fruitless arena, leaving it to people not pursuing divinization as their primary realm. The radical separation of the realm of divinization from all other realms betrays the incarnational theology that makes asceticism attractive, especially in the postmodern world where such distinctions no longer hold. Incarnational theology demands the interconnection of every person, thing, and realm so that everyone and everything may reveal the presence of the divine. Withdrawal, however, did not necessarily exist as a means to denigrate the entanglements with public affairs and family, for example, but rather to create a space and energy for creating something new, something different, something firmly established in a divinized identity and a divinized way of relating not yet realized and instantiated in the ascetic's current life.

It is true that once the ascetic desires to pursue divinization, an immediate need emerges for a psychological, social, and political space for the new, divinized person to develop. One cannot simply add divinization in this sense to an old identity, because divinization requires a complete deconstruction of the old identity in order to construct and create a new, divinized one. The process of deconstructing the old identity, old social relationships, and the old symbolic universe does indeed separate a person from those past patterns of behavior, relationship, and understanding. But the deconstruction and construction process takes place firmly in the context of the daily life of the ascetic. The ascetic withdraws in order to transform or remake the self in the context of its mundane and routinized living. Ascetic withdrawal inaugurates the process of transforming and reconstructing that mundane and routinized living. It is not withdrawal from it, but the renewal of daily entanglements from the perspective of divinization.

In the postmodern world ascetic withdrawal should be understood in terms of entering the ascetic imaginary. The ascetic withdraws from the imaginary of the world as it is currently lived; enters into the process of imaginatively constructing a vision of the divine and of divinization that compels attention; and then enters into the divinized and ascetic imaginary as the site for the deconstruction of the old and the construction of the new pattern of living. In other words, the space is not a place, a geographical withdrawal from city to desert, but the space for withdrawal is an imaginary space where the compelling images of divinized living transform the basis for imagining and living life in any place. The creative use of imagination, of entering into a divinized imaginary, enables the ascetic to experience the same sort of withdrawal that ancient monks experienced in withdrawing from city to desert, but without denigrating the sanctity and potentially revelatory nature of all existence and all patterns of life. Ascetic withdrawal, then, has a very positive role: the construction of a divinized person who is capable of living, relating, and understanding a completely divinized view of the self, society, and universe.

54 / The Divine Mystery

T HE DIVINE IS A MYSTERY. Despite thousands of years of effort to know and to describe the divine in human language, every theologian and religious practitioner ultimately and finally concedes that the divine remains a mystery. The divine, by virtue of operating beyond the categories of human imagining, simply stands beyond human comprehension. The mystery of the divine, however, does not conclude searching and the will to articulate, but rather draws the believer and the seeker into the desire to know the mystery more and more, to grasp at the ungraspable ever more intently, to peer into the ultimately unknowable in order to challenge the very basis of human knowing. That creates the wonder of the mystery.

The Christian tradition maintains a threefold approach to the divine: the kataphatic, the apophatic, and the unitive. These methods of gaining more and more experience of the mystery, and hence more knowledge of the divine, have provided a means of encountering and organizing that which is beyond experience and organization. They provide lenses through which the seeker may apprehend beyond the normal human means of knowing and studying.

The kataphatic way (the way according to speech) explores the nature of the divine mystery by adducing the various attributes of the divine in human language. Seekers know the divine as the creator of all things, the subsistence of all humans, the energizer of everything that is good, the opponent of evil, the sustenance of the poor and weak, the healer of the sick, the advocate of justice for all, the glue of every religious community, the end of all effort, the ruler of the universe, the energy that guides evolution, and many more attributes accumulated to present a verbally and intelligibly articulate description of the divine. Of course, these all remain verbal approximations, because the divine remains ultimately beyond the human capacity to verbalize.

The apophatic way (the way of negating speech) practices a discipline of negating everything that may be postulated regarding the divine. If, for example, one stipulates that "the divine is the creator of all things" is a kataphatic statement, the apophatic response says "the divine is far beyond any category of creation." The negation of categories recognizes two factors: first, that all the categories remain firmly rooted in human language and therefore remain inadequate; and second, that all human conceptualization cannot ultimately comprehend or articulate the reality of the divine, which far surpasses human understanding. The apophatic way works to bring the seeker to an experience of the divine that substitutes for the inadequate and limited language about the divine. The apophatic experience stands as a primary experience of a mystery beyond human categorization.

The unitive way builds on the apophatic, and strives to move beyond mere verbal experience of the divine to the sustained relationship with the divine beyond known human categories. The unitive way attempts to meld the postcategorical human experience of the divine and the real presence of the divine into one composite and united state of being. In the unitive way the divine and the human not only meet, but mutually enjoy the other's real presence.

In the tradition these three ways form a sequence, with the kataphatic way for beginners or novices, the apophatic way for the more advanced, and the unitive way for adepts in the ascetical life. In the postmodern context these three methods should be treated as different lenses through which the human may come to comprehend the reality of the divine. Furthermore, from the postmodern incarnational perspective, the relationship of human and divine begins from the unitive. Since there is no separation of human from divine, no divide to be filled by human intellection and action, the divine dwells in the human person as a reality and as an impulse animating the thoughts, actions, and relations of the person. The unitive way founds the incarnational basis for all understanding and action, both of the individual and the social body, and therefore becomes the foundation of both kataphatic and apophatic means of knowing.

All of this, even in the postmodern situation, firmly rests on the mystery of the divine. That is, even the unitive way recognizes that the relationship of human to divine, and the divine reality and presence itself, ultimately and finally defies understanding. The divine remains mysterious and draws humans into the contemplation and consideration of the divine mystery, a divinity that far surpasses the human mind to comprehend.

55 / Charting a Way .... ∽

T HE PATHS TOWARD divinization are infinite. They depend not only
on the number of people and groupings of people who pursue
them, but also upon the variability resulting from the revised visions and images of divinization that occur along the way. This may
cause consternation among those people and groups who need absolute
surety about their direction and action, and a sense of unchanging or
eternal properties. But the ascetic rejoices in pursuing a path toward divinization, albeit variable and changing as knowledge and experience
shift, that unites, not in content but in practice, a wide assortment
of people and groups throughout the world and throughout history.
The pursuit of the way of divinization valorizes the effort for the
ascetic.

Thus charting a way toward divinization for an individual or a community becomes an important process; the chart gathers up various
experiences, desires, images, and aims and sets a direction for initial
action and contemplation. The ascetic knows that these paths are interim and temporary, but still the charting of a path organizes and
directs the energy toward divinization.

Many factors implicate the process of charting a way. Individual
ascetics must assess their particular gifts and resources, their peculiar vision of the divine, their personal experience and knowledge. The
path will be tailored to the way in which individual ascetics operate
in the world, and hence each path will be different from every other
path. Individual ascetics' own promptings and inclinations form an
important basis for charting a way, and give incarnate reality and particularity to the path being pursued. But individual ascetics do not live
in a vacuum. They are part of religious, social, and political groups
that also impinge upon the process of charting a way. Individuals, as
part of groups, join their vision to the various groups in which the individual participates, and contrarily, groups have a profound influence
on the way individuals know and experience the world, and the way
they operate in society and the cosmos. The assessment of the social
gifts and resources, as well as an honest appraisal of the needs of the
world and universe, begin to set a direction not only for the individual
but also for various groups of seekers of all sorts. Individuals in their
social and communal contexts begin to chart a way toward divinization, looking not just to the divinization of the individual, but also to
the paths that individuals chart together as social groupings.

Charting paths toward divinization, however, displays a dynamic alternating between solid, clear direction and the chaos that follows from its dissolution. As a path toward divinization is charted, it imposes an order on the process, expectations, and specific practices. That order provides the structure and direction for pursuing the aims articulated by individuals and groups. Following the charted path provides important information, which emerges from unfolding experience and growing understanding of the people, the groupings, and the environment of divinization; this information requires adjustment of the charted path. The adjustments begin the contrary process of dissolving the order and direction, and plunging ascetics and communities into a process of reconsideration and revisioning. Again, the factors involved in charting a path come into play and new directions, with new paths, are pursued.

The dissolution of the charted path, like the deconstruction of the habituated person, remains a positive phenomenon. The dynamic of charting a path and its dissolution forces ascetics continually to orient themselves not to a specific, universal, and unchanging path, but to the continual reflection upon the interior divine impulse and the presence of the divine in the existent universe. The dynamic of order and chaos shifts attention from the proximate and intermediate stages to the ultimate state of divinization.

56 / Exercises

T HE CHRISTIAN SPIRITUAL TRADITION, as well as many other religions, specify daily prayer and meditation. The tradition called these spiritual exercises, and promoted them as the bedrock or foundation for the religious life. Unfortunately only professional religious practiced these spiritual exercises — such as male and female monks or priests — whose position both required these daily exercises and provided significant time to accomplish them. Because of the time necessary to perform these exercises the layperson, generally a working person, was exempt from performing them. Even with that caveat, the pattern of daily spiritual exercise demands attention, even if only for the purpose of learning the tradition and retrieving whatever parts of it might work for seekers in the postmodern context.

The cycle of these traditional spiritual exercises patterns itself on the course of the day. In the morning, upon rising and before anything else is done, the ascetic turns the mind to the divine in praiseful morning prayer. This pattern of morning prayer frequently includes the recitation of the psalms; the regular cycle completes the entire Psalter in the course of a week or a month. Morning prayer also includes readings from scripture, prayers for the consecration of the day and its labors, intercessions for personal, social, and worldwide needs, and a hymn of praise to the divine. Various arrangements of these elements exist in different Christian denominational traditions. Sacred reading follows immediately upon morning prayer. Sacred reading involves a meditative reading of a spiritually classic text. The ascetic reads a section, meditates on its meaning and significance, applies it to the ascetic's own life and context, and then turns in prayer to the divine for guidance and direction. This meditative reading brings the spiritual tradition into the context of an individual's life and labor. Both morning prayer and sacred reading present the ascetic with the path toward divinization, and provide the ascetic an opportunity to live in the imaginary of that path, actualized and realized in the present moment. They set the direction and tone for the day.

According to the tradition, the working part of the day is filled with "pious practices," devotions intended to keep the mind and effort focused on the process of divinization while performing one's daily work. These practices include bringing the memory of the divine forward; saying cyclical meditative prayers, often using beads that organize and present the fruits of previous meditative sessions; prayers before and after various tasks; prayers before meals; the recitation of litanies; lighting candles before sacred images; and many others. These pious practices intended to bring the fruit of morning prayer and sacred reading into active play during the day in order to extend the benefit of the ascetic's morning exercises throughout the day. They were infinitely varied and the choice of them was left entirely to the ascetic or seeker.

In some traditions, there is a comparable evening prayer that complements the task of morning prayer after the completion of the working portion of the day. These evening prayers are often more meditative, but they consist of the same elements as morning prayer: recitation of psalms, reading of scripture, prayers and intercessions, and a hymn. Their intention, however, is to bring to a close the active part of the day in order to turn to the evening as a time of leisure and relaxation.

The cycle of prayer concludes with the prayers at the end of the day, and the process of self-evaluation and examination. These concluding prayers often consist of psalms appropriate to the end of the day, prayers for a restful and divinely directed sleep, hymns appropriate to the evening, and intercessions that commend the concerns of the day to the divine. After these prayers, the tradition directs the ascetic to the examination of the self, to the exploration of the successes and failures of the day, and to set resolves for the following day. This examination is not intended to create guilt or to condemn the ascetic, but to place the day into the context of the effort toward divinization, and to set the tone and direction for the following day. Thus the ascetic always has some bearing upon the direction and content of the progress toward divinization.

These traditional spiritual exercises may not be applicable in a postmodern context, but the principle of regular and consistent patterns of prayer offers postmodern ascetics the opportunity consistently to turn the mind and effort to the divine in the midst of a seemingly endless flow of information, demands, and responses. The interruption of that flow of energy in order to redirect attention toward the process of divinization has great potential. The specific pattern of these exercises, however, needs to be adjusted to the individual ascetic's personal and social context.

57 / Living in Community .... ᘒ

THE CHRISTIAN MONASTIC TRADITION, particularly in the West, recognizes the particular difficulty of living in community. Thus it established the exercise of living in community as a specific ascetic discipline. The tradition recognizes that being born into a community, or choosing to live in a particular community, does not actually equip a person to do so effectively. The demands of living with so many others, whether of one's choosing or by one's birth, are so great and so distracting that they need to be regulated by particular training. Anyone who has ever tried to live in an intentional community knows the difficulty and the challenges of doing so. The tradition correctly stipulates that to live effectively in community demands particular training.

The problem, and the joy, of living in community focuses upon the loss of one's center. When alone, the individual person imaginatively creates and lives a life entirely from a personal perspective, and then organizes social relationships and tasks from that highly individual place. But when many such individuals come together to live in community, then the center or focus must shift, because an intentional community cannot exist simply as a conglomerate of individual attitudes and directions.

The discipline of living in community demands that the individual ascetic makes space within the self for alternative and conflicting perspectives experienced as one's own, even though they originate outside the self. The boundary of the self must become sufficiently permeable to admit the presence of alternative identities that intrude and, perhaps conflict, with the central focus of the self. The ascetic, already adept at constructing a personal social body, will quickly learn that this process resembles that of constructing a communal social body; the ascetic then learns to live with the ambiguity and multiple directions of such a communal body. In community, however, the construction of a communal body has less to do with the center of one's own self and more to do with living with people who have their own social bodies, which they present to the corporate body. The more fluid and permeable the boundaries, the more these other people and their social bodies will be able to become part of the ascetic's own body. In short, a community is formed as one opens oneself to the existence of others within the orbit of the individual self.

From the perspective of the community, the various selves and their social bodies must cohere in such a way as to open the lives of each to the lives of the other, not as separated and isolated beings but as part of the self. The community constructs a communal body consisting of the individual and social bodies of all its members. That social body of the community, then, begins to take on the same dimensions and directions as an individual's social body; it begins to set a course toward divinization and to pursue it with energy and devotion.

Each individual ascetic living in community learns to adjust the self to the patterns and directions not only of each other individual in the community but also to the community as a whole. Life in community demands constant attention to the permeability of the self and the expansion of one's perspective to accommodate that of many others. This forms the heart of the ascetic task of living in community — the adjustment of the self to include others and to merge with others in processes and activities leading toward divinization.

In traditional language, this process consists in the rejection or suppression of the ego or the will. That is not entirely correct. It is not really a rejection or suppression but a matter of making room, of accommodating the lives of others, within the self. The expansion of the self demands that the ascetic work with his or her own attitudes and deal with the conflicts created by others, but this process does not in itself constitute either a suppression or a rejection. This expansion rather represents a deliberate permeating of the boundaries of the self to include and involve others.

58 / Spiritual Direction ....

T HE ASCETIC TRADITION almost universally recommends spiritual direction. It advises that each seeker, each novice ascetic, establish a relationship with what the tradition calls a "spiritual director," an experienced and advanced guide of persons toward divinization. The tradition contends that this formative relationship is central and critical to the process of advancement toward divinization, and it cannot be circumvented. Although the tradition links such a relationship and its import to the submission of the individual seeker to the authority of another person who represents both the institutional and divine hierarchy, the postmodern seeker will find that such a relationship provides important access to the understanding of his or her own self, the knowledge and exposure to otherwise unknown parts of the ascetic tradition, and engagement with a sure and tested companion on the way toward divinization. The relationship of seeker to spiritual director, though potentially dangerous, constitutes one of the central relationships for the seeker's advancement toward divinization.

The spiritual guide focuses attention on the particularity of a seeker's constitution; this describes the chief advantage for the seeker. The guide brings to one particular seeker the entirety of the tradition and knowledge of the ways of advancement. It is precisely in this particularity of the seeker's constitution that the most pronounced advancement may be made, and so the guide assists in tailoring the path toward divinization to the particular character, sensibilities, desires, and inclinations of the seeker. Therefore the seeker must choose a guide well advanced on the path of divinization, whose struggles and contexts mirror those of the seeker, and whose character and bearing embody for the seeker the seeker's own vision of the divinized life.

In choosing a guide, the seeker must understand the guide's role. The guide is a loving advocate of the seeker's progress toward divinization. The guide's advocacy spurs the seeker to continue along the way of divinization even when progress seems small or ineffective, but the guide does so in a way that lovingly understands both the frustrations of the seeker and the ways of progress. The guide also stands as a frank and honest companion. When the seeker attempts to delude the self into thinking that progress has been made, or that a problem really need not be faced, or that the impediments on the way are not real, or that the progress that has been made is not sufficient, the guide engages the seeker as an honest companion who will speak the truth of the situation as the guide perceives it. This honesty, especially from a loving advocate, enables the seeker to delve deeper into the seeker's own constitution and proclivities in order to further the process of advancement. The guide, then, functions as one who enables the seeker to progress by probing all the underlying desires, patterns of behavior and reaction, impediments, and advancement. The guide directs the seeker to probe deeper, to plumb the depths of the seeker's own character and propensities, gifts and demons, in order continually to make progress at the deepest level of the seeker's constitution and life. Finally, a guide must be a person knowledgeable in the tradition of divinization and capable of communicating that knowledge to the seeker in effective ways. That knowledge of the tradition must be extensive, so as the seeker progresses and discovers the need for different forms of prayer and meditation, or different practices, or new ways of relating to others and to the world, the guide, knowing the tradition, will be equipped to offer the riches of the experience of the past to the seeker. The guide may also be able to develop new ways of praying or acting that will more specifically accommodate the unique character of the seeker. This ability to tailor the tradition to the particular seeker requires that the guide know the tradition thoroughly.

The seeker, on the other hand, must understand the nature of the relationship to the guide. The seeker's choice of guide should be based on an affectionate respect. The affection arises because the guide embodies an image of divinization, or more properly an image of progress toward divinization, that attracts the seeker. The respect comes from the recognition that the guide holds necessary knowledge and experience valuable to the seeker. The seeker, moreover, must have an expectant trust in the guide. The relationship is a particularly intimate one, and therefore it must be founded on trust that the guide seeks only to advocate for the divinization of the seeker. That trust incrementally increases as the relationship develops and deepens. Finally, the seeker must be vigilantly pliant toward the guide. The guide directs the seeker in the transformation and reformation of the self on its way toward divinization, opening new and different avenues of advancement while closing off avenues of less success or opportunity. The seeker's pliancy allows the movement in new directions, often just prior to comfort with that new direction, pushing the edge of the seeker's own growth just noticeably beyond the current horizon of knowledge and understanding. But that requires vigilance as well. The seeker must be careful that the guide's prompting will maintain the health and sanity of the seeker, a health and sanity that only the seeker may affirm.

There are also serious dangers in the relationship of seeker to guide, and potential for harm. The intimacy and the sure knowledge of the seeker could be abused, and the intimacy move in directions not conducive to the seeker's progress and health. Discernment regarding this relationship must always be exercised.

59 / Sodalities

T HE LITERATURE OF ancient Christian monasticism often portrays the early monks as seeking companionship. Texts reveal monks seeking other monks, or groups of monks, who lived a similar life and sought the same goal of divinization. These groups often differed significantly, and so offered a perspective on living the ascetic life and advancing toward divinization from a different perspective and in a different context. The tradition, that is, often relates the importance of engaging alternative readings and understandings on the practice of the religious life aimed toward divinization.

For the ancient monks, this involved a number of differences: a geographical difference (they traveled to a different part of the monastic world to engage their colleagues); a theological difference (they sought the counsel of others whose direction was similar but whose practices and orientations differed); and a practical difference (the monks learned different techniques for the conduct of lives aimed toward divinization). These monks formed temporary sodalities of like-directed people; they submitted their manner of life to the scrutiny of others and learned from those who lived in divergent and distinctive communities but pursued similar aims and goals. The connection between these different groups of monks, which came into existence in a temporary sodality, offered both groups an opportunity to discern the veracity of their practices; to review the effectiveness of their own practice; to re-image the final divinization and the paths that lead to it; and to revise their own manner of living to conform more articulately with their common goal.

Standing outside one's own common relationships and viewing one's own ascetic practice from the perspective of other, supportive but very different ascetics provide the seeker with important information. Entering a sodality of like-directed people, the seeker becomes part of a larger movement toward divinization in a context at once unfamiliar and foreign but also consistent and mutual. This affords seekers an opportunity to view their own lives and practices from the perspective of others, to discern the ways that are most helpful and productive, and to discover new and different ways of achieving mutual goals. Additionally, seekers find comfort and support in the pursuit of similar objectives among a wider assortment of ascetics, so that the difficult labor of instantiating the divine and seeking divinization of self, society, and cosmos may be experienced as part of a larger movement and something far beyond one's own personal endeavors.

The creation of sodalities, however, does not simply provide comfort, encouragement, a time of renewal, and discovery of new techniques. Sodalities also provide important discernment. By engaging with like-directed people outside the normal orbit of social and religious relationships, these sodalities hold up a mirror to the direction and practice of seekers. That mirrored reflection enables all members of the sodality to discern the health and authenticity of the lives of the other. In these sodalities a potential exists for the discovery of error, delusion, and abuse of the ascetical practices and aims. It also provides a means of addressing and redirecting the interim steps toward eschatological divinization. Sodalities, even very temporary ones, provide the means of authenticating and evaluating the ascetic life and protect the various groups from straying too far into unhealthy and misdirected ways.

The refreshment experienced by the ancient monks was a refreshment based not on relaxation but on authentication. By submitting their lives to the scrutiny of others, which enabled both a correction of erroneous practices and the endorsement of effective means, the monks became confident that their efforts were indeed bearing fruit and that their divinization was in fact being accomplished incrementally. That knowledge from an outside perspective refreshed their lives and encouraged them on the road toward divinization.

These sodalities must be distinguished from communities. A community consists of an increment of homogeneity, a commonality that is built and supported consistently over a long period of time. Communities become part of the fabric of daily and habitual living. A sodality, on the other hand, represents an alternative and preferably critical association that remains more temporary. The alterity of the sodality is central: in seeking to form a sodality an ascetic should seek out those whose perspectives and orientations are critical and significantly different from the ascetic's own. Without such a perspective from outside one's community, no true discernment can take place.

60 / Stages

THE CHRISTIAN ASCETICAL TRADITION has articulated three stages of growth in the religious life: the purgative, the illuminative, and the unitive. The tradition supposes a wide distance between the person and the divine; thus the stages describe the gradual progress toward becoming more and more godlike over the course of a seeker's life. In other words, the tradition founded itself upon an understanding of the religious life that does not take incarnate reality seriously, a perspective not acceptable in the postmodern context.

In the postmodern context the stages of the religious life may be conceptualized as modalities of responding to the presence of the divine in person, society, and universe. The stages, that is, do not describe levels of achievement, as in the older tradition, but ways in which the person responds to the incarnate divinity.

The initial stage, comparable to the purgative of the tradition, describes the first awakening of the knowledge and experience of the divine presence. The seeker comes to know, either suddenly or over a period of time, that a divine impulse operates within; this impulse calls the seeker to live in a different way. The awakening of the knowledge of the divine presence creates in the seeker a desire to cooperate with that divine presence and to pursue a path of divinization. This stage of discovery simultaneously looks back with sorrow over the seeker's prior life, a sorrow based not on a sense of unworthiness but rather on a sense of having lived an unfulfilled or unsatisfying life. That sorrow feeds the desire to explore more fully the parameters and implications of the divine presence. This initial stage is exploratory; the reality and meaning of the divine presence begins to take hold, opening new possibilities for the manner one conceives of self, social relationships, and one's place in the universe in relationship to the divine presence now known and perceived.

The intermediary stage, comparable to the illuminative of the tradition, describes the first efforts at instantiating the divine in self, society, and universe. Based on the experience of the divine presence, the seeker attempts in this stage to deliberately refashion the self, to transform social relationships, and to reconceive the nature of the universe. Images of the final eschatological state begin to take form with implications for daily individual and corporate living, and the seeker grasps hold of those images as goals. The continual formation and reformation of the images, and the consequent constant redirection of one's efforts and thoughts, characterize this period. Gradual growth toward divinization becomes evident in the seeker's life, in the seeker's relationships with others, and in the seeker's way of living in the universe. This stage actually accounts for most of one's ascetic life because it is the most discursive and the most active.

The final stage, comparable to the unitive of the tradition, is the stage of rest. Incrementally over time, the seeker begins to know and to experience the divine presence and its impulse toward divinization not as an action but as an alternative way of life in which the seeker simply wallows. The seeker enters into the experience of the divine presence and rests there, knowing that in the end, resting in the divine signifies the eschatological aim of complete divinization. This rest may not be a permanent stage, and may be intermittent in both the initial and intermediate stages, but over years of struggle and work, the sense of simply resting in the divine presence takes on more and more of the modality of response.

These stages — awakening, striving, and resting — describe both modalities of response to the divine presence and also states of being that cohere one within the other. The seeker does not awaken to the divine presence without a sense of the call to divinization that such an awakening constitutes. The awakening is the initial rest in the divine that enlivens and activates, but it is still an encounter with a divine center of being that reveals itself in an initial moment of resting in the divine. Similarly, in rest, there is an awakening to the larger and more profound implications of the divine presence and impulse that compels the seeker to act on newly emerging images of divinization occurring in that rest. And the intermediary stage of activity spans the other two stages, moving continually from image to action, and finding rest in the divine presence as the seeker continually and incrementally moves toward divinization of self, society, and cosmos.

The tradition intuited and structured a system of stages in order to assist the seeker in gradually achieving a more godlike state. This retrieval of that system of stages aims to explain various modalities of response to the divine, not as a chronological sequence of levels of perfection, but as modes of response and fulfillment that accompany the effort toward divinization.

61 / Generosity and Hospitality .... ᔧ

T HE POPULAR IMAGE of ascetic monks of the ancient period is one of isolation. The image portrays monks as completely absorbed in the practice of their own religious life and its attendant asceticism, and both restricted in their relationships with outsiders and fearful of engagement with other people. In other words, the image, fallacious as it may be, portrays monks as stingy with their time and resources and fearful of the encroachment of the nonmonastic world into their sphere of personal work. This image cannot be further from the truth; in fact, the tradition highly values an ascetic's and a monastic's sense of generosity and the necessity, if not the sacred obligation, of hospitality to strangers. Generosity and hospitality define important traits of the ascetic, and the practices of generosity and hospitality, linked to the presence of others in the orbit of the seeker's life, stand at the center of the seeker's proper progress toward divinization. This is especially true in the postmodern context.

Generosity involves the "pouring over" of the boundaries of the self and society in order to enclose the presence of others. It consists of a "pouring over" because the boundary of the self, and the boundaries of society, expand to include the lives and needs of others within their orbits. Seekers, both individual and corporate, pour over the boundaries in order to enclose others within themselves. The purpose of this enclosure of others, however, does not function simply to make others part of the self or the society, but to give them the benefit of the resources of self and society. Generosity in this sense encloses others within self and society to bestow upon the other the riches and the blessings of the self and the society. The other is no longer experienced simply as other, but as an other united fully to the self and deserving the full benefits of being part of the self and the society. By generosity, the outsiders become insiders, others become part of the self, and foreigners become part of the corporate entity, the society.

Hospitality is the shifting of the center of the self, or correlatively the society, to another self or society in order to put the necessities and desires of others first. Whereas generosity maintains the self and expands its boundaries, hospitality relocates the center of the self itself and places it in the other. This relocation bestows upon others an increment of honor and respect and makes the needs of the other primary to the self. It is a dislocation of the self that both honors and ministers to the other from within itself. Likewise, the social grouping displays its hospitality as it shifts the center of its life from its own agenda to that of the stranger, foreigner, or simply outsiders who come within the orbit of the society's life and activity.

Both generosity and hospitality, precisely as mirror images of one another, open the self to the world and to the people around it and places a high valuation upon those others, those outside the orbit, those extraneous to the seeker's own ascetical activity. Both generosity and hospitality, thus, disrupt the set path of divinization in order to accommodate the needs and desires of others who interfere and intervene in the seeker's life at the most unexpected and (usually) most inconvenient moment. Especially when it is inconvenient and disruptive, the seeker puts aside personal pursuits and activities to expand the boundaries of the self to include others (generosity) and to locate the self in an exterior person (hospitality) in order to minister to another's needs as though they were the seeker's own.

These disruptions of one's personal ascetical regime, or of a community's pattern of working toward divinization, play an important role in the progress toward divinization. The disruption derails the process and forces both individual and corporate seekers to accommodate the lives of others. The disruption, that is, brings a new perspective on one's own personal and social practice and way of living, and that new perspective creates the chaos out of which new images of the divinized self, society, and world may emerge. These disruptions, brought about by the practice of generosity and hospitality, prevent individuals and communities from concentrating on themselves alone, from becoming myopic in their understanding of divinization and its demands, and from becoming so self-absorbed that they become obsessive. This is the reason that generosity and hospitality were enjoined upon the ancient monks; this is also the rationale for practicing generosity and hospitality in the postmodern context. In the postmodern context especially, corporate hospitality to people of different religions, different sexual orientations, different attitudes toward the world, different cultures and mores stands as the most critical of all practices, given the capacity of war to destroy the very fabric of life on the planet.

To be disrupted and prevented from pursuing a set path by the need for generosity and hospitality prevents individual and corporate seekers from their own narcissism. It pours over the boundaries of self and society to enclose another in safety; it relocates the center of the self in another to minister to the needs found there as the seeker's own.

62 / Penance

T RADITION LINKS the practice of penance to self-examination, to the sacrament of confession, and to actions and states of mind that repair the damage of sin. In the postmodern context where sin is defined as living as though the divine were not present and active, the concept of penance makes good sense.

The occasion for penance arises in the acknowledgment that the seeker has been unfaithful to the presence of the divine, and in the desire to retrain the self in order to repair the damage. This postmodern self-examination offers many opportunities for evaluating and understanding the ways in which the seeker has advanced toward divinization, or has been stymied in growth. Negative growth or hindrances do not remain simply as descriptors but become an occasion for retraining and reformulating actions and thoughts that will repair the damage done and move the seeker on the path toward divinization.

The seeker's reparation ought to take place in a number of different arenas of human existence. First, the mentality of sin, the patterns of thought and reaction that suggest that the divine in fact is *not* present or active, must be directly addressed in meditation and reimaging. The imagination that is capable of denying the presence of the divine must be transformed into an imagination of the vital and ever-present activity of the divine in the person, society, and the universe.

Second, the seeker must make reparation to self, society, and the world. Life lived as though the divine were not present and active creates the illusion that a person is isolated from others and from the world. It creates the illusion of distinction and individualism divorced from relationship with the wider world; hence, it creates literally a selfish orientation. Penance addresses that selfishness by turning the sinful person to the needs and desires of others, by pouring out the self to the sick, the friendless, and the needy. By doing so, seekers become agents for others' transformation in the process of transforming their own selves and moving toward divinization. Likewise, reparation of the physical world will take place when seekers clean the environment, or organize a recycling program for neighbors, or clear a blighted area in the city, or do some other action that repairs the physical environment. In transforming the world, seekers also transform themselves.

Finally, the seeker must repair the seeker's own self. The patterns of behavior that trigger the fantasy that there is a life divorced from the divine must be rigorously reconsidered and revised. Penance addresses the triggers to sin and failure directly, so that those places within oneself that seem to resist the presence of the divine become the arena of intense self-reformation. It is not enough simply to understand failure and to imagine anew a different kind of life. The seeker must also train the self to recognize failure and to habituate the self to new patterns of living and reacting. These new patterns must be consistent with the fundamental reality of the presence of the divine in and around and through the self, society, and world. Penance provides the opportunity for that reconstruction of the self, society, and world.

Penance must not be identified solely with introspection and psychological analysis. Penance arises in self-understanding and self-analysis, but it moves far beyond simply understanding the psycho-spiritual dynamics of sin and failure. Penance moves into specific and definite actions to redress those sins and failures directly. Penance moves the analysis and understanding into actions that move the seeker more solidly into the ways of divinization. Penance retrains the mind and the imagination and performs acts and deeds that repair the damage of sin, while at the same time it trains the seeker in new ways of living, ways that counteract the effects of debilitation and harmful habituation.

63 / Renunciation and Reconstruction .... ⌒

P ROGRESS IN THE SPIRITUAL LIFE demands serious effort. Progress results from an active engagement and transformation of the self, society, and the universe that aim toward divinization. In the postmodern world the common term "spirituality" tends to have passive meanings: of withdrawal into quiet prayer and meditation, of a reflective stance in relationship to the self and world, and of an entirely interior and personal discourse of the spirit that disengages from the activities of daily living.

Such a passive view of spiritual progress reflects the myopia of an unhistorical perspective on divinization. Actually, the ascetical tradition values an active repudiation of a former way of living, and an active reconstruction of the person, society, and universe in conformity with the aim of divinization. In the tradition this renunciation and reconstruction were signified in the term "mortification," a process of actively putting to death the old person distanced from the divine, and of consciously and deliberately constructing a person faithful to the divine. Mortification will be explored under the terms renunciation and reconstruction in order not to invoke the dualistic polarity of the spirit fighting the flesh that the term mortification implies.

The seeker after divinization must actively renounce all patterns of thinking, acting, responding, and living that reflect the imaginary of sin, that is, that reflect patterns of living that function as though the divine were not present and active. The seeker must actively repudiate; understanding alone does not suffice, nor analysis of the situation alone, nor even the critical identification of debilitating patterns. Once recognized, the seeker must reject these patterns. Once the seeker realizes that activities, or patterns of thought, or certain social circumstances, or consumer activities blind the seeker to the reality of the presence of the divine, then the seeker must repudiate those patterns and circumstances. The seeker must reject the pattern of thinking, or avoid entering deadening social circumstances, or cease to practice the consumer activities that lead the seeker away from progress toward divinization. The renunciation is active and intentional with respect to the imaginary of sin. It is not at all a passive process.

An equally active reconstruction of self, society, and the universe accompanies the act of renunciation. Renunciation working alone does not accomplish the divinization, but a process of renunciation complemented by a process of reconstruction. The seeker actively renounces deadening patterns and creates patterns of thought and practice that lead directly toward divinization. In one sense, the reconstruction replaces the deadening thoughts and activities with those that lead to life. This is a simple understanding of the process, but an effective one: the seeker renounces old and deadening patterns and creates a new identity, new social relations, and new attitudes toward the universe. These new ways reflect the presence and activity of the divine. Gradually in reconstructing the self, the seeker conforms self, society, and universe to the image of the divine toward which the seeker moves. The seeker appropriates the attributes of the divine, according to the projected image of divinization, and imprints them on the emerging person now oriented toward divinization. The seeker takes on the attributes of divinity and manifests them in the self, in social relationships, and in attitudes toward the physical universe; the reconstruction of the person becomes a means of advancing toward divinization.

The tradition recognizes that divinization cannot simply be added to an already formed person. Divinization does not, that is to say, simply follow logically and directly from the given patterns of living and thinking provided in any hegemonic society. The tradition stipulates that divinization follows from a reconstruction based upon a deconstruction. The deconstruction and renunciation of debilitating patterns establish the basis for the reconstruction of a divinized person, society, and universe. The renunciation creates the free space for the construction of a divinizing self, a divinizing society, and a divinizing universe. The construction, however, must be based on a new and firm foundation consonant with divinization. In this sense, the movement toward divinization does not encompass a natural movement, but a supernatural activity that transforms patterns of living into life-giving and divinizing structures.

64 / The Body Transparent .... 𝒽

THE TRADITION MAINTAINS that a holy person ought to look and act like a holy person. No disjunction should exist between the appearance of the person and the person's values, manner of life, and spiritual advancement. The ascetical tradition addressed these issues under the rubric of "personal comportment" or "custody of the eyes and lips," which formed an important part of the beginning of the process of self-transformation. The issue, as petty as the traditional system seemed to make it, remains an important one, especially in the postmodern context where ideological perspectives may stand as completely disembodied. For example, a disjunction appears when a person speaks about a high regard for peace but continues to act aggressively toward other people or groups. The tradition valued the complete integration of values and comportment in a way that postmodernity might term "the body transparent."

The concept of the body transparent is really very simple. One ought to be able to read the body of a person, or a society, or a physical environment in such a way as to see and understand the underlying values. The body ought to bear the marks, or point the way, or indicate somehow the values it bears. In this understanding, another person ought to be able to read the peaceful nature of a person by the person's demeanor, or the value of freedom and justice for all in the lives of the poorest members of a society, or the commitment to clean air and water by the purity of the air and water in a specific location. The body — whether of person, society, or the environment — ought to reveal the inherent values operating within it. Incarnational reality makes the body transparent to what operates in and through it.

Although the concept of the transparent body is simple, making the body readable takes significant effort at training and retraining the senses, modes of communication, patterns of daily living, and ways of relating to other people. The process of training begins by looking into a metaphorical mirror to read one's own body. What does one's comportment say about one's commitment to divinization of self, society, and world? Can that commitment be read in speech patterns, or in the manner of dressing, or eating, or treating other people? Or do the modes of communicating and relating to others reveal a dichotomy between deep values and bodily living?

After looking into the mirror to take metaphorical stock of oneself, the seeker must begin to adjust and reform patterns of speech and communication, systems of relationship to others both close and far, and ways of operating in the physical environment. This reformation of behavior need not be dramatic, but simply mark incremental changes that eventually add up to a significant and transparent shift that reveals the deep values of the person. For example, if the value one wishes to express is the inclusion of all people, regardless of their race, gender, or class, in the path of divinization, then the seeker must learn to pattern speech and actions in such a way that this inclusive goal becomes evident. Racist and sexist language must be weeded out and inclusive language developed in order to reveal verbally the value of inclusive divinization. Likewise, if the seeker deeply values peace and the treatment of different people with justice, then every violent and warlike pattern of behavior and speech must be weeded out; new patterns of peaceful speech and actions that reveal justice must be developed. Moreover, if the seeker values provision for the poor and hungry, and yet eats rapaciously or never gives money or food for the relief of the hungry and poor, the dichotomy between value and being becomes manifest and tangible. There can be no divorce between the seeker's apparent and real values.

At one level, the road to divinization becomes the most difficult at this very tangible and concrete level of the transparent body. The articulation of values is a far easier task than their embodiment in concrete action and speech; and conversely, it is far more difficult to live out the path toward divinization than to talk about it or to theorize about it. The discourse about divinization must eventually lead to the actual living out of a divinized way for the individual, societies, and the physical universe. The discourse must at some point become thoroughly incarnate in particular ways of living and relating. The word, that is, must not only become flesh (John 1:14), but it must also become completely transparent.

65 / Passions

HUMAN PSYCHOLOGY informs asceticism. The ascetical tradition has always acknowledged the depth of human psychology in psychological systems consistent with the historical period in which the ascetical program developed. Historical ascetical theologians most often use the term "passions" to discuss the psychological dimension of ascetical formation.

Passions are physical movements or appetites of the human person that generally command strong emotion and have a physical effect on the person. The Western tradition holds that there are eleven passions: love, hatred, desire, aversion, joy, sadness, courage, fear, hope, despair, and anger. The tradition aimed to moderate the passions so that the seeker was neither consumed nor obsessed by them; neither was the seeker to be indifferent to the potential positive direction of the passions toward the love of the divine. The tradition set a goal of perpetual equilibrium and tranquility with respect to the passions, which neither denied their destructive tendencies, nor surrendered human agency to their control.

The postmodern person would experience that equilibrium as lifeless and sterile. The strong emotions that the ancient passions describe seem already dulled in the postmodern world where the constant flow of information wears off the edges of any strong emotion, and the constant interaction with problems too big to solve or with groups too large to encounter seems to anesthetize both individual and society from any strong emotion. If anything, in the postmodern world the passions need to be revived as worthy dimensions to pursue the rehumanization of seekers whose humanity has been diminished by living in a postmodern context. The strong energy of the passions — of aversion and hate as well as love and courage, for example — proclaims the indomitable human spirit and points to the strong power of the divine impulse dwelling in every person and society. The strength and power of the passions animate the seeker to pursue divinization thoroughly and to respond as strongly to that which thwarts the divinization of self, society, and the universe. In the postmodern world where passivity and receptivity remain the dominant human reaction to the world, strong and energized reactions provide an important antidote.

Rather than equilibrium, the postmodern seeker needs to practice discernment. When is the strong energy of love transformative and moving the seeker toward divinization, and when is it compulsive and controlling and thwarting the divinization of self and others? The same applies to anger. When does anger express the logical and godly response to the injustices and dehumanization of other people that thwarts their movement toward divinization, and when does it express a vengeful and hateful reaction to a person or situation that stifles the seeker's own will? This same discernment must be applied to each of the passions, to every strong reaction, not with the intention of neutralizing them but with the desire to establish how these strong reactions and emotions relate to the immediate and important project of divinization.

This discernment, however, also relates to the tradition. The historical treatment of the passions revolved around submitting to reason. The tradition employed intellectual faculties as a means of neutralizing the passions. In the postmodern context, reason alone does not necessarily contextualize strong passion, but the relationship the passions have to the project of divinization does. The passions, however they are understood, take their meaning and significance from their relationship to the more immediate goal of divinization.

The postmodern understanding of the fully present divine impulse within the human person, society, and the universe itself means that strong emotions and reactions that emerge from the human condition relate to the divine impulse. The passions, if they are to be called that in postmodernity, have a relationship to the divine impulse and therefore they must be honored and respected as part of the reality of human existence that moves toward divinization. The postmodern seeker does not begin with a negative view of the passions and strive to transform the negative into a positive, but rather begins with the assumption of the divine relationship to all human passions and strives to manifest in them the fullness of the divine presence. Unlike the historical work with the passions that begins with a negative view of human existence as far distant from the divine, the postmodern person begins with a positive anthropology emergent from the indwelling divine impulse and moves toward the manifestation of that divine presence in every aspect of human existence, sociality, and responses to the physical universe. The passions form an important part of the divinization of self, society, and the cosmos.

66 / Study and Curiosity

THINKING AND STUDY is the highest form of worship. Parts of the ascetic tradition hold this view because the connection between the human and the divine exists in their common rational faculty, the *logos.* Other parts of the ascetical tradition hold thinking and curiosity in suspicion, since they lead the person into uncharted and uncontrolled areas that may distract the person from a singular pursuit of the divine.

In periods of intense religious conflict, as well as in times of battle between groups holding different ethical and moral standards, each faction tends to maintain ideological positions and to suppress study and curiosity in favor of already established patterns of thinking and acting. Such polarization of positions and marginalization of thinking and study pose a serious threat to the pursuit of personal, social, and cosmic divinization.

The goal of universal divinization demands the highest and most intense effort of individuals and groups. Divinization is complex and difficult; it gathers up every aspect of human individual and social existence and affects the lives of every living creature including animals, plants, and all forms of life in the physical universe. The complexity of divinization, therefore, requires thorough knowledge and understanding of the human person, the biology of living creatures, physics and the sciences of the created universe, oceanography, and every other body of knowledge that influences the current way of living and that plays a role in the divinization of all life. This complex divinization demands study, the advancement of knowledge, and the pursuit of even difficult and problematic ways of thinking.

The glory of divinization resides precisely in this intense pursuit of study and knowledge. In the postmodern context there can be no bifurcation of arenas between religion and science, spirituality and knowledge. Since everything is united into one complex understanding of human existence, and everything must be brought into the project of divinization, study and the pursuit of knowledge provide important and different avenues toward divinization. Rather than avoid knowledge or problematize study, the seeker eagerly pursues the advances of the life of the mind in order more fully and completely to bring every aspect of life into the project of divinization. Although study presents serious problems or difficult issues or even seemingly impossible and insurmountable impediments, seekers pursue it with the full vigor and strength of the human mind. Study in this way becomes an instrument of the contemplation of the mystery of the divine presence. Study becomes a form of prayer.

Study, as a spiritual discipline and form of contemplation, naturally leads to the central role of curiosity. Curiosity is a vital correlate to study. To be curious about oneself, or one's responses to the world, or the mystery of biological life, or the vastness of the universe, expands the horizons of one's understanding and widens the arena of contemplation. Curiosity stretches the mind beyond what it is capable of knowing into new and different avenues of knowing. Curiosity focuses attention on that which casually appears to the mind, begins to break down older patterns, and explores habits of thought previously unexplored. Curiosity presents the mind with unbounded or unfamiliar questions that lead to deeper knowledge. To be sure, curiosity cannot be controlled — it will lead where the mental intuition directs and into places the mind has not yet conceived. But such shattering of the edges of knowledge, such pushing the boundaries of knowledge outward opens vast new areas for the exploration of the meaning and significance of divinization. Curiosity leads, that is, to the creative and generative chaos that at once moves individuals and groups toward different ways of knowing and divinizing self and society, and at the same time destroys the habitual patterns of thinking that may inhibit real and dramatic movement toward divinization.

Although the postmodern situation does not permit a connection between human and divine located only in the rational faculty, the postmodern affirmation of the divine presence in all living creatures makes the connection even stronger. Anchored in the reality of the divine presence, the human mind freely roams into every arena of human existence to explore every troubling and problematic phenomenon and to follow the lead of curiosity into the exploration of unbounded and uncharted geographies of human and social existence.

67 / The Deadly Sins

THE ASCETICAL TRADITION developed the "deadly sins." Over many generations, the ascetical tradition tabulated the chief or principal impediments to progress in the religious life. The Western tradition codified them as seven sins: pride, anger, envy, greed, gluttony, lust, and sloth. The Eastern tradition codified them as eight sins, adding as the eighth, *akedia,* religious ennui or listlessness resulting from boredom. The traditions connected these deadly sins to the practice of self-examination and confession, so that the seeker might have a structure to organize the thorough examination and evaluation of his or her progress toward union with the divine. These deadly sins, in other words, provided the principal faults one had to counteract in the process of moving toward union with the divine.

Underlying the codification of sin into principal faults is a particular concept of sin. It defines sin as the transgression against divine law and the simultaneous usurpation of the majesty and authority of the divine. The sinner confronts these principal ways of offending God's majesty and disobeying God's command and begins to make progress toward union with the divine. The hierarchy of a humanity and world divorced and separated from the divine invests these chief impediments with the authority to keep humans (and other living creatures) far away from the divine. Sin's ability to effect this separation has ultimate and eschatological significance. The attempt to codify the sins, however, was a serious and important step toward making progress toward union accessible and possible, and it is to be honored as an important part of the process of divinization.

These particular faults or sins, however, do not necessarily jibe with a postmodern perspective. This is not to say that anger, gluttony, and greed, for example, do not have serious import in the postmodern situation, but rather to say that they are not the *principal* postmodern faults. The codification of principal faults ought not be denigrated in a postmodern world; even with the postmodern plurality of perspectives, it is possible to lay out particularly thorny faults that speak to Western Euro-American cultures. That list of faults easily would include the following seven postmodern principal faults:

1. ennui in the face of (a) the enormous needs and problems in the postmodern context and (b) the constant and overwhelming stream of information;

2. diminishment of human value and effort as well as the devaluation of all living forms;

3. spinning information, which gives the pretense of truth to that which is a lie and reveals a preference for ideology over reality;

4. a preference for hierarchy and its patriarchal structures;

5. an anti-ecological stance in which humans refuse to recognize their connection to all other living beings in the universe and deny their interconnectedness with the physical universe itself;

6. waste of human and physical resources in an attempt to satisfy the immediate needs while ignoring the needs of future generations;

7. a hatred of people who express difference from the tradition, those who are poor, or those who are disenfranchised.

Although these particular seven principal faults begin the conversation about ordering and structuring postmodern spiritual sin, they do not necessarily speak to everyone at every time. The discourse about the larger and more pervasive framework of impediments to divinization must be examined thoroughly, not for the sake of creating the list alone, but to assist people in advancing toward divinization. In other words, the codification of impediments makes it easier for subsequent seekers and future generations to understand the impediments of their forebears, and it trains them in a system of analysis that will aid in their own advancement.

The identification of the traditional deadly sins continues to structure the processes of self-evaluation long after those particular faults lost their central place in spiritual formation. Codifying principal faults gives structure to the process of self-evaluation; the results must of necessity be critically evaluated on a regular basis. Any new codification of alternative postmodern principal impediments must not stultify critical self-examination and social critique by becoming a pervasive system that distorts the advance toward divinization. The postmodern principal impediments ought not exemplify the same deadness they are intended to combat.

68 / Attention

THE PRACTICE OF THE RELIGIOUS LIFE depends upon careful attention to details. The process of attending to the smallest details of a seeker's prayer, or thoughts, or relationships, or actions trains the mind to observe deliberately and to seek the divinization of everyone and everything at the most concrete level of existence. Attention, then, involves an increment of meditation and concentration, as well as a careful focus on the most minute element of self, society, and universe moving toward divinization. Attention involves other skills as well, such as reading the present moment or incident for signs of the presence of the divine, or for signs of a particular impulse toward divinization, or for signs of the dire need for conversion or transformation, or for signs of a new direction initiated by the divine impulse and captivating the divine imagination. Only careful attention to the details of existence makes such reading of the signs possible. By deliberate delving into the realities of the present moment, the ascetic at once develops skills of attentive engagement and full participation in the concrete and basic elements of daily living. Then the ascetic can link the present moment in its most minute detail to the eschatological process of divinization.

One can most easily understand attention from the perspective of the use of language in prayer both private and corporate. Those who pray with familiar and often-used words often tend to move quickly over the words to capture the general sense or direction of the traditional words. In fact, corporate worship often suppresses the deliberate use of language to the more general inattentive use precisely in order to provide a common basis for the community's experience and knowledge. But taking the same words and attending to them carefully imbues the words with particular meaning and opens them to complex interpretations. By attending to the details and depth of the words, the seeker internalizes them and thereby makes the common and traditional words part of the seeker's own path toward divinization.

This same skill of attending to the particularities of speech and action applies to social relationships. By careful attention to the meaning of words, the seeker begins to transform the nature of the relationship, because every word, carefully chosen and spoken, operates out of the striving for divinization. No detail of language stands as superfluous to the process of divinization, and no spoken word operates outside the struggle to divinize self and society. By deliberate attention to the words and expressions of communication, the seeker begins a kind of habitual mode of response that operates in the present on the basis of the eschatological orientation. It is true also in relationships. In relating to others with attention to the details, and by carefully reading the signs within that relationship, the seeker begins to see the arena of divinization at its most concrete level. Social interactions, read as texts, begin to reveal the degree and direction of divinization — or its lack — and provides the basis for transformation. By interacting and relating deliberately in a new manner with others, the seeker begins to instantiate the divine presence in new ways. But such an instantiation is not possible in general, it must be accomplished in the details of the present moment.

The same attentiveness must be practiced in relationship to the physical universe as well. The attention to details and the careful attention to the implications of every act sets the stage for a serious engagement with the universe. At the most basic level, seekers reveal their theologies and their progress toward divinization in the smallest details: the consistent practice of recycling paper, plastic, and glass in order to save the physical environment from degradation and trashing; the constant attention to putting litter and trash in a proper receptacle and maintaining the cleanliness of the environment; the conscious and deliberate use of natural resources such as automobile fuel, natural gas, water; the general care taken not to pollute the environment; outfitting the home with environmentally friendly fixtures that preserve the environment; and many others. The central point here is that the divinization of the physical universe demands attention to details and, for those dedicated to divinization, can only happen through careful modification of actions on a daily basis.

The practice of attention, though difficult at first, gradually becomes easier, because the training of attentiveness in one arena translates directly to other arenas. Learning to pray deliberately leads also to deliberate attention to the dynamics of prayer, on the one hand, and careful attention to the implications of one's actions in the environment, on the other. The skill remains the same, while the arenas of attention change. The development of the skill significantly enhances the movement toward divinization because the seeker, holding the vision of the eschatological divinization in mind, acts in the details of daily existence and relationship with the most deliberate attention. In this the seeker links the present moment in its most concrete sense to the final instantiation of divinization.

69 / Engaging the Tradition

TRADITION HOLDS A SPECIAL PLACE in ascetical theology. The Christian church's spiritual, intellectual, and theological tradition must be considered from a postmodern perspective. That tradition consists of the various interpretations of Holy Scripture from previous generations; the theological and spiritual formations throughout the history of the church; liturgy and practices of prayer; the canons of the church and its councils; as well as the multitude of practices both major and minor that have developed over the years (such as fasting, or memorializing the dead, or celebrating a saint's day or a name day, etc.). The tradition of the church grows and develops, like an amoeba continually expanding, to engulf ever newer practices and thoughts, and over generations it forms a large repertoire of information, thinking, practices, and functions available to subsequent generations.

In the modern imagination, and especially in contemporary church political arguments about sexuality, the family, and other difficult issues, tradition has become a static thing. It is conceptualized as a boundary to acceptable behavior, thought, and practice; it is understood basically as an unchanging and unchangeable treasury, which limits human religious response and conforms contemporary church life to that of the historical and past activities and thoughts. Such a conception of tradition misses the point and must be rejected. Tradition does not serve the function of keeping everything new out of the practice of religion, nor does it limit potential human responses to the divine by insisting upon the replication of only already established responses. Such conceptions not only deny the validity of a living relationship with God, but also deny the living nature of God, consigning God to replicating only past revelations and delimiting God's ability to act anew in new historical and personal contexts.

A more appropriate way of understanding the tradition is as a repertoire of potential guides from previous generations that suggest ways of structuring and responding to the activity of a living God in new circumstances. Tradition consists of a treasury of human responses and conceptualizations and practices that have been successful and helpful to previous generations. They point to what has worked before and suggest ways that one might consider relating to the divine in one's own time. Tradition makes present and immediate the workings of the past in order precisely to assist in the reformation and reformulation of ways of thinking, responding, liturgizing, and praying in the present historical context.

To engage with the tradition, then, involves steeping oneself in the rich treasury of the past in order to enter into the deep meaning of previous generations' way of understanding the workings of God, to consider both the specific practices and the principles that underlay those practices, and to seek to understand the way previous generations have articulated their individual and corporate relationships with the divine. Then, having steeped oneself in the knowledge of the past, and guided either by the past's successes or its failures, the postmodern believer is equipped to look at the current needs of self and community and to begin to put proper responses into place. The past tradition does not limit, but suggests, while the new practices extend the realm of tradition in ever-new and different ways. The connection to the past makes suggestions, but does not limit the new. The consideration of the past links past and present in ever-new ways of engaging with a living God.

The continual sense of the ascetic remains that God is always active, that the divine presence inheres in the human condition, and that such has always been the case. Ascetics in previous generations marked their way, having steeped themselves in their ancestral ways, and they left a trail to be followed not slavishly, but with a generosity of knowledge that recognizes the capacity of the divine to work in new and wonderful ways that differ significantly from past activity. God is capable of doing new things, and the ascetic, whose eyes have been trained to see the new things emergent in past traditions, blazes a new path to respond to the current situation, and opens new ways into the future. Engagement with the tradition at once guides, suggests, and describes the past, but also simultaneously frees the ascetic to pursue new and uncharted territories of human existence for ways to respond to the divine presence.

70 / Seeing Double

ONE OF THE PREPARATORY and preliminary practices central to meditation is "seeing double." The "seeing" part of this practice relates to the concentrated attention to the present moment. The "double" part is the placement of the present moment in two contexts simultaneously: (1) the remote context, which is an immediate relationship to the eschatological pursuit of divinization of self, society, and the universe and (2) an immediate context, which is an attentive relationship to the current event or person fully appreciated on its own. The practice of seeing double relates to the process of simultaneously approaching people, events, and actions from a dual perspective: from the perspective of appreciation for the immediate context — the fullness and the richness of the present moment — and from the perspective that recognizes the present moment already exists in the eschatological reality of the divinization that is yet to come.

The present moment — the person or group before the seeker — can never be devalued in relationship to eschatological divinization. That would betray a fundamental tenet of incarnational theology. Seekers live in the present, honestly dealing with themselves, other people, events, and the physical environment with the full assurance that the divine is fully present and fully active in this very moment. The seeker approaches the present with the full knowledge and experience of the divine indwelling and instantiated in the present time.

However, the seeker also experiences the present moment, the present relationship or community activity, in the context of an eschatological divinization that still evolves and is yet to emerge fully. The present moment simultaneously functions in itself and in relationship to a divinization not yet fully understood and not yet fully actuated. The practice of seeing double relates to this remote sight, the eschatological one, and to the proximate sight, the presence and activity of the divine in the present moment. Seeing double is seeing both the remote and the proximate at the same time, without valuing one above the other and without discounting the reality and importance of either. Seeing double bridges the remote and the proximate into one practice of apprehension.

Another way of discussing double vision relates to the traditional language of the divine immanent (the proximate) and the divine transcendent (the remote). Seeing double apprehends the divine simultaneously from the two discordant and often contradictory perspectives as fully immanent and fully transcendent. The divine in fact operates in both ways simultaneously, and seeing double enables the seeker to experience the divine in the oppositions of immanence and transcendence without distorting the reality of either.

It is this apprehension of the divine as immanent and proximate as well as transcendent and remote that makes seeing double a meditative art. Meditation, or the practice of mental prayer, imaginatively takes seekers, or communities of seekers, or sodalities, into new apprehensions and understandings of the ways of the divine and the application of those ways to the lives of the seekers or communities. At the heart of the meditative practice stands the seeming opposition of a divine presence immediately apprehended and yet far surpassing the capacity of the seeker or community to apprehend. The paradox of this dual apprehension draws the life of the person into the contemplation of both poles — the remote and the proximate — in order to create the chaos out of which new experience and understanding may emerge. The mind, that is, by focusing on the two poles at once stretches to unite what would be significantly distant under other circumstances. The mind conjoins what appears to be impossible to join; it does so because the divine operates in the world and above the world at the same time. The apprehension of the paradox, the bridging of the dualities, the simultaneous seeing the remote and the proximate realities of the present moment train the mind to live fully now, but also to live fully in the divinized state that is yet to come. Such a way of perceiving constitutes the beginning of the practice of meditation, because it begins the process of thinking in a way that engages the seeker's desire to know the divine fully and to move incrementally toward divinization.

71 / Sin

POSTMODERNITY HAS A PROBLEM with sin. The question of sin is a particularly thorny one in the postmodern context because the concept of sin denigrates the human person and operates in a worldview foreign to contemporary thinking. The tradition distinguishes two kinds of sin: venial sins, which occur when a person transgresses the divine law; and mortal sins, which are crimes against the majesty of the divine. The tradition characterizes both venial and mortal sins as states or actions enacting a willful turning away from the Creator of all things to the creature. The tradition describes each in such a way that they differ in degree only. Venial sins are minor and momentary lapses in an otherwise well-ordered life; mortal sins are (as the name implies) deadly and serious affronts to the majesty of the divine, such as murder, fornication, extreme hatred of other people. In the postmodern context mortal sins would include racism, sexism, heterosexism, and the intentional pollution of the natural resources of the earth.

To retrieve a concept of sin, the seeker must begin with the fundamentals and work out from them. The fundamental reality informing the religious belief and practice of the postmodern seeker is that the divine is indeed incarnate, present, active, and pervasive in the lives of individuals, societies, and the physical universe itself. Sin, then, denies this reality in a variety of ways and in varying degrees. Sin occurs when the seeker chooses to live, act, think, and respond as though the divine is not fully present and operative. Sin is acting outside the presence and activity of the incarnate divine.

But is it possible to act as though the divine were not incarnate and present? In fact it is not. Sin lives according to a fantasy that is not real, a pretension that denies the reality of the foundation. Sin operates as a lie that posits that the divine is not present and active, that the person may live outside the basic premise that the divine indwells the person, that society is in fact neutral to the divine agency, and that the physical universe exists outside the divine impulse. In a sense, sin creates the opposite and problematic imaginary to that which leads toward divinization. In the imaginary leading toward divinization, the seeker engages with the divine impulse in self, society, and the universe and works toward their gradual and incremental transformation. But sin creates the opposite imaginary, that there is no divine presence informing and transforming the self, and therefore the person may act and live as a totalizing agent apart from all others, independent and isolated from connection to other people, other groups, and the basic elements of the universe.

The seeker must actively oppose sinful inclinations — not because sin is transgression of a specific law or an affront to the divine majesty, but rather because it denies a fundamental reality of postmodern existence: namely, that the divine impulse indwells and is active in every realm of human, social, and physical existence.

Just as there is a felicitous and gracious benefit to living in the imaginary of divinization that unifies the seeker's efforts in a transformative whole, so there is a debilitating effect of habitually living in the imaginary of sin. The effect of living in either of these two imaginaries has serious consequences for the manner of living for individuals and society and certainly has a significant potential impact on the physical universe. The habit of living in one or the other solidifies the imaginary in the life of the person. The habit of thinking and reacting according to one or the other eventually takes hold for good or for evil within the person and establishes itself as the norm. This is the reason that the tradition feared the habitual performance of even venial sins — they habituated the person to a way of living that was a fantasy and a lie, and eventually that fantasy and lie came to be lived as though it were the only reality. The same fear exists in the postmodern context, and that possibility makes the election of one imaginary over the other all the more significant. The seeker, in avoiding the imaginary of sin, must continually turn to the foundational reality of the presence of the divine and live there, even when tempted to imagine otherwise, so as to build up the personal and social resources aimed toward transformation and divinization.

The language of turning from the Creator to the creature is also problematic in the postmodern context. In postmodernity it is a good thing to consider the created universe, and all the creatures in the universe, as participating in the divine impulse toward divinization. There can be no denigration of creaturely status; that leads to pogroms, hatred, pollution of the natural universe, ethnic cleansing, and all the other evils that have plagued the modern world. To turn to the creature means to realize that the same divine impulse and presence resides in other people, animals, plants, the air, the earth as dwells within the person. Acknowledging that is to honor that reality. The postmodern concept of sin, therefore, must resist the language of "turning from Creator to creature" and stay the course on the pervasive indwelling of the divine.

72 / Playfulness

THE PROCESS OF CONSTRUCTING a spirituality has been a serious endeavor in every era of human history. The vast theological and religious literature on the religious life attests to the seriousness of living a life oriented toward God. Play and playfulness did not find much room in the tradition. When reading the biographical tradition and especially the sayings of the desert masters in Egypt, it becomes evident that the monks did play and tease one another, they did enjoy good humor even while struggling to divinize themselves. Despite the seriousness of the objectives and the task of divinization, these monks found time to play.

Playfulness is an important ingredient in the construction of a postmodern spirituality, and it does not in any way denigrate the serious effort toward divinization of self, society, and the cosmos. Play accomplishes a number of things. First of all, play relieves the tension and tedium of being a seeker focused on divinization. The intensity of being fully aware of the relationship of concrete actions and thoughts to the divinization of self and others creates in the seeker a sense of urgency and devotion that organizes and directs energy and activity. That intensity is not bad, but it should be tempered with times of sheer relaxation and playful inattention to the process of divinization.

Secondly, in the process of relieving the stress and pressure of divinization, playfulness unbinds the operative categories of the seeker's life and relationships. These categories, molding as they do the structure and content of divinization, hold sway over the life and activity of the seeker to such a degree that they dominate all other categories. Playful interactions loose those categories and enable the seeker to encounter them not in their hegemonic authority, but in their creative and energizing reality. To play within the context of active work toward divinization is to realize that the process is far more expansive than categorical organization allows it to be experienced. Play, then, advances the process of divinization by challenging the primary categories of a seeker's life and thought.

Thirdly, play creates space for the expansion of the mind. This is a correlative point to the previous one. In challenging the hegemony of even good categories, playfulness creates a mental space for lively exploration of alternative ways of moving toward divinization. Play in this sense functions much like the process of chaos in other parts of the ascetical system. Playfulness opens up the mind and spirit of the seeker to new possibilities, different ways of seeing and experiencing the road to divinization, and other forms of relationships to others in society and to the universe itself. These new ways may alter the direction and focus of the process of divinization.

Finally, play provides a time for seekers simply to enjoy the fruit of their labor and effort. The work of divinization deserves the seeker's highest efforts; the playful and restful enjoyment of the progress and the effort, of the incremental transformation of selves and society, and of the progressive repair of the universe provides the seeker with a new vantage point, which is based in playfulness and relaxation. Divinization ought to be as enjoyable as it is transformative and restorative, and playfulness brings out the joy of efforts well intentioned.

In structuring a spiritual manner of living and in constructing a spirituality, time for playfulness must be included. It invokes the rest and the play of the seventh day, the sabbath, the day of rest in the midst of creative and serious labor. It invokes the holy fools whose playfulness provided a serious criticism of the dominant religious categories, practices, and theologies. And it invokes the need, particularly in a postmodern setting, to step out of the continuous onslaught of information and knowledge in order to enjoy the fruit of one's labor. Seekers ought not to be seduced by the seriousness of the divinizing project into thinking that all of living must be intentional and directed. Playfulness interrupts the process and offers a fresh view precisely to allow seekers to experience joy and relaxation and perhaps to redirect the effort. Playfulness, like chaos, is a holy tool of the seeker's gradual divinization.

73 / Emotional Ecology

THE DEADLY SINS (pride, envy, anger, gluttony, lust, sloth, avarice) connote inordinate passions or strong emotions wrongly directed. According to the spiritual literature, the remedy for such strong passions revolves around moderating all strong emotions or subordinating them to equally strong positive emotions. The positive opposites include respect for others, rejoicing in the success of others, anger only at injustice, moderate eating, subordination of sexuality to marriage or to the religious life, active working, and satisfaction with one's own person and property. These remedies certainly are not mistaken, but often they do not speak to the postmodern situation.

The regulation of strong emotions in the postmodern world suggests emotional ecology. Emotions, especially strong emotions, operate within a context that gathers up an individual, connected to other individuals in social groupings, which in turn connect with other social groupings and with the wider physical universe. In other words, strong emotions do not operate in a vacuum isolated from many other factors. Emotions have contexts within a seeker's own life, community, and cosmos.

The expression of strong emotion, as well as its meaning and appropriateness, must be understood in wider contexts. It is not that all emotion and fervor must be tempered, or modulated at all times, or even suppressed. Rather, strong emotional reactions must be understood in context, with discernment based on that context.

To say that emotional ecology has a context also suggests that this emotional ecology connects with the unfolding divinization of self, society, and the physical universe. The context comprises not only the local, but also the eschatological. To explore the context of emotions demands not simply that the seeker explore the relationship to the circumstances of individual, society, and cosmos, but also that the seeker explore the relationship of strong emotions to the incremental and gradual divinization of all people, groups, and universes.

So as the emotions emerge — anger, fear, lust, envy — they must be explored not simply from the perspective of the person expressing the emotion, but also from the perspective of the community in which the person expresses that emotion. And their appropriateness will be determined in both an individual and a corporate context. The community's discernment, however, will also explore the significance and meaning of these emotions in relationship to the larger project of divinization. The emotions — again, for example, fear, anger, lust, envy — may have a significant role to play in the divinization of the individual or community, or they may move others to establish justice, or they may spur a lagging community to begin stronger efforts at cleaning the environment in the face of a very highly motivated neighboring community. The expression of strong emotion has a context both local and eschatological, both of which must be taken into account in discernment.

The ecology of emotions also has another important dimension. Emotions point to the truly visceral and foundational flash points of people's lives. Strong emotions signify the deeply held convictions and fissure points for the individual, or the community's corporate fault lines. Strong emotions act as ensigns of the emotional structure of the seeker and the community, just as fault lines indicate the deep movement of the plates of the earth's crust. As ensigns, these emotions, and their ecology, must be studied and interpreted as important indicators of the structures that undergird the apparent layer of one's individual life, or the visible appearance of a community's life. In reading the ecological environment, then, the interpretation must take into account a wide set of perspectives both within and outside the person and society.

It is not sufficient simply to talk, as the tradition does, in terms of moderation, suppression, or substitution of strong emotions. That strategy assumes a consistent and universal mode of behavior and moral and ethical standards that do not exist in the postmodern context. Rather, the ecology of the emotions must be studied, analyzed, investigated, compared, and contextualized in order to understand not only the immediate cause and circumstances, but also the significance and importance in relationship to the eschatological context as well.

The meaning cannot reside in only one of the dimensions of strong emotions; the entire ecology of emotions must be explored and understood. Then, and only then, can a proper remedy, or understanding, or channeling, or transformation of the emotion occur.

74 / Holy Energy

ENERGY GETS SHORT SHRIFT in the ascetical tradition. Little is written about the energy expended on behalf of sanctification or divinization. It seems as though the tradition assumes that energy expended toward sanctification is good energy, and energy used for bad things, or sinful things, is bad energy. Energy, which seems to be neutral in itself, takes on moral character in relationship to its object. That kind of neutral view of human energy and effort does not translate well into a postmodern worldview. From a postmodern perspective, all energy, all human effort and activity, is holy; that is to say, all energy has a positive role to play in the process of divinization because all energy participates in the divine presence. Energy participates in an unfolding mystery and thus has a positive direction, even when it seems to be operating in modes and arenas not geared to divinization.

Holy energy permeates the universe in unfolding the mystery of the divine presence. The extension of the mystery into the physical universe mirrors the recognition that God is larger and more complex than anyone can understand. Christian incarnate living demands that Christians recognize that the one God may be manifest in every other religious tradition and belief, despite its distance and difference from Christianity, precisely because other traditions participate in the articulation of holy energy. Incarnate living demands that Christians trust the mystery and complexity of God among religious peoples of the world, even when they cannot comprehend how. Rather than looking to convert or to put other religious people into Christian categories and patterns, Christians should accept the mystery that God is at work throughout the created universe in diverse ways, using mysterious means to bring about the complete transformation of the created universe. Holy energy literally energizes all religious belief wherever it may be manifest. So Muslim, Buddhist, Hindu, even nonreligious people and atheists, all live in a universe where the divine is at work in supporting, sustaining, and transforming the peoples of the world. The incarnation so changed the nature of the cosmos and human existence that the mystery of God may be manifest in places humans never dreamed God could be present and active.

The Jewish rabbis have the concept of "repairing the universe." That summarizes what incarnate living manifest in holy energy aims to achieve. Christians are called to mirror the activity of God in the world and to repair what has gone amiss, to become the holy energy that repairs the world. The repair begins in the common, daily, and mundane events and tasks of the day. The repair of the universe begins with the solid centering of the person in God, in concentrating holy energy, and in dedicating the self to the work of God in the world. The repair of the universe begins in daily work and action. It is in the regular writing of letters of protest against national and international injustice; the regular donation of food, clothing, and money to the relief of the poor and afflicted; the kindnesses shown to a neighbor who is grieving; the constant care for an elderly parent; the visitation of the sick and homebound; bringing comfort to those in social isolation; the attentive conversation with a person going through a difficult time; the conversation at dinner with spouse and family; being with friends gathered to watch a favorite television show; the smile to a stranger passing by on the street. The incarnation makes each and every one of these activities an arena for incarnate living, a place for the manifestation of holy energy.

Through holy energy the universe becomes resplendent with the glory of the knowledge of God, and people are transformed by living in a world in which the ways of God are manifest and real. The mystery of the incarnation creates the glory of the world, so that the mystery of God may be seen, known, eaten, smelled, touched, heard, and understood by all.

75 / Holiness of Resources ....

THE POSTMODERN WORLD knows that resources are limited and often nonrenewable. This reality has led to an important emphasis on conservation of resources and preservation of the natural environments of air, water, and earth.

The ancient spiritual traditions taught that the human person also had limited physical resources, which needed to be conserved and preserved throughout a person's life. There was fear that an unnecessary expenditure of energy and resources would deplete the human ability to live fully and to cope with crises. This is the concept that underlay the theory of the deadly sins, which are also known as the "capital sins." Since there is a limited stock of emotional energy, all that energy must be used for proper purposes. Love, for example, ought only to be used for procreation and propagation of the human species and not wasted on lesser things. Or, in the case of the monk who renounced marriage, love was to be focused on God alone and nothing else. All other "loves," whether sexual or emotional, would deplete the person's capacity for full living and at the same time waste precious human resources on unworthy and lesser things. This view of human emotional resources does not ring true to experience. For example, love, anger, and envy seem to create a surfeit of energy and magnify the emotional energy and activity of the person. The emotions seem, in fact, to be renewable and unlimited.

Stepping back into the postmodern context, one can see that there are elements of both the ecological and the emotional truths that apply. Human and environmental resources are indeed precious commodities and ought both to be conserved and preserved. They should not be squandered and wasted. Both the physical and human resources, however, well up from a common source deep within physical existence: they both share in the common divine impulse and energy that dwells in both humans and the physical universe. That divine impulse and presence is inexhaustible, unlimited, and perpetually renewable, and it operates within human persons, societies, and the physical universe even when those arenas are unaware of its presence. In other words, the source of all energy and resources is the incarnate divinity whose presence energizes and transforms all living creatures and impels them toward their eschatological divinization. Whenever humans, or societies, or the physical universe expend energy for any purpose, they draw upon the wellspring of divine energy infused into all. This is part of the great mystery of living, that the divine not only transcends the self, the community, and the world, but also dwells deep within it, animating and bringing fullness of life to all.

So energy already has a divine element. The question raised in the tradition about the proper use of energy and the issue raised in ecological circles about the preservation and conservation of natural resources bring the seeker to a different understanding of the holiness of energy and activity. It is not that energy expended for good things is good and energy expended on evil things is evil. All energy participates in the divine impulse. The question then turns on discernment about the relationship of the expenditure of energy and the use of natural resources to the plan of divinization. The relationship to divinization determines the proper use of resources both human and natural. Those resources already have a direction and impetus toward divinization that humans and communities may either thwart or enhance. Energy either moves toward divinization, or it does not; if it does not, that energy is not evil, but simply wasted. The expended energy becomes useless and ineffectual in the face of the great potential for divinized use. Energy is wasted.

But wasting resources need not be permanent. It is possible to connect all energy and every activity to the larger project of divinization and to change the course of one's own life, one's communities, and the physical universe itself. That same mysterious divine impulse in the physical universe can work to transform and to change. The waste is only temporary, provided that seekers begin to conform their use of their human and physical resources to their proper and naturally divine purposes.

So with regard to the deadly sins, they are indeed "capital" sins. They squander the human capital that humans are capable of investing and developing. They take capital away from their divine purpose and apply it to things that are ineffective, useless, and ultimately insignificant. Anger, lust, gluttony, sloth, and the other deadly sins simply waste the divine capital that dwells in humans and their communities. The remedy to the capital sins revolves around centering the expenditure of resources in the process of divinization. And from that centering comes an endless supply of resources for the repair of human, social, and physical universes.

76 / Temptation

EVERYONE KNOWS TEMPTATION. Any seeker who has ever begun the process of sanctification, or pursued a religious goal, has experienced temptation, the testing of the mettle of the seeker's will and devotion to the cause. Temptation in the context of an ascetical system plays an important role in the seeker's own divinization, as well as in the divinization of communities and the physical environment.

Temptation involves the active engagement with the imaginary of sin, which promulgates the fantasy that the divine is not present. Temptation, that is, pretends that all of the efforts toward divinization by individuals and groups really do not count, because the means and the striving are not real. Temptation denies the reality that the divine indwells human individual and social existence; therefore aiming for divinization is a fantasy and not a real possibility. Temptation challenges the reality that lies at the foundation of the ascetical struggle for divinization. Temptation tests, challenges, questions, denies, and attempts to ignore the presence of the divine in the eschatological process of divinization.

The testing of the process of divinization plays a positive role, however. By challenging the dominant modality of existence — the pursuit of divinization by individuals, communities, and the cosmos itself — temptation strengthens the vision of total divinization. The testing of the reality strengthens the hold of reality itself, so that the temptation to live as though the divine were not continually present in fact strengthens the notion that in reality the divine presence inheres without interruption. Temptation, precisely as a fantasy, enables the emergence of a stronger vision of the movement toward divinization.

Temptation, then, has an educative function. It directs the seeking person and the seeking community to the points of vulnerability, to the weak points of divinization. Temptation displays the very points where divinization has not taken hold, where the vision is not sufficient to sustain energy and commitment, and where the person or community is most likely to deny the very realities that inspire the movement toward the transformation and divinization of all life. These weaknesses and vulnerabilities provide important information and experience to the individual and communal seekers because they point to the very places where needs exist and must be addressed in the process of divinization. The same may be said of the physical environment where, in a sense, the temptation is most evident: people and communities treat the environment as though it were neutral, or that the divine was not incarnate and present in it. So they pollute it, trash it, manipulate it as though it were not important in itself, but only important in satisfying the needs of individuals and communities. Such a view of the environment is a fantasy that leads to the destruction of the ultimate divinization even of the physical universe. But these weaknesses and vulnerabilities educate seekers about the places where the resolve for divinization must be strengthened.

The means to strengthening the resolve, to resisting temptation, rests with a renewed commitment to the contemplation that follows a period of temptation. After a bout of temptation, an urge to enter the imaginary of sin, the seeking individual and community looks back on the experience and realizes that the temptation showed weaknesses, but not the reality of the presence of the divine. This looking backward begins a process of looking forward to a new imaging and contemplation of the meaning and implications of the divine presence in human, social, and cosmic life. Temptation leads naturally to contemplation of the reality of the divine presence, which in turn leads to a reconsideration of the direction and path toward divinization. This new path is now based upon a realistic appraisal of the weakness and vulnerabilities of the individual and the community. Temptation not only educates seeking individuals and communities, it also leads to a renewal and redirection of efforts through contemplation.

A phrase in the Lord's Prayer points to this mystery of temptation. The traditional language translates the Greek as "Lead us not into temptation," while the modern translation says, "Do not bring us to the test." Here the denial of the value of temptation seems to reign. But the original Greek words have a more profound sense to them. English translations suggest the final test, the eschatological judgment at the end of time. But there is another way of interpreting that testing, that temptation. The Greek may just as well suggest that the prayer says, "Do not make this (merely) an experiment." This interpretation of the Lord's Prayer asks that the divine honor the reality of the divine's own presence and that all the human and corporate effort at divinization be real and not simply an experiment on the divine's part, an experiment that might be abandoned. Stated in a positive sense, this interpretation of the phrase in the Lord's Prayer asks God to make the struggle real. The role of temptation is to validate the reality and power of the divine presence.

77 / Consolations

DIVINIZATION DEMANDS significant effort by individuals and communities. It demands not only energy expended in self-formation and communal activities aimed toward the divinization of self and society, but also the intellectual and emotional energy to pursue an existence far beyond the capacity of any individual or group to achieve.

The eschatological state attracts seeking people and communities, propels them on a glorious road, and demands significant effort to transform the known world into the divinized world God has planned for all living beings. Divinization is hard work.

The divine presence, both immanent and transcendent, provides times and experiences of consolation; that is the joy of the work. These consolations bring refreshment and joy to the seeker as the seeker works diligently to divinize the self, and it brings rejuvenation and elation to the community gathered together for worship and conversation in the midst of hard work.

Consolations may be understood as periods of time, or simply moments, when the individual seeker experiences the self as completely connected to the larger divinized world. It is that moment when everything seems to fit together and to make sense, and the seeker understands the self as a part of the whole and holy, divinized cosmos. Or it may be the point at which the individual seeker comes to experience the self as part of a community fully engaged in divinization and working toward the repair of the universe. Consolations for the individual seeker connect the single person to the larger context and provide in the present moment a glimpse and experience of the end product. Consolations are experiences of anticipated joy that bring refreshment and renewal.

Consolations also come to communities. After periods of intense internal struggle or community tensions, or after periods of strenuous work that seemed to demand more than usual amounts of energy, or after deaths of beloved members whose lives were central to the community, or after setbacks or failures in particular projects that held great promise but which could not be realized — at these turning points (among many others) there comes a grace of consolation to the community. These allow the members and the corporate body as a unit to experience the sense of well-being that comes from being a small part of a much larger divinizing whole. As with the individual, the community catches a glimpse and experiences the eschatological end in the present moment, despite failures, setbacks, and losses. Consolations refresh the community and bring joy in the work even when the work does not seem to progress as planned or succeed as projected. Consolations renew the community by anticipating the eschatological joy.

Consolations also come to the physical environment and the universe. Here over generations there have been setbacks in the form of pollution of the air and water, the degradation of landfills with nonbio-degradable products, the strip-mining of the countryside in pursuit of ores and minerals used to sustain a market economy, and the felling and burning of valuable rain forests for economic growth, among many other degradations of the earth. From the perspective of the use of natural resources, one could say there is little chance of the divinization of the physical environment because the pattern of abuse has been so great that it thwarts the physical universe's repair and transformation. Yet in the midst of that, rivers are gradually cleared of the pollution that killed the fish in them and made them dangerous to those living near them; now people may swim in them and fish may thrive. In the midst of the degradation, one sees the polluted air in metropolitan areas gradually begin to clear, ever so slowly, so that breathing might again become a literal inspiration of the divine breath. These and many other small and incremental successes in transforming the world serve as consolations to the physical universe in its growth and movement toward divinization. This consolation connects the universe to the refreshment and renewal of individual and communal seekers engaged in divinizing self, society, and the cosmos, and it is indeed a consolation of the physical environment.

The task is supernaturally difficult but consolations come to encourage and strengthen, to refresh and rejuvenate those people and communities working toward divinization. Consolations come not only from within the individual seeker or the community — that is, from the divine presence known and experienced there — but also from the transcendent divinity that stands at the eschatological end drawing all people and every living creature to the ultimate divine One whose own divine presence animates all life. These glimpses of the whole and the holy energize creatures to pursue that which will bring them the ultimate joy, only partially seen and experienced in these consolations.

78 / Aridity

THE MOST PERVASIVE METAPHOR of the ascetic tradition is going into the desert to pray. That sense of willingly entering a barren and lifeless place described the experience of setting out to discover within oneself the divine spark of life, to encounter the very limits of human capacity to know the divine, and to find the divine inhabiting an arena of intense isolation and human struggle to stay sane. Aridity metaphorizes the struggle to know God in the least likely places and to build a vital and vibrant life upon that knowledge discovered in aridity. The desert, with its aridity and isolation, metaphorized the ascetic struggle to be divinized — both for the individual who retreated to the desert to find God and for the communities of ascetics who found in their common struggle the support to sustain their efforts at personal divinization.

That experience of aridity, of dryness and lifelessness, however, also describes periods of time in a seeker's spiritual life when nothing seems to be happening. These are periods when the divine seems distant, unrelated, not real, and the efforts at divinization seem rote, and meaningless, and boring. Aridity in the spiritual life happens frequently, but it is not without its benefits.

Aridity most often occurs when a seeker has been actively pursuing a path toward divinization and has achieved some advancement. The expectation is that such a pace and success will continue indefinitely and that progress toward personal and communal divinization will move quickly. Success, however, does not continue, and progress begins to slow down and to stop. The very energy and excitement that propelled the enthusiastic pursuit of divinization wane, and the dry and sterile realities of apparent stagnation begin to be the dominant reality. The very juices of living divinization seem to dry up, wither, shrivel, and diminish the flow of divinized life. The seeker has entered into dry times that seem to stifle the spiritual life.

In times such as these, the metaphor of entering the desert takes on new meaning. Dry times do not speak of the reality of the absence of the divine, but of the reality of the lack of connection with the divine reality that is always present and active. The lack of connection, the isolation and disconnection from the very source of life, define the desert experience into which the seeker must enter. It only appears that the divine is not present; that appearance is not correct. Like the desert monks, their aridity and isolation become the still place where new and different encounters with the reality of the divine spark dwelling in every living creature can be explored. The aridity of the desert highlights the general lifelessness of the place, but also allows the very small and infinitely small traces of the divine to be seen and known in the smallest signs of previous life. In other words, the desert experience strips away all the outward signs of success and moves the seeker toward noticing and holding on to the very smallest indicators of the divine presence. The contrast between the vitality of the fully engaged divinized life and the sense of dry and arid isolation trains the eye to begin to read the small and seemingly insignificant signs of the divine presence traced on the parched landscape of the soul.

So the seeker lives into the aridity by embracing it with whatever level of enthusiasm the seeker might muster. The arid times in the spiritual life provide the seeker an opportunity to strip away the interior and exterior detritus of the soul in order to make new paths, to forge new directions, to transform the sight and sense, and to experience the divine in ways not yet conceived or understood. Aridity in the spiritual life presents an opportunity for exploring the depths and limits of one's own being and activity. Standing alone in the desert or perhaps in the company of others who stand bereft in their arid places begins a process of stripping away and building anew.

There are some practices, however, that might accompany the seeker into the desert. The habitual practices of prayer and meditation, even if they seem not to have the energy and enthusiasm of other times, ought to be continued. Dry, lifeless prayer, bereft of enthusiasm and warmth, still connects the seeker to the divine, despite the feeling that the divine is absent. The habit of prayer becomes a lifeline to the divine presence, even when that presence is not part of the seeker's current experience. Likewise meditation should continue to be part of the seeker's luggage in the desert. Meditation keeps the imagination operating and active. It keeps the eyes alert to potential signs of life and energy, even when that life and energy seem distant and dormant. Meditation creates a space that may become an oasis in the desert.

In addition to prayer and meditation — the habitual daily activities that are the center of divinized life — the seeker must search for the other burned-out ones in the desert. There in the deep sense of isolation and aridity, the seeker connects with others who have achieved but have become stagnant. There is a community of people living in the desert whose experience is similar in its dryness, and that community also becomes an oasis. In the discourse of aridity, the seekers and the arid communities of seekers begin to refresh one another and to encourage one another even in the despair of isolation. That refreshment and encouragement, even among the lifeless ones, is a sign of the divine presence.

Communities of seekers know when one of their own individual members enters into the desert. Although not themselves arid, their life somehow seems foreign to the person experiencing aridity. The community ought to keep space open for these alternative experiences, holding the person in the community, not seeking to diminish the reality of the aridity that the seeker is experiencing, but rather affirming that even in the midst of a dry life in pursuit of divinization, the divine spark remains vital and active.

79 / Discerning the Divine Mind .... ⌇⌐

THE FIRST TOUCHSTONE for knowing the mind of God in the present is to ask, "Is this consistent with the way God has acted in ages past?"

Christians have the scriptures, which provide the chronicle of God's activity first with Israel, then with Paul, Jesus, the apostles, and the church. The scriptures are not rule books — they are far too inconsistent to be able to provide a clear set of rules — but they chronicle relationships and provide the information necessary to observe God's reactions to human activity. They allow seekers to view some of God's past plans that people tried to follow, or to hear God's speaking to people who sought guidance in the past. The sacred scriptural books provide the first place to understand God's ways in the past. But the past does not rule the future. These books describe the past and provide a basis for discernment in the present, but they do not impose a pattern on the future. Such an imposition would imply that God either does not exist in the present, or that God cannot engage in new ways with humanity, or that God's ways are rigid and unchanging. The scriptures themselves portray God's ability to change and adjust the plan for humanity. In the end, such an imposition implies that God is not a living God of the present, but a dead God of the past. So searching the scriptures begins the process of discernment, not to discover rules, but to explore historical patterns of God's interaction with humanity. This searching can reveal bases for action and reflection in the present.

Tradition and history also chronicle God's interaction with humanity. They cannot be ignored. Tradition transmits to the present the accumulated wisdom of the past so that humans may understand the ways past people have engaged with God and understood God's ways. History chronicles both the successful and unsuccessful ways that the people of God have acted in various times and circumstances;

in history seekers may discern the consequences of their action. Both history and tradition link the present situation, which is in need of discernment, with the past.

The third major touchstone to discernment is human experience. God has been active not only transcendently in the scriptures, history, and tradition, but God has been active and present in the human experience. A wide diversity of people have experienced God in their daily lives and they have acted on those experiences. Likewise, human experience guides the capacity of a person to know and to understand God. In experience, Christians in particular may call upon the scriptures to ascertain ways of God in familiar circumstances. Christians are called to serve the sinful, the rejected, the disenfranchised, as well as to repair the universe through a self-giving and self-transforming love that connects all people perceived as both sinful and good. This comes from the model of Jesus' interaction with other people in healing, forgiving, gathering, feeding, clothing, and restoring people to their God-given human dignity, while despising oppressive regimes both political and religious. Reflection on human experience through the scriptures tells Christians that they are not doing the things of God when they reject, condemn, judge, harm, or oppress other people. Even though the scriptures portray God as having often acted in harmful ways in the past, the common humanity that links all people in the postmodern world makes it clear that to reject or condemn or kill another is simply not the way of God in modern times.

The Western tradition maintains that Jesus as a human being had three kinds of knowledge: beatific knowledge of God face-to-face; infused knowledge of God through the mystical understanding of all natural and supernatural orders; and experiential knowledge he developed during his earthy years of human living, a knowledge of the truths that the human mind may also know through gradual and progressive reflection on his experience. The system of discernment presented here reflects that threefold division and applies it to the postmodern situation and to the believer. Seekers may also know God face-to-face in the sacraments and in prayer; they may also contemplate the knowledge of God transmitted through history and tradition that shows the underpinning of God's presence in the natural and supernatural worlds; and they may also know God in their own experience as it unfolds in the course of their lives.

These kinds of knowledge, not rules, lead to discernment of the mind of God. It is risky business: it takes energy and commitment to explore the ways of God anew in each generation, in each circumstance, among divergent people, and even among people who believe differently. It is difficult: there can never be a sure foundation upon which all people of faith at all times may stand, in order to know an unchangeable mind of God. It is arduous: looking back while affirming that God is engaged with humanity and the created order now, and looking back yet knowing God is so very present that at every moment God stands ready to make all things new. The foundation is not in the rules, but in the relationship to a living God among an active and thinking people in a world desperate for repair.

80 / Discernment of Spirits

THERE HAS ALWAYS BEEN a need for the discernment of spirits. The Christian tradition discerned the sanctity and propriety of actions and thoughts through the evaluation of them on the basis of three primary dichotomies: whether they were of the flesh or of the spirit, from the self or from God, from the devil or from the holy angels. The location of an action, thought, or relationship on one side or the other of these polarities established whether it was good or evil, of God or of the devil, spiritual or libidinous. The tradition clearly defined criteria for each of the categories, and it maintained that the systems of values used for discernment had universal and eternal authority. The system functioned effectively until the Enlightenment, and postmodernity questioned the validity and authority of these polarities and dichotomies themselves.

Discernment in the postmodern context relates primarily to one question in three arenas. The question is simple: Does this action, or thought, or relationship advance the person, the society, or the universe toward divinization? The central point of discernment concerns the relationship of everything to the eschatological end, divinization. The three primary arenas of discernment invoke the three primary arenas of divinization: individual, society, and the physical universe. The question for the individual's discernment revolves around whether the actions and thoughts of the person move that person toward divinization. Likewise for the society: does the work and orientation of the society move that community toward divinization? And probably most importantly, from the perspective of the physical universe: does the action or attitude repair the universe and restore it to its proper place in the scheme of divinization? No easy answers to any of these questions exist. The questions may be simple but the response and the discernment prove even more difficult in the postmodern context than in prior times. No human or social action can ever be fully known and simply related to any one concept; discernment works to begin to explore the fundamental direction of every human activity and thought, both individual and corporate.

Discernment cannot be static. The process of discernment constantly shifts between different understandings and interpretations of actions and thoughts in relationship to a constantly shifting understanding of divinization. Self-understanding and communal self-awareness do not happen naturally or easily; discernment continually works through the changing views and understandings to question whether even in the context of continual change an action or thought may be viewed as an advancement toward divinization.

Moreover, discernment cannot be universal. The context of a person or community plays an important role in the discernment process. That contextual frame for discernment invokes class, gender, race, and other social locations. The rich with vast resources and multiple life-options discern differently from the poor, struggling with fewer or no resources and significantly diminished life-options. Likewise women may discern differently from men, as well as the differences raised by different cultures and races. The systems of discernment accommodate themselves to this vast array of specific contexts. Just as the image of divinization shifts in each of these contexts, so does the question of discernment. This means that discernment is highly contingent upon the context and social location of the person and the society, and that contingency reflects the complexity of divinization itself.

The reality that discernment is neither static nor universal, that it is rather changing and contingent upon social location, makes the process very complex. Discernment does not simply happen once and for all, but it must continually delve into the complexities of people, societies and cultures, and knowledge of the physical universe. Divinization itself in its continual process of revision of the image and the substance of the divinized self, society, and cosmos, demands that discernment adjust to its own changing reality, so that discernment becomes directly linked to the emergent and changing process of divinization.

Delving into the fundamental direction of an action or thought, even in this changing and contingent context, provides important information for the conduct of life and the evaluation of thoughts and relationships. Because the standards and the means shift, the self-understanding of the person and the self-awareness of the community become more nuanced, more precise, more subtle in their comprehension of the depths of human and corporate capacities for divinization. The complexity of discernment thus in itself advances the process of divinization and moves it ever forward until God be all in all (1 Corinthians 15:28).

81 / A Living God ....

G OD LIVES. The systems of ascetical formation both individual and corporate rest on an important foundation: God lives, acts, and engages in the lives of individual people, communities and societies, and the physical universe in which they all live.

No one would dispute that this description of God pertained to the past. Most religious people can easily trace the activity of God from the creation of the world through the founding of their particular religion. The supreme witness to this divine engagement stands written and preserved in the sacred writings, for Christians in the scriptures of the Old and New Testaments. Surely, the holy scriptures encapsulate and communicate the living God and the mind of the living God for all ages. Some religious people could go a little further to argue that the living God has also worked in the history of the church, especially the church of the early ages of the first two or three centuries or so of Christian history. These formative years produced the doctrinal foundation for Christianity as established in the doctrines of the human and divine natures of Christ, the divinity of the Holy Spirit, the nature of the Trinity. Not all Christians accept this next move, but many do. Still fewer Christians can accommodate the presence of a living God active in the church throughout the ages, especially in the Protestant Reformation and the Catholic Reform of the sixteenth century. Even fewer go further into acknowledging the presence of a living God in the contemporary life of the church. As the understanding of the presence of God moves further from the foundational documents in the scriptures, some believe that the ability of God to do new things decreases.

Rigid thinkers tend to use tradition and scripture to put God into a box; that is, they have made God incapable of doing new things, effectively declaring God to be vital and living primarily in the past, a past that must at every turn be replicated in the present. The sense that God has already spoken and set forth a plan for all eternity, a plan made known only in the scriptures and the tradition of the (primarily early) church, declares that all God could envision for humanity, society, and the physical universe has already been established in the past. God limits and restricts the divine activity in the future based upon God's own activity in the past. God can only be described and understood in patterns of living, language, and thought that replicate the past. According to this view of tradition and this understanding of the role of scripture, God cannot do anything not already revealed and, therefore, God cannot do anything new, be thought of in new metaphors, be present in new things (especially science and the environment), and act in bold and new ways responsive to the way that humans, societies, and the physical universe have evolved over the past millennia.

Obviously such an understanding of God would render all ascetical striving meaningless. Striving to become a divine agent, to manifest the divine presence, and to divinize self, society, and the physical universe demands that God be so living and active as to be able to move all creation toward a new point yet unrealized in human conceptuality. Ascetical activity defines itself not as a return to the past, but as a movement ever into the divinization that the divine has set forth for all creation. That divinization requires that God be more than the past reveals; that God dwells in new ideas and new ways of living; that God lives in the present and acts in a wildly variable way to divinize even more wildly different people and societies. Divinization, the aim of ascetic endeavor, rests upon the human capacity to envision a God living in a plural world, among very different people who think very differently from one another, who believe in the divine and live it out according to the cultures and contexts in which they live, who pattern their lives according to the latest knowledge and understanding of themselves, society, and the physical universe, and who can envision a God divinizing everything and making all things new.

A living God means exactly that to a seeker — a God living and true, dwelling in the midst of individuals, communities, and universes eagerly awaiting their transformation into creatures who know God to be all in all. This living God, dwelling in the creation that God has created from before time and forever, energizes the world to change, to move, to think unthinkable thoughts, and live lifestyles never before considered divine. This living God is capable of engaging in new things, in transforming new sciences into agents of divinization, of promoting new ways of thinking as worthy of those moving toward divinization, of imagining new social arrangements valued because of their transformative and divinizing presence, of imaging the physical universes as the vast expanse of space in which God will be all in all (1 Corinthians 15:28).

Without a living God, asceticism becomes mere obedience to the past, a lifeless effort related to a dead God. With a living God, however, asceticism moves eagerly and dramatically into the future making manifest the divine presence and glorifying a God living and true, active and engaged, and ever-present in the lives of individuals, societies, and cultures, and the outer reaches of the galaxies of the universes. This is indeed a living God, one known in past revelations, but experienced more and more in the new things that God is doing.

82 / Illumination

THE SELF, SOCIETY, and the physical universes yearn for illumination (Romans 8:19–23). There comes a time in an individual's life and in the life of a community as well when the spiritual life shifts from a modality of struggle to divinize to one of settling into a lifelong pattern of divinization. This shift represents an important point of transformation. The seeker's struggle to habituate the processes of divinization into the thoughts, emotions, actions, reactions, and relationships begins to take less effort, and becomes a way of life. This illuminative life has adjusted to the chaos that the discursive practices create by being able at once to celebrate and embrace the chaos and constant shifting of images of divinization and to stay firm in its resolve to move steadily into the future as those images change. This illuminative life has already become adept at recognizing and resting with the interior divine impulse and presence so that it is no longer a process of remembering the divine or even of struggling to bring that divine presence into operation in life and thought, but rather the seeker is able to rest and enjoy the divine impulse and presence as a constant

companion on the way. The illuminative life accepts the connection
between one's prayer and meditation and the transformation of self
and society, so that the seeker assumes that everything and every creature interconnect and cohere as elements of a larger divinized whole;
then the seeker can rejoice in the glory of such intercommunion of
elements.

The same illuminative way of life comes to communities. The
struggle to experience community life as completely infused with the
divine presence becomes a deep and abiding awareness that the divine presence impels the community to reach beyond its limits to the
service and ministry to the poor and disenfranchised. The struggle of
the community to live with diverse members and different perspectives of their roads to divinization becomes a relishing of the diversity
and difference within the community and an eager desire to manifest
greater diversity by embracing and drawing into the community even
more diverse and different people to become a part of the communal
movement toward divinization. The illuminative community adjusts
to the reality of its divine mission to be a community for others and
recognizes the deep and abiding connection between its interior life of
prayer and liturgy and the exterior life of service and ministry. This
connection of interior and exterior leads to a constant interplay between the work and needs of the exterior world and the even stronger
impulse to divinize and to transform all social relationships. The illuminative community moves into a kind of comfort with its mission
and identity as a divinizing agent and thereby becomes more adamant,
intense, and intentional about proclaiming and manifesting the divine
presence in the world.

And even the physical environment has an illuminative life. The
universe itself begins to be experienced as resplendent, radiating the divine presence in noticeable ways. Parks and green space provide places
for the physical environment to reveal the inner beauty of the divine
presence. Clean air and water, restored to their purity by personal and
communal efforts, manifest the divine impulse to gather together a
diversity of human creatures, birds, fish, and other animals to enjoy
the wonder of the physical universe, and in the process to experience
the divine life there. Places that were trashed and filthy begin to reflect
the divine life as they are cleaned and the detritus carried away, and
the world begins to manifest the beauty of the divine presence.

The move from struggle to a comfortable reflection of the divine
does not mean a move from activity to passivity, but rather one from

activity to enjoyment of the fruits of one's activity, an enjoyment that leads to further reparation and restoration of the universe. In other words, there comes a time in the spiritual life when the seeker and the community move away from a modality of struggle to a modality of adornment. Adornment of the person, the community, and the physical universe builds on the foundation of the initial struggle involved with divinization and extends the work of divinization to greater and more diverse arenas. In the individual, the move toward adornment that accompanies the illuminative life suggests ways that even peripheral aspects of the person's life may reflect connections to the divine presence and impulse toward divinization. One's clothing, way of commuting to work, manner of speech, habits of eating begin to take on more importance and interest as places for the manifestation of the divine presence. In time these peripheral adornments also become habitual and the process of divinization seems to advance almost with an energy of its own. The whole person becomes a living image of the fruits of the struggle and the joys of having stayed the course in order to become an example of a divinizing person.

The same applies to the community. The illuminated community adorns itself with the health of a community completely alive in the divine presence and resolute in its living for others. The community itself becomes an adornment of the divinized social world and an example to be imitated. The process of moving toward this adornment and refinement indicates that the person, the community, and the universe have moved to a different level of their spiritual and religious life. And in that they each should rejoice.

83 / From Discourse to Affection .... ৯৲

DISCURSIVE PRAYER builds the foundation of the spiritual life. This foundation stands upon several processes: training the mind and emotions to understand and to relate to the divine impulse that inheres in individual and communal bodies, reformulating social relationships in a manner consonant with the divine presence that imbues every relationship with a sanctity and divinized aspect, and learning new ways of relating to the physical universe as a place resplendent with divine energy and direction. The discourse involved in building this foundation revolves around an active use of imagination and analysis to introduce the mind, emotions, and relationships to the concept that they manifest a divine presence and impulse, a concept which often seems contrary to the dominant understanding of humanity, community, and the physical universe. Entering the imaginary of divinization engages the seeker in a process of rebuilding and reconstruction, deconstruction and reorientation, that moves the seeker more and more into the actualization and manifestation of the divine presence in every aspect of living.

As this foundation is laid, however, the seeking individual and community begin to branch out into different ways of praying and responding to each other and the world. The discourse, that is, takes deep root, and it is not so much the imagining of a divinized self, society, and universe that holds attention, but an affective relationship with it that becomes primary. That affective relationship involves now an active living on the other side of divinization, a transference of attention from the foreignness of divinization to the engaged entrance into a divinized world as the primary base of operation. This is a subtle shift in focus. In building the foundation, the seeking individual and community continually enter the imaginary of divinization in order discursively to change the conception of individual, corporate, and cosmic living. That discursive transformation demands significant expenditure of mental, physical, social, and engaged activity. There comes a point, however, when that discourse has built such a foundation that it demands less energy to enter the imaginary. Then the seeking individual and community begin to live more actively in the imaginary of divinization and to relate to self, society, and the cosmos from a more solidly divinized perspective. Now the divine presence comes not in memory, but as a constant companion to the seeker — a companion with whom the seeker may, throughout the day, enter into affective conversation and fully conscious partnership in the divinization of every arena of life.

It is the sense of fully active partnership and engagement that defines the affective state, which follows upon the discursive. The divine impulse and the divine presence have taken such a hold of the imagination of both individuals and communities that they are capable of working together in a fully united fashion. What was previously experienced as an effort to delve into the depths of the divine presence in individuals and communities, has now become a relatively permanent fixture of life. And this sense of the permanence and fully conscious relationship with the divine presence moves seeking individuals and communities into new and different ways of working toward divinization. Since divinization now has become a permanent aspect of human and social effort, seekers live in a divinizing world that commands their energy and attention in moving more fully into the complete divinization of self and society.

This new direction emerges from the shift from discourse to affection. The seeking individual and community come to love the divine presence with strong emotion and affect. Divinization can no longer simply exist in the imaginary, because seekers now want to live in that world they have been struggling to construct and to stay there permanently. Their desires for the consummate divinization of self, society, and universe, and their will to work tirelessly for the divinization move them from engaging the imaginary of divinization to enfleshing the imaginary of divinization actively and with passion. The imaginary of divinization defines their reality and centers their affections and desires. The shift from discourse to affection may be described as a shift from imagining divinization to a love of divinized living. Having entered into an intimate partnership with the divine presence, seekers may no longer simply imagine a life lived in accordance with it, but must now live fully in the divine presence that animates and transforms all existence.

This affection for the divine presence also frees individual and corporate seekers to explore more fully, more graphically, more radically, and more effectively the direction and image of divinization. The affection for the divine presence enables a person and a community to leave behind the constrictions of the imagination to envision a more completely divinized self, world, and cosmos, because the partnership, now firmly rooted in the divine presence, engages them in a different way of relating to the world. This partnership provides a more active desire and need to enflesh that which has been imagined.

84 / Affective Contemplation

S EEKERS STRIVE FOR affective contemplation. There is a point in the contemplative practice when the seeker seems able through contemplation to live in the reality of a divinized self, community, and cosmos. It is a turning point: what has been known and imagined as potentiality actually begins in the imagination to take on a reality so graphic, real, and articulated that the seeker desires to live there. Contemplation affords the opportunity for a limited period of time during the day to leave the nondivinized and divinizing world to enter into a fuller communion with the divine presence, into the divinized life of one who lives in communities already in the imagination divinized, and into a physical environment already radiating the divine presence. This form of contemplation is called affective contemplation, because the seeker enters affectively into the reality that is contemplated. It is a form of contemplation that begins to develop over time, as the image of the divinized world becomes more tangibly real in the imagination.

In the tradition, such affective contemplation focused solely on an event from scripture, or the life of Jesus, or the deeds of a saint, or a mystery of Mary, the Mother of God. In contemplation, seekers would place themselves into the scene and actively participate in the events. They would engage in conversation with the characters, observe the details of the environment, and become completely absorbed in the event. Often the senses of taste, touch, smell, and hearing would be brought into play so that the seeker would experience the event or scene as immediately present, and not as an event in history, by imagining what aroma the event would produce, or what tactile sensation it would involve, or how the event might invoke particular taste or sounds. The objective was to have the seeker enter into a new reality and to live there with the affections fully engaged in the process of meditation. This sort of meditation holds validity even in the postmodern context.

The postmodern context, however, goes one step further. Affective contemplation does not focus simply on a scriptural or historical event from the distant past as the basis of meditation or contemplative practice; it also extends to the future and to the eschatological divinization. In the postmodern context the seeker enters into the transformed and divinized world as a means of experiencing affectively in the present the state of persons, communities, and the cosmos when each has become more fully divinized. The seeker contemplates the reality of a fully divinized self and begins to live (at least for the duration of the meditation) as a fully divinized person. That image of how the fully divinized person will look and live in a particularly divinized way evokes patterns of interaction, of reaction, of thought, and of being. The contemplation opens up for immediate experience the imaginary eschatological state of the person so that the experience of divinization becomes an experiential reality in the psyche of the person.

In a deep sense, communities also engage in affective contemplation whenever they gather for worship. The worship makes manifest and experiential the collective contemplation of the way social arrangements and responsibility operate. The community envisions the way the world should look, how social relationships should be structured, and how the divinized cosmos will appear, and it begins to live it out in its common liturgical life. The reason these communal seekers gather, in a sense, is precisely to experience the social dimension of the eschatological divinized world in the emerging and struggling divining moments leading to it. Communal life experiences that eschatological life affectively in the way it patterns itself in the ritual actions of worship, so that in liturgy the newly articulated understandings of self, society, and the physical universe find affective and concrete expression.

The objective in affective contemplation, both for individuals and for communities, consistently enfleshes and articulates affectively the future reality in the present moment. Affective contemplation enables seekers to enter fully into the world that is to come, to experience fully the reality of a divinized self, and to wonder at the majesty of a divinized physical universe not as something merely hoped for in the future, but as something real and concrete in the present moment. This form of contemplation energizes seekers to pursue divinization even more ardently because the experience of living the divinized life, in a divinized community and universe, has taken on a new dimension. Such contemplation, however, does not end the process of continual revision and reimagining of the eschatological realities, because having lived in the new world, seekers continually revise their understanding of the shape, direction, and experience of divinization. Contemplation bridges the two worlds and makes the eschatological one immediately experienced, but it does not in itself effect the final divinization of people and living things. Through affective contemplation seekers are afforded a moment of transcendent reality in the immanent imagining of a fully divinized world.

85 / Divine Virtue

VIRTUES ARE POWERFUL EXCELLENCES. They describe patterns of behavior that manifest or reveal the powerful and effective divine energy that recreates and transforms human and corporate activity. Virtue comes from the Latin word for power and translates the

Greek word for excellences. The combination of power and excellence, transformed behavior and divine energy, becomes a hallmark of progress in the religious life. The manifestation or representation of virtue in the seeker's life, in the community's life and activity, and in the physical universe attests to a more advanced stage of progress toward divinization.

In the early stages of movement toward divinization, the individual and community seek to habituate themselves to the divine presence and the divine impulse that dwells within them. Seekers train themselves as individuals and communities to attend to the divine presence and to live, think, and act according to the reality of that presence. The training, that is, habituates individual and corporate seekers to live according to the interior reality of the presence of the divine, and these habits form and reform them, more and more manifesting and revealing the divine presence in their patterns of life and thought.

As with any habitual practices, they become easier over time. The training takes deep root in the person and in the community, and the capacity for living in accordance with the divine impulse and presence becomes a way of life. The training literally has become a "second nature" to the person and to the community so that these habitual practices not only become easier to perform, but they become habitually the norm for the individual and the community. The change, the transformation and divinization, has become a way of life habitually oriented to the divine presence that activates behavior and thought in persons, communities, and the physical universe as well. The power, the virtues, and excellences of life lived in accordance to the divine presence and impulse have become the normative way of life.

As that habitual conforming of life to the divine presence and activity continues over the course of time, there develops an alignment of personal, corporate, and cosmic agency with the divine impulse and presence. This alignment comes naturally as the exterior patterns of behavior conform more and more to the divine impulse and presence, as the virtues of living the divinized life become more and more natural to the person and the community. The seeker begins, then, to act as one, in complete unity, with the divine presence. The distinction between habituated virtuous living and the direct action of the divine presence through the person becomes so blurred that they can no longer be distinguished. They are at one, indistinguishable, undifferentiated in action or thought, because the habituated behaviors of divinization have become a second, more divine nature, to the person.

The same applies to communities. As communities conform themselves more and more to the divine presence, and their interior lives and actions begin more completely to manifest the divine presence in their relations, actions, and corporate identities, they begin more ardently and directly to manifest the divine presence by their normative activities and services. The line between their exterior life and the interior divine presence has been broken down by habitual efforts toward divinization so that others may see the divine presence immediately and apprehend the divine impulse directly through their actions and interactions. The virtues of corporate living become revealers of the divine presence and agents for the divinization of the nondivinized world around them.

The divine virtues, as they are developed over the course of a long struggle for divinization, become a sacrament of the divine presence in the physical universe and every living creature within it. The lives of individuals and of communities, habituated to the virtuous life of divinization, witness to the transformation and eventual divinization of all life in the physical universe. The efforts of individuals and communities become transparent to the divine presence and impulse. Those looking in from the outside see people and communities vibrant with divine energy. They begin to see the interior and inward grace outwardly displayed in patterns of behavior and relationship conforming to the divine presence. The virtues become a sacrament of the divine presence in the physical universe. These divine virtues sacramentally display the reality of the divine presence in the actions and thoughts of individuals, in the corporate lives and ministries of communities, and in the effective repair of the physical universe. The divine presence becomes sacramentally visible and apprehended in the concrete actions of seekers whose lives more and more reveal evidence of divine presence.

86 / Representation ....

T HE CONCEPT OF REPRESENTATION operates within the Christian religious life. This concept, sometimes raised to a doctrine, states that within a hierarchy of being, the higher rung on the hierarchy more fully represents the presence of God, or Jesus Christ, to the lower rungs. The broadest conception of that hierarchy is threefold: Christ, the church, the world. Within that threefold hierarchy, archbishops and higher prelates represent Christ to bishops; bishops represent Christ to priests or other ministers; and priests represent Christ to lay people in the church, who in turn represent Christ to nonchurch-goers or nonbelievers. At each lower stage in the hierarchy, there is less and less Christ to be represented, so that the closer one is to the higher level of the hierarchy the more representative of Christ or God the person is.

Three unfortunate correlates attend this theory of representation. The first gives the impression that the divine presence does not pervade every person and being in creation. The hierarchy distances the divine from the so-called nonbelieving world and creates a dichotomy between the realm of the divine and the realm of the secular or profane — anything that is not directly related to the hierarchy of divine presence. In other words, such a hierarchy implies that the divine does not fully dwell in the lower rungs of the ladder and that parts of reality do not relate to the hierarchy at all. Incarnational theology, however, stipulates that in the divinity's taking on of human flesh and dwelling in the world, all creation and every creature has been taken into the divinity's own being, transformed into a new ontological agent and being, and set on the path toward complete and total union with the divinity at the end of time. No room exists for representation in a system in which the divine is fully present and accessible to every person and every creature equally.

The second unfortunate correlate is that such a hierarchy led to obedience to authority rather than faithfulness to the divine presence. Since agents or institutions above the seeker in the hierarchy always represent the divine, seekers may only properly respond with obedience and submission. Disobedience or working toward divinization in a way unauthorized by the higher representatives constitute a denial of the presence of the divine and betrayal of the divine impulse. This submission to authority denigrates the full participation of the divine in every creature and person.

The third is that this hierarchy and orientation toward obedience imply that the divine may be known only in categories and patterns that already exist. It implies that those representatives on higher rungs of the hierarchy already know all the ways of the divine and all of the paths leading to divinization; and, therefore, those who stand on the lower rungs must restrain themselves accordingly. This in turn implies that the divine's historical operation takes precedence over the operation of the divine presence in the immediate moment. The seeker cannot operate beyond the historical patterns of divine revelation; the divine is not sufficiently immediate and present to allow new things, new patterns, new revelations, new understandings, because the seeker is limited both by the history of revelation and the hierarchy of revelation.

In an ascetical system representation operates in an entirely different way. Beginning from the premise that there is nothing in creation that has not been redeemed by the incarnation of the divine, the question of representation becomes significantly democratized. The role and function of each person, community, and even the physical universe revolves around revealing to one another the divine presence and the divine impulse that operates within the created order. In other words, the seeker must represent the divine presence to the seeker's own community, to all other creatures, other people, other communities, and the environment in which the seeker lives, as well as the wider physical cosmos in which the seeker is placed. Likewise for communities and societies, they must, each in their own unique and particular way, reveal the divine presence in their interior communal life, in the relationships among members of the society, in their actions toward other individuals and groups, and in their way of living in the physical universe. Each community represents the divine presence and manifests the divine impulse in relationship to everyone and everything with which it comes into contact. Representation, then, does not descend a hierarchical ladder, but rather emerges from an already regenerating divine presence, which has entered into the created realm and opened the way to divinization to all creation. Representation of the divine may be accomplished in ways both old and new, astounding and normal, significant and insignificant, radical and traditional all at the same time because the divine presence and the divine impulse operate in all people, in every historical and contemporary society, and in the physical universe from its inception to the present moment. This articulates not a hierarchy of representation, but a democracy of manifestation.

87 / Receiving the Mystery .... ⟨ↄ⟩

THE DIVINE LIVES IN ALL. This incarnate theology that lies at the base of ascetical theology acknowledges that the divine presence and the divine impulse inheres in all creation. Nothing operates outside the movement toward the eschatological divinization that will make God all in all (1 Corinthians 15:28). The great joy of the ascetical life involves the discovery of that divine presence within and the engagement with the divine impulse toward divinization in order to begin the wonderful process of divinizing self, society, and the cosmos. Each seeker, awakening to the glory of this divine presence, begins to move ever so slowly into a transformation and recreation of self, relationships with others, and the environment that displays for others the fruits of one's progress toward divinization. As seekers move from the awareness of the divine presence in themselves and their own communities, they also become aware that the divine mystery unfolds in manifold people and circumstances all around them. The mystery of God discovered within themselves and their communities also permeates every other person and community in the world.

Seekers respond properly to this unfolding mystery of the divine all around them by cultivating a receptivity to receiving the mystery from without. Seekers develop a capacity to look for the mystery unfolding in the lives of other people, other communities and social groups, and especially in other dimensions of the physical environment. Since all of those places, people, and communities participate in the unfolding of the divine mystery present within them, they become revelatory of the divine presence in new and different ways. To receive the mystery from without, to recognize the same divine presence and impulse in others, transforms the personal and corporate efforts at divinization into a wonderful menagerie of divine revelations. The divine presence and impulse come not only from within, but also from without in myriad and manifold ways.

Attention to the unfolding mystery, and receptivity toward it, often becomes most dramatic and confounding when the mystery unfolds in people who differ radically from the seeker and the seeker's own communities. The difference confounds the normal categories and forces individual and corporate seekers to move beyond the confines of their own thinking and understanding to account for different and mysterious revelations of the divine from other quarters. As the divine mystery impinges upon the understanding and lives of seekers from without, seekers at once become part of the larger process of divinization and at the same time struggle with the holy chaos that redirects and informs personal and corporate divinization. The divine mystery unfolding all around in myriad ways continually upsets the categories of divinization in order to expand the perspective and to redirect attention and effort to an unknown and unpredictable level of inclusiveness.

It is in fact the uncontrollable nature of the unfolding divine mystery that has the greatest value, since it forces upon the awareness of seekers that the divine impulse toward divinization far surpasses the imagination or even the understanding of any one person, or any one community, or any one understanding of the physical universe. The mystery in which seekers engage cannot easily be comprehended or comprehensively articulated from only one perspective, but rather must be expressed in the language of mystery and the language of diversity, which shatters the preconceived and developing ideas of unity in divinization that develop over the course of striving.

As time goes on, seekers find themselves less dependent upon their own images and understanding and more fascinated and interested in the unfolding mystery around them. The divine presence moves from something personally valuable to a phenomenon that opens seekers to the mystery of the divine and the wonder at the unfolding of the divine plan in people never before considered agents of the divine, in societies and customs often deemed outside the realm of the holy, and in a universe often seen as simply a backdrop to a human drama. That unfolding mystery begins to open seekers to the immensity of the project and turns their efforts into prayer, transforms their relationships with others, especially very different others, into a meditation on the divine mystery and finally brings them to utter silence before the awesome majesty of the universe. Seekers find a kind of rest here — not a rest of relaxation and disengagement from action, but a rest in the mystery unfolding, a stepping back to observe the way the divine presence moves and acts throughout all creation and in every person, a meditative rest that enables seekers to stay connected to the unfolding mystery while at the same time enjoying the vision of divinization unfolding. This receptivity to the mystery confounds, redirects, mystifies, energizes, transforms, and utterly engages seekers who understand themselves as a small part of a very large divine project whose limits and boundaries know no end.

88 / Singularity and Integration .... ⟡

THE ASCETIC IS ONE. A consistent value of the ascetical tradition is that the ascetic be "singular," or a "single one"; the Greek word (*monachos*) refers both to the spiritual state of being "single" and the social state of being a monk in a monastery of religious. That singularity, probably understood more properly in modern language as integration, revolves around the need for the seeker to gather up all the fragments and multidirectional aspects of the personality into one unified and singular whole. The single one in this respect opposes the "double-souled" person, who seems to present the self as conflicted and moving in multiple directions under the influence of various incompatible forces. The single one acts as a unified and integrated person under the direction of the divine presence. The single one advances toward divinization with a purposeful and steady determination. The single one appears to have achieved a unity between the interior presence of the divine and the external drive of the divine impulse. This unity encompasses every aspect of the human personality so that the single one appears to be at rest, or at least at peace, knowing both the self and where the self is heading. That is, the single one is fully integrated not only with its own self, but also with the divine presence and impulse toward divinization.

The same integrity or completeness extends to communities. The interior life and values of the community, oriented as they are to the corporate divine presence and to the repair of society through divinization, become fully visible in every action, thought, liturgy, and service of the corporate body. The community's life becomes a kind of visual sacrament of the integrity and determination of the members of the community to move toward divinization not only of themselves as members of a community of faith, but also of every society and culture in the world, and of the physical world itself. The sacramental and revelatory (or at least revealing) quality of a community's life will display whether the community is singular or two-spirited, whether the community has internalized the divine presence sufficiently to manifest it clearly and directly in its social relationships and in its relationships with other communities and people, whether there are contrary tendencies and impulses working in the community that thwart the advancement toward divinization. The same singularity and integration, socially under the sign of integrity, operate within the community as within the individual person.

Singularity, however, is not obsession. When the seeking individual and community become obsessed with their mission, when it becomes a mania, that is not singularity. Each may be uniting all effort into one steady activity, but such obsession does not lead to divinization. The singularity of the ascetical tradition relates instead to the full integration of every aspect of the self, in conjunction with the integration of selves into holy communities, and the sure placement of holy communities in a physical universe resplendent with the radiance of the divine. In other words, the integrative processes move the person outward into union with other people and societies and into full communion with the created physical universe. It does not move a person into the obsessive completion of his or her own personal idiosyncratic agenda, or a community's ideological program. The singular integration of person and community gathers up the fragments in a flow of effort moving toward a divinization that cannot be fully comprehended by any one individual or one community, but is far greater than all the parts.

The movement toward unity explains why in the ascetic tradition the easiest way to become singular necessitated becoming a monk. Contemplative monasteries organized themselves around the primary work toward integration of the self with the divine presence. Joining that community, with its established structures oriented toward divinization, enabled the individual seeker more easily to enter the flow of energy toward divinization and to focus all attention on that one goal. It is not so easy with postmodern people, who need to live out their personal, familial, and professional lives in a complex and often very demanding world. Singularity requires more effort in the postmodern context precisely because the impetus of the postmodern world draws individuals and groups more toward fragmentation and decentering than toward unity and singularity. This spiritual integration flies in the face of the fragmenting normality of the postmodern world, and it makes singularity all the more precious.

Singularity and integration, however, are not that difficult to achieve for either the individual or the community, especially when it is approached not as a comprehensive whole, but as small incremental efforts to hold all the disparate parts of one's life in relationship to the divine presence. Turning to the divine presence in memory, when action is undertaken, or when a thought occurs, unites what appears to be disparate into a singular whole. Integration occurs not by will, but by relationship to the divine presence, and singularity follows closely upon that integration.

89 / World and Self ....

S PIRITUAL TRADITION profoundly distrusts both self and world. The Western spiritual tradition particularly and seriously distrusts them. The Western tradition problematizes both to such a degree that seekers must at once despise themselves and withdraw from the world, which is the site of degradation and separation from God. The effect of these dual renunciations has been to drive seekers away from the tradition and into spiritual traditions more accepting of the value of both self and world. The Western tradition, however, is not uniform in its renunciation, and there is room for exploring alternative and more positive ways of conceptualizing the value of both the world and the self.

The world presents the arena of divinization. In fact, it is more than that: the world founds the place where divinization must occur for both individual and corporate bodies. The culture, even popular culture, becomes the place of transformation, and because it is the arena of divinization, it must be embraced and valued. If divinization cannot be perceived and manifest in popular culture, perhaps it has not occurred or is not in the process of occurring. The cultural environment, like the corporate environment of a religious community, bears sacramental significance; it points to the realities that lie deep within it. If those realities seem antithetical or at odds with divinization, then seekers must begin to baptize them into divinization. If elements in the culture exist that tend toward divinization, even if not directly related to any effort toward divinization, then seekers must embrace them. Slowly over time, the world will begin to reflect its engagement with divinization, as seekers begin to direct and mold the cultural environment. Withdrawal from the world, from popular culture, from the social associations not intentionally oriented toward divinization, simply abandons the public and cultural aspects of divinization; that is unacceptable. It is precisely in the world that divinization must be seen and known, and thus the world is an important and vital element in the progress toward eschatological divinization.

Likewise the self must be embraced as a similar arena for the divinization of the world. Divinization simply cannot occur if individual seekers do not accept the self as a primary site for effort. The treatment of the self as suspicious, prone to evil, abject in its depravity, or problematic to divinization's mysterious transformation simply inhibits the potential for growth in divinization. The self, even in its failure to respond to the divine presence and to move under the influence of the interior divine impulse, remains a vital and central site for the eventual transformation of the self, society, and world. Recognition of this central role for the self puts pressure on the seeker continually to work with the self, to overcome hindrances, to train the self in divine ways, to accept limitations when necessary but to pursue possibilities when opportunities arise. There can be no eschatological divinization without the divinization of individual selves.

Affirming the value of world and self, however, does not imply that everything that the world is or that the self desires will lead to divinization. Discernment still remains a vital function to determine the value and importance of various factors in a seeker's personal, social, and cultural contexts. That discernment requires not only sifting through the elements in self and world to discover that which cooperates with the divine presence and impulse and that which seems unrelated, but also sifting through the language, images, and music of the culture and the self to discern what enhances progress toward divinization and what inhibits it. Because visual, linguistic, and musical images have such a profound impact on the self, social groups, and the culture, seekers must exercise a custody of the senses that keeps them aware of the implications of patterns of sound, sight, and words. The value of popular cultural images and songs can be weighed and measured according to their relationship to the divine presence and their potential for cooperating with the divine impulse. Even images, music, and language seemingly antithetical to divinization may ultimately play a positive role in the divinization of self, society, and the physical environment, because they begin to direct individual and corporate seekers to an understanding or a way of living, which advances progress toward divinization.

Living with a complex world and with an even more complex self does not in itself create problems for the seeker. Both self and world are to be highly valued as important sites for divinization, but their value must be carefully weighed in relationship to their capacity to respond to the divine presence and to cooperate with the divine impulse. In the end and at the end, divinization must be visible and perceived directly and obviously in the self and the world in order that both may reveal the interior energy of the divine that inheres in all creation.

90 / Rest .... ॐ

O NE OF THE MOST ANCIENT articulated goals of the spiritual life
is rest (Hebrews 4:1–11). The struggle for divinization and the
difficult work of transformation of self, society, and the world demand
significant effort and energy. These divinizing activities, both mental
and physical, demand enormous exertion by individuals and groups to
sustain momentum toward the point when God will be all in all (1 Corinthians 15:28), when all things are finally restored to the fullness
of the divinity, and when divinization of individuals, of every society and community, and indeed of the whole physical universe will be
achieved. In this context the emphasis in the spiritual literature on rest
takes on both an immediate and an eschatological significance. Like
anticipated joy, this rest anticipates the final rest that all divinized beings will find when God is all in all; that is, at the final restoration of all
things to the divine. This eschatological rest, which culminates in the
eschatological divinization of every living creature, creates momentary
and proximate experiences when the individual and the communal
seekers may glimpse in passing moments that which will be the permanent state of all living beings in their divinization. The glimpse
of eschatological rest in the present, even fleetingly, energizes and re-
news the steady advancement toward the final divinization and rest of
all things.

This ascetical rest, however, is much more than the cessation of
effort toward fully achieved divinization. Rest actually functions as a
very active way of living. For the individual, rest marks the time when
the seeker has accepted the seeker's own foibles and limitations and
can live with them and incorporate them into the movement toward
divinization. The seeker comes to rest with the self and its specific
constitution as simply part of the life where the divine is present
and through which the divine impulse operates. This rest signifies the
seeker's capacity to forgive and accept the self, even in its weakness
and disorientation toward the divine. The seeker acknowledges and
heals those destructive memories and experiences that every human
person accumulates, by an active process of the healing of memories
and experiences, and by releasing the self from operating under their
destructive influence. So the self, healed and accepted in whatever
state it is in, rests in an anticipation that (in the end) all things —
all memories, every experience pleasant and harmful, and every other

aspect of human existence — will find their final consummation in eschatological divinization. And finding that rest in the self, the seeker accepts the foibles and limitations of others, resting in the knowledge that all other seekers experience the same debilitating and destructive experiences and act out of them in the same way; the seeker can forgive and accept others as being in the same situation as the seeker's own self.

The same applies to communities. Corporate bodies also find rest in their work toward the divinization of themselves and other groups and cultures in their sphere of influence. Communities experience this rest as a kind of equanimity combined with magnanimity. The equanimity of rest describes that steadiness of acceptance of other individuals and groups as being equally propelled toward divinization. Acceptance solidly locates a community in a stream of other communal efforts moving toward divinization. Equanimity provides a context for the community's rest, knowing that in every circumstance its own efforts and those of other communities succeed and fail, advance and progress, while the most important experience is to remain constantly in the divine presence and to conform to the divine impulse. This equanimity leads to magnanimity, the capacity to pour out the communal self generously to others, sharing the benefits of the divine presence and impulse with other communities and individuals who differ significantly from one another. In other words, the seeking community rests in itself, knowing that ultimately God will be all in all and rests in relationship to other communities, even very different communities, because at the final restoration of all things these communities will also rest in their divinization.

This eschatological rest, then, frees seekers to accept, to forgive, to heal, and to stand before the divine presence with the full assurance that divinization will come even through feeble and ineffectual efforts, even through failure and hurt. The rest enables seekers to enter into that other place where already the self, communities, and the physical world are divinized and whole, and where all others who have similarly struggled and found limited success stand as well. And standing there, seekers rest in the sure mystery of this comprehensive divinization, which drives all creatures to find their ultimate fulfillment and joy in the divine.

91 / Faith, Hope, and Love ....

FAITH, HOPE, AND LOVE, these three (1 Corinthians 13:13), define the more advanced movements of seekers toward the divine; the tradition labels them as the theological virtues. These theological virtues form the foundation of the more advanced spiritual life by connecting seekers more closely and habitually to the activity flowing from cooperation with the divine impulse.

Faith describes an attitude of trust in both the divine presence and the divine impulse. Seekers at first awakening to the interior presence of the divine continually remind themselves of that presence and strive to cooperate with it in daily life and thought. Eventually, seekers come not only to knowledge of the divine presence, but also to a sense that the permanence of the divine presence and the vitality of the divine impulse form the core of their being. Seekers come to trust in that presence as a firm foundation for all other actions, thoughts, reactions, and relationships. When seekers come to that point of trust, relying and depending upon the foundational reality of the divine presence, they have come to faith. Such faith undergirds all spiritual endeavor. The same applies to communities of believers. Communities strive habitually to rely upon the divine presence and upon the divine mission they have been given. At first, communities must remind themselves of their divine origin and direction, but eventually, gradually, and even incrementally, that divine presence becomes the defining reality of the community. The community's coming to such faith frees it to become even more radically an instrument of divinization and restoration in the world. Faith describes the solid trust in the divine presence in self, society, and the physical universe.

Hope describes an attitude toward the future. Firmly rooted in the security that comes from faith, hope opens seekers to the potential of the future and to the unfolding of the process of divinization of self, society, and the cosmos. Hope expands seekers' horizons in order to see the divine presence unfolding in myriad and mysterious ways. Seeing the unfolding mystery, seekers — both individual and corporate — have confidence that the divine impulse directs and inspires the future. Hope acknowledges that the eschatological divinization at once draws all creatures to a fullness of life not yet conceived or conceivable and at the same time restores all creation to the fullness of life possible because the divine is present and transforming. That openness to the future, to what is coming and not yet fully perceived, defines hope. But hope is of particular importance because it sustains seekers when the struggle for divinization becomes difficult, or opposed by others, or confused by the normal and continual chaos of revisioning the direction and nature of divinization, or even exhausting by the sheer demands put on faithful individuals and communities. Hope sustains the faith and opens seekers to the unrealized and yet real future divinization.

Love describes the capacity of seekers to embrace all that currently is. Emerging from faith, and founded in hope, seekers begin to embrace and hold sacred all that currently exists. Seekers begin to embrace other seekers, and even opponents of divinization, as caught up in the plan of salvation. Seekers begin to cherish even their failures at advancing toward divinization because the divinizing impulse operates despite failures and deficiencies. Seekers embrace communities that bear the potential for divinization as well as those communities that actually work toward divinization and restoration. Seekers embrace the physical universe, in all its wonderful beauty, and even in its polluted reality, as the arena in which God will be all in all. This embrace has two directions: seekers embrace the divine presence that dwells within them; they love the divine presence that has taken deep root in their lives, and they rejoice in that love. But seekers also embrace the divine presence in other people and communities. It is not simply a love that looks inward, but an embrace that looks outward in an acceptance of the reality of the divine presence, which permeates all relationships and people. Love turns seekers toward the embrace of the infinitely productive divine presence and toward the embrace of everyone and every community because of the faith and hope that the divine plan of restoration advances even through failure and hurt. Love forms that capacity to embrace, even when embracing makes no sense, because the divine presence seeks to unite every creature in which it dwells.

Faith, hope, and love, precisely as theological virtues, display the fruits of advanced labor on behalf of divinization and the fruits of personal and corporate cooperation with the divine plan for divinization. They signify the deep roots that the divine presence has formed in the life and labor of people and communities — roots that enable seekers alone and together to confidently trust in the divine presence, to be open to the unfolding mystery of divinization, and to embrace the advancements and failures as instantiating the divine in the world.

92 / Humility ....

THERE CAN BE no engagement with asceticism and the spiritual life without taking up the question of humility. The word "humility" relates to the Latin word for "soil, dirt," and usually means close to the core, low to the ground, near to the soil; humility means humble, earthy, lowly, and a poor image of oneself. Theologically, humility parses the account of the formation of human beings from the soil, Latin *humus*, in the biblical book of Genesis and constructs from that account of creation an understanding of the human condition as low, humble, deeply physical, and contingent. At the same time the biblical parsing also acknowledges that although humans were created by God with the dirt of the earth, God blew the spiritual breath of life, the Holy Spirit, into humans to give them life and fullness of being (Genesis 2:7).

Although the recognition of the simultaneously contingent and divinely inspired status of human beings has been affirmed throughout the ascetical tradition, spiritual masters tended to emphasize the abject poverty of human resources, characterized as derived from dirt and very lowly, in comparison with the fullness and glory of the divine presence. The divide between human and the divine took on more importance than their union and cooperation, resulting in a view of human life as abjectly poor, worthless, and inadequate before a divinity that was surpassingly rich, valuable, and capable. Humility became a means of denigrating human existence and effort.

In the postmodern context, however, humility takes on new and important significance as a return to an earlier sense of the deeply contingent and yet divinely inspired nature of human being. Now humility, as an orientation toward oneself, others, and the cosmos, readily admits the very limited perspective that any one human being, or any group of human beings, has regarding the unfolding mystery of divinization, which drives all creation. In recognizing that they cannot know the full glory of the divinization that evolves in other people, in communities, and in the physical universe, seekers recognize that they form part of a wonderfully complex and even more wonderfully mysterious unfolding of a divine impulse in creation toward divinization. Humility describes the sense that the mystery of divinization is larger than any human conception. Humility acknowledges that the impulse toward divinization shows human thought and effort to be contingent upon the unfolding of a mystery far greater than any one individual might conceive. Humility recognizes that the categories of human existence, the capacity of the human mind to comprehend and the ability of humans to emotionally experience the divine presence and to cooperate with the divine impulse cannot be comprehended by any one person or group. Humility soundly proclaims that no human can know the mind of God. The mystery far exceeds the existent categories and transcends the capacity of any person or group to understand.

To the extent that no one and no community can know the divine mind, humility allows seekers to know their place in society and in the universe. Seekers have the divine presence and cooperate with the divine impulse toward divinization. This gives meaning to seekers' lives, efforts, and relationships, but in every way that meaning depends upon an unfolding mystery in which seekers participate not as the center or the focus, but as members, single elements among an infinite number of others. Such humility, however, does not denigrate the efforts or the humanity of the seekers. Humility rather takes seekers deeper into the mystery of which they themselves experience only dimly, a glory and majesty that is to come (1 Corinthians 13:12). Humility does not prevent seekers from experiencing in a small way the eschatological glory now, nor does it hinder seekers from working toward divinization as they understand it and may enact it. Humility simply locates seekers in the larger unfolding of the divine mystery of divinization and gives context to their efforts and thoughts.

In the physical universe, to be made of dirt, to be created out of the elements of the physical universe with all the complexities and mysteries to which scientists have been pointing for decades now, is a wonderful thing. Humans consist of the same elements and forces that live in the earth, the air, stars, and galaxies. The divine presence, infused as it is in these elements and processes, drives creation toward a divinization not oriented to human beings alone, or limited to particular religious groups alone, or defined by any one galaxy alone, but toward a divinization that will gather all the physical universe into one divinized creation in which God will be all in all. Humility glimpses this reality and rejoices in it, knowing that the divine presence and the divine impulse ultimately can never be comprehended.

93 / Simultaneity ....

T HERE COMES A POINT in the spiritual life when the capacity for
simultaneous attention and action begins to take place. It is a
time when the process of seeing double, that is seeing the daily and
normative actions and the efforts toward divinization, becomes a simultaneity. Simultaneity refers to that ability to attend at the same
time to divinization and to all the other thoughts and tasks of the day.
Simultaneity no longer distinguishes between that which attends to
the interior presence and impulse of the divine and all other activities,
thoughts, and relations of the day. Divinization has been so thoroughly
integrated into seekers' lives that simultaneity erupts. This integration of divinization into daily living stipulates that there is nothing
that takes place unrelated to the divine presence and unrelated to the
divine impulse toward divinization. Simultaneity recognizes that no
person, event, thought, or relationship stands outside of the divine
presence or is alienated from the process of divinization.

When seekers achieve simultaneity, some aspects of their lives also
change. In the first place, the distinction between discourse and prayer
disappears. Seekers who have been engaged in a discursive process
with themselves, their communities, and the physical environment,
and who have attempted to make this discourse habitual and normative in their lives, now find that the discourse has gradually become
a continual referral of self, society, and world to the divine presence.
The discourse that once was characterized by the remembrance of the
divine presence has now become a continual conversation with the
divine presence and impulse that no longer needs articulated effort.
Discourse has become prayer, a continual prayer of individual and corporate seekers whose lives, thoughts, and actions are oriented toward
the divine presence.

When seekers achieve simultaneity, they also begin to live simply.
This simplicity takes on many forms, but all of them relate to an
attention to the heart of all matters, the divine presence. Seekers find
themselves capable of looking into complex and difficult matters and
finding evidence of the divine presence and the modality for moving
toward divinization. The simplicity is not simple mindedness, nor is it
naive, but rather an ability to recognize the most important elements
in oneself, society, and the world. This simplicity recognizes the divine
presence without difficulty while simultaneously embracing all life and
relationships as part of the divine plan.

Another way of articulating the fruits of simultaneity is to speak of the unity in seekers' lives. Unity, the capacity to live a fully integrated and divinizing life while also being fully engaged in the world, comes from the gradually developed singularity of being and purpose founded in the interior presence of the divine. Over the course of a seeker's life, the capacity simultaneously to stay related to the divine presence and to move the world toward divinization gradually becomes the unified modality for all living. The unity emerges from prolonged orientation toward the divine presence and from the concerted efforts at divinizing self, social relationships, and the cosmos. That unity signifies the capacity of the seeker to live simultaneously in the real world of daily existence as it moves toward divinization and the real world of the eschatological divinization that is yet to come.

Finally, simultaneity moves seekers further and further into the sense of a transcendent divine presence that seems to draw everyone and everything into its orbit. Simultaneity enables seekers to see the final divinization from a transcendent perspective, from the perspective of the convergence of many different or even conflicting strands of divinization, in a point where God will be all in all. Simultaneity focuses the attention at the same time in the concrete and manifold events of daily life and in the mysterious unfolding of the divinization of all things that far exceeds the capacity of seekers to comprehend. Simultaneity conjoins immanence and transcendence in one moment, connecting the most contingent and mundane with the most sacred and divinized, the most particular with the most universal, the most similar with the most conflicting, all with the deep sense of the divine presence mysteriously working out the plan of salvation for all existent beings.

Although simultaneity comes later in the religious life and marks the life of the more spiritually developed and mature, there are glimpses of that simultaneity earlier in the religious life. The divine presence opens the mind to see beyond its confines and allows seekers the sense of the great mystery that surpasses all understanding. While this is momentary early in the religious life, it becomes more habituated over time, and seekers gradually grow into a deep sense of simultaneity, of simplicity, unity, and deep focus on the most important reality of life, the divine presence and impulse toward divinization.

94 / Contemplation .... ᘒ

T HE TRADITION has always reserved the contemplative life, and contemplation itself, for the very few. Contemplation in the Western spiritual tradition represents the highest level on the hierarchy of spirituality, correlative in the Eastern monastic tradition to the indwelling of the uncreated divine light in the advanced monk. Both Eastern and Western spiritual traditions aim to regulate and control access to such extraordinary experiences of unmediated access to the divine energy and presence both by restricting access to the contemplative arts and by withholding validation of a truly contemplative experience.

In reality, however, the unmediated and profound contemplative experience can neither be regulated or controlled, nor even limited to the more advanced seekers in the religious and ascetical life. The divine presence, fully operative in all creation, operates and activates experiences without boundaries, without restriction, and without training. Contemplation, the indwelling of the divine light, constitutes a reality of the spiritual life that should be widely understood.

Contemplation is simply the act of seeing oneself, communities, and even the physical world from the perspective of their fully divinized status. In a sense, contemplation steps to the other side, to the divinized world and gazes back over all creation seeing that which is hidden and invisible within it, the presence and activity of the divine. Contemplation looks upon the self and all relationships not seeing the struggle, not struggling to see the divine, not focusing on the effort, but seeing with the deep sense that divinization has already been accomplished. In contemplation the eschatological state already exists in the present. Seekers in contemplating themselves, as well as all their social associations, and the physical world, see them already divinized, already at rest, already manifesting the divine light. For these seekers, the struggle has ended; they rest in the reality of an already fully divinized status for all creation. Experiencing the world from the divinized side, seekers simply rest in that reality, finding neither their emotions nor affective states activated, finding a passivity in the face of the full reality of things that appear only to be in the process of divinizing.

Contemplation may be metaphorized as the divine presence bursting into flame within the person, warming and enlightening the interior life so that the seeker completely identifies with the interior radiance. It is a way of being united fully with that interior flame and becoming a warming and transforming flame in the world, among other people, in the physical environment. No longer struggling to stay related to the divine presence, the divine presence itself seems to burst forth into the fire of love that transforms and transports the seeker into the divinized world as it will eventually be fully realized. To the seeker that fire seems to come from outside, combining with the interior sense of the divine presence, and bursting into flame within the seeker, but in reality it is simply the divine presence becoming more and more the center of the seeker's or the community's life.

From the Eastern perspective, contemplation may be metaphorized as the indwelling of uncreated divine light within the seeker. The divine energy, understood as light, inhabits the universe. As the seeker begins to engage with that divine energy, both inwardly in the person and outwardly in social relationships, the divine energy begins to take hold of the seeker's experience. It is experienced as though the divine energy has a life of its own, enters into the person, and begins to radiate divine energy from within the seeker to other people and to the outward world. In fact, however, the divine energy is not coming simply from without into a void within a person or community, but rather it has been present in the individual and corporate seeker all along. The contemplative experience, however, connects the individual knowledge and experience of the divine with the presence of the divine in others and in the physical universe in such a way that the seeker comes to understand the self as fully united with all other divine elements. It is a union of all the seemingly disparate elements of divine presence into a solid and unified whole, of which the seeker is part. That sense of the union of all divine energy, taking deep root within the person and within communities, describes the contemplative experience.

Eventually that contemplative experience of complete union with the divine energy and of the capacity to experience the world from the perspective of its divinization will come to all. Some seekers, both individual and corporate, seem naturally more disposed to these experiences, but the contemplative life does not come from natural disposition, or even from training. It is a sense that comes from the sudden, often unpredictable, projection of the self and community to the eschatological end, the final restoration of all things in the divine. The tradition correctly understands contemplation as unusual, but that does not restrict the contemplative life to the few. Contemplation remains available to all, and the divine energy moves seekers toward the experience of unity in mysterious and complex ways, which surpass human understanding and regulation.

95 / Transparency ....

MATURE SEEKERS BECOME TRANSPARENT. The mature ascetic and the seasoned spiritual seeker have a particular social role that they must perform: to become transparent to the processes of attending to the divine presence and cooperating with the divine impulse toward divinization of self, society, and the physical universe. Others ought to be able to read the seasoned seeker as though reading a text on divinization, so that in observing that seeker they may learn the integrated way of abiding in the divine presence. Others observe the minutiae of a seasoned seeker's life in order to experience directly the energy of divinization. They observe the manner in which the seeker processes information, responds to circumstances and other people, analyzes and articulates the issues involved in an individual's or community's attention to the divine presence, engages with the problems of society and the world, and begins gently and directly to move people and circumstances toward the central purpose of their lives in divinization. The seasoned seeker becomes transparent to divinization for others.

That transparency, however, emerges from habituated and long-term attention to discernment. As seekers sift through the issues of their own lives, the lives of their communities, and the state of the physical universe around them in order to discover the divine presence and to energize the divine impulse toward divinization, they become adept at understanding the manifold ways and complexities of divinization in various circumstances. That discernment forces seekers to interpret often conflicting and opposing directions toward divinization and to experience them as part of a mysterious and transcendent movement toward divinization. Discernment, that is, leads seekers to understand and experience the complexity and mystery of divinization in the myriad problems and events of daily living. A seasoned seeker begins to understand difficulties, to perceive the peculiarities of various individuals' and communities' personal relationships with the divine presence within them, to understand that multiple and manifold paths will eventually converge in the universal plan of divinization even when that convergence seems wildly impossible and implausible, and to operate from a deep trust in the continuing mystery of divinization even when it seems to be making no progress or advancement toward any consensus. In sifting through all the detritus of human experience as it strives toward divinization, the seasoned seeker becomes wise, and becoming wise, communicates that wisdom in every action, reaction, and thought throughout the day in order to model responses to the divine presence and to assist others in pursuing the divine impulse.

Transparency eventually takes on a life of its own. It comes to seeking individuals and communities not as a learned skill, but as a grace developed over years of striving to be faithful to the divine presence in the midst of one's own problems, joys, pains, struggles, triumphs, and desires. It is the grace of maturity that shows the way by simply living out what has become a natural way of responding to the circumstances of living a life with attention to the divine presence and devotion to the divine impulse. Seekers do not choose to become transparent, they become transparent because of the way they have lived, and continue to live, their spiritual life. They become transparent because their habituated responses to the divine presence have taken such root in their behaviors and modes of thought that they cannot be otherwise.

The corporate transparency may be seen in communities of faithful people who have lived the religious life for many years. In such communities may be found elders (not necessarily in age, but in experience) whose depth of discernment and wisdom guides the community by their example, and whose depth of knowledge of the ways of the divine are such that no problem or new issue seems to confound them. Communities, under such leadership and guidance, become flexible, responsive, inclusive, transformative, energized, and renewed by the confidence built over years of discernment and struggle. So the borders of the community continually expand to include the lost, the hungry, the homeless, the institutionally disenfranchised; the orbit of the community's life shifts more and more from the enjoyment of its own relationship to the divine to the enjoyment of the fruits of its effort in the embrace and protection of others. The community becomes transparent to its divine presence and impulse, and models for others the way to that mature perspective.

The transparency here does not mean that the individual or corporate seekers disappear, or that they are erased so that some other force takes them over. The contrary is true. Seekers become transparent precisely through their particular and peculiar ways of responding to the divine in the myriad circumstances of their own lives over many years. It is precisely their particularity that models the way toward divinization. Their transparency comes from the unity of purpose and being that derives from years of faithful attendance to the divine presence in themselves, others, and the world around them.

96 / Visions of Deification .... ৵৲

E VENTUALLY ALL SEEKERS have visions. Over the course of prolonged and sustained attention to the divine presence within and without, seekers begin to develop an intuition regarding the final state of all things. The effort and energy put into working toward the divinization of the self, of the communities and social groups to which the seeker is connected, and of the natural world in which the seeker is located take deep root, forming the imaginative and intuitive understanding and knowledge of the way in which divinization occurs. The seeker begins to glimpse the magnitude of the divinizing process and the complexity of divinization converging from so vast and different a conglomerate of peoples, societies, cultures, nations, universes, and galaxies. And glimpsing the magnitude, the seeker begins to have visions of the full and ultimate reality of divinization. These visions of deification, surpassing as they do the particularities of one person, or one society and culture, or one galaxy, cause the seeker to contemplate the mystery of eschatological deification, the restoration of all creation to the divine presence.

It is precisely the hard work of a lifetime of struggle to divinize oneself that finds and establishes these visions of deification. Knowing the personal struggle, and the complexity of one's own attempt consistently and persistently to attend to the divine presence and to choose courses of action and thought that move oneself, and the communities in which one lives, toward divinization, the seeker acquires an experiential as well as a reflective theoretical knowledge of the ways of deification. Taking those individual and personal learnings to the communities in which the seeker participates, the seeker comes to understand deification not only from his or her personal perspective, but also from the conglomerate of perspectives and experiences manifest in the community. These communities in turn communicate with other communities and societies, and the way of divinization and restoration becomes infinitely more complex and rich. Seekers who persist in learning, studying, and searching for the knowledge of the varied paths toward divinization begin to form almost instinctive and mostly intuitive knowledge of the ways that divinization comes. Over time, the seeker comes to have an experiential knowledge of the unfolding mystery of divinization in various and complex peoples, circumstances, and groups.

These visions of divinization emerge from a kind of yearning for union. Seeing the ways of divinization and experiencing both the glory of success and the pain of failure, while at the same time growing in wisdom and knowledge of the ways of deification, the seeker achieves a capacity to attend continually to the divine presence and a less-labored effort at cooperating with the divine impulse. As these experiences, combined with the wisdom gained through prolonged effort, take root in the seeker, the seeker yearns more and more for living completely in the divinized state, in the divinized societies and communities, and in a physical universe made alive and restored by divinization. The yearning moves the seeker toward a desire to live out the glory of eschatological divinization. It is now no longer a mere vision of God that propels the seeker, but a vision of the full and eschatological divinization of all creation, including all peoples, all nations, all cultures, and every dimension of the physical universe.

Only the mystics of various religious traditions seem to have preserved this experience for future generations. The visions of the final end, the restoration and divinization of all creation, have compelled mystics to sing rapturously of the glory of union, not only with the divine, but with all others who have the divine presence implanted within them. It is a vision of unity and of completion that unites the disparate and conflicting aspects of human and created life into a completely divine whole. That mystic vision, however, should not be reserved only for the select few, but ought to be an experience and a perspective held out for every seeker and every seeking community to experience. It becomes the logical end to the smaller yearnings for attention to the divine presence and impulse that fills a seeker's life, and over time these lesser yearnings should lead toward the full vision of the goal that comes through effort. Always, the union and the vision will transcend the perspectives of any one person and community. The mystery of divinization far surpasses human understanding, but the yearning for the ultimate union with all others in a fully divinized world draws the seeker more and more into the mystery. In this sense, every seeker and every seeking community become mystical participants in the eschatological divinization of all creation. Every seeker eventually contemplates the visions of divinization, built upon the infinitely small and incremental first steps toward divinization, combined with the intuitions of divinization that develop over years, mixed with the imaginative and contemplative grasping of the totality and complexity of divinization emerging from all creation, and joined into a yearning for union with all the energies of divinization manifest in the world.

97 / Prayer Beyond Words ....

SOMETIMES IT IS DIFFICULT to imagine prayer without words. The use of words in individual prayer and corporate worship seems so much a central aspect of converse with the divine that words themselves become the vehicle of communication. But that is not necessarily always the case. The history of Christianity and indeed of other religions as well provides evidence for prayer beyond words, a form of prayer that moves beyond the discursive and enters into a direct apprehension and communion with the divine.

When words function as the primary vehicle of communication with the divine at once immanent, dwelling within the seeker, and transcendent, dwelling in others and in the universe and even perhaps outside the universe, the focus of attention revolves around making meaning. Words are instruments for the construction of meaning and the meaningful communication with others. Prayer using words, then, becomes a process of establishing a common meaningful relationship mediated by the words. The divine presence and the human person connect with each other through words that transmit meaningful messages from one to the other and that create a significant relationship between them. This is the sense in which prayer using words may be described as discursive: it creates a common discourse that connects two people through a common linguistic medium. And such prayer lays the foundation for all other prayer — words help create and sustain the initial intimate relationship between the seeker and the divine presence both immanent and transcendent.

Once that discursive prayer has taken deep root within the seeker, the seeker may begin to move toward prayer without words. Here the seeker prays to enter into union with the interior divine presence and to connect affectively and experientially with the divine presence manifest in others, in circumstances, in nature, and in events. In other words, the seeker begins to commune with the divine presence by simply living in the presence of the divine without words and extending that communion outward to all the other manifestations of the divine surrounding the seeker. This prayer apprehends the divine presence in the self, in society, and in the cosmos directly and immediately, without the intermediary of words.

This kind of prayer moves from words to wordlessness. It moves from establishing the category or understanding of the divine to the intentional transcendence of the posited category in order to move into direct communion with the divine beyond it. An example will help. The seeker prays using the word "Creator" and focuses on the meaning and significance of the divine characterized as creator by considering the manner and means of the divine energy creating all human beings, all societies and cultures, and all the stars, galaxies, and even the unknown universes. The "Creator" takes on rich meaning and significance, and the seeker may think and reflect on this richness for a long time, coming to a deep understanding and communion with the divine through the conceptual frame. The seeker, however, remains fully present to this form of prayer in that it revolves around the contemplation and consideration of the category. The seeker understands self and others from the perspective of their relationship to the "Creator." When moving beyond this category, the seeker moves beyond the discourse about the "Creator" to a direct apprehension of the divine in negating the category "Creator." The divine creates, but is much more than simply the "Creator," because the category "Creator" does not adequately describe the divine. So the divine is "Creator" and yet "not Creator," "Sustenance" and simultaneously "Not Sustenance." The process continues positing a categorical description of the divine and negating it in order to move beyond the category, beyond the word, to a direct experience of the divine without any mediation.

This prayer beyond words aims to create immediate experience of the divine by moving beyond discourse into union. The seeker moves beyond the mediating words and concepts into a direct experience of the profundity of the divine presence that seems to baffle every attempt at comprehension and description. This sense of the union of agency, the union of direction, the union of wills between the seeker and the divine presence, unmediated by any connecting vehicle beyond the relationship of seeker to divine itself, enables the seeker to experience the unity and singularity of the divine presence not only within the seeker's own self, but also in others and in the physical universe. The divine presence becomes a naturally functioning part of self, society, and cosmos so that the seeker becomes one with the divine presence everywhere and communes with that universal divine presence in a mystic, sweet communion. The discourse, that is, gives way to immediate communion, so that the seeker, disengaging the categories the mind creates, clings to the divine in self and others directly and lovingly.

98 / Divine Energy .... ⟩⟨

MATURE SEEKERS enter a spiritual marriage. The spiritual tradition describes a state of union of the more advanced and mature seeker with the divine called a transformative union or spiritual marriage. It is a stage in spiritual seeking when the divine presence seems to take control of the person, fusing the divine energy with the effort and energy of the seeker. The seeker's will, imagination, actions and thoughts seem to be driven by the divine presence and taken over by the divine energy. No longer does the seeker strive in the same way as earlier discursive attempts, but now appears to respond to the direction and force of the divine presence whose guidance seems irresistible. In the tradition this stage represents an intense unity of being between the seeker and the divine presence, but now the energy, direction, modulation, and expression of the seeker comes from the divine energy. The union of seeker and divine presence totally overshadows all the individual and corporate efforts of the seeker, so that the divine energy expresses itself directly and immediately through the seeker.

This union, which in itself appears beyond the yearning and will of the seeker, extends the seeker's life and being into the eschatological state. The seeker in this sense bridges the interior divine presence and eschatological divinization, connecting the divine present now in the life of the seeker with the fully divinized universe of the end-times. This state of union recognizes such a level of conformity flowing from the person and the interior divine presence that the effort toward divinization takes on a divine energy that moves it almost effortlessly toward eschatological divinization. The divine energy carries the seeker toward the union not simply between divine presence and the seeker, but now toward union with the final goal, the fully divinized world. In traditional language, this articulates a mystical union of seeker with the totality of the divine; in postmodern language, this union signifies the complete conformity of energies between the seeker and the divine presence and impulse.

What characterizes this union as appropriate only for the more mature is the fact that it emerges only after the discursive practices of the earlier stages. This union with the divine energy, and the flow of the seeker more and more into the final divinized state of the entire universe, no longer rely upon the exercise of the imagination, which images and configures scenarios for the achievement of divinization. The seeker no longer relies upon the visionary imaginary of divinization, which gave substance and direction to earlier actions and reactions aimed toward divinization. The seeker no longer depends upon envisioning and planning the means toward divinization, sometimes because these divinizing patterns have become completely habituated (such as a complete habituation toward recycling and cleaning the environment) and sometimes because the plan of divinization has so surpassed the imagination that the divine energy takes on a life of its own. Finally, in this union the seeker no longer needs to conform the will and action by intention and articulated direction of energy, because the will and the direction have been conformed so intently on the divine presence and impulse that a distinction between them no longer exists. This union, then, is beyond visions, beyond imagination, beyond planning and intention, because the union manifests a divine energy and life of its own, moving the seeker more completely into an eschatological divinization that is yet to be fully manifest to the rest of the universe.

The traditional metaphor for this union is spiritual marriage, a metaphor that does indeed help to explain the nature of the union. In a mature relationship, each spouse knows the abiding and complete love of the other; there is no longer need to prove or to test the depth of love. Over many years of living together in harmony, having worked out the various kinks of difficulties, couples appear to live in a harmony and unity of existence that defies separation. The two have indeed become one person, one flesh. Often such spiritually united spouses even begin to look alike, to take on the appearance of the other so that even in appearance they operate as one person. But even more, their lives have been so conformed to one another that the daily patterns of living and responding have flowed into one common modality of living and responding. That union of two into one has been the primary descriptor of the most advanced state of spiritual formation, spiritual marriage. Spiritual marriage describes the point at which two agencies flow into one modality of being and action; that modality is the divinizing energy and the divinizing reality of the eschatological goal. It is a union that comes only over time and only through a lifetime of effort, when the divine energy becomes all in all within the person fully conformed to the interior divine presence.

99 / Recollection, Silence, and Ignorance ..... ‿⟩

T HE NEED FOR DISCOURSE in the spiritual life never really fades away. Given the complexities of postmodern existence and the speed with which new phenomena both come into existence and change people's way of life, there will never really come a time when discourse — engagement with ideas and new things, with social connections and social interactions, and with concern for the physical environment — will dissipate. Discourse is a reality in the postmodern spiritual life. But discourse does not solely define the modality of the religious life. There are also times when seekers become capable of moving beyond the discourse into silence and into holy ignorance.

Recollection is the foundation of this movement beyond words and knowledge. In habitually recollecting the self in the divine presence, the seeker allows the divine presence to permeate life and thought. In the memory of the divine presence, in calling to mind the interior divine presence, the seeker connects with that divine source of life and begins to cede to the divine presence the priority of expression and centrality. The depth and transformative power of the interior divine presence takes on a central role in the life of the seeker. Recollection, in this sense, remains a discursive practice, because in recollection the seeker directs the attention to the divine presence and actively attempts to remain connected to the divine presence while thinking, relating, or acting. And recollection is also a passive state, because the seeker rests in the divine presence and finds there solace, peace, and renewal. Recollection bridges the discursive activity with the contemplative inactivity.

When the seeker enters into the divine presence and rests there, the seeker experiences a great silence. This silence draws the seeker into experiential relationship with the divine, putting the mind and its work aside in order to rest in that which ultimately is beyond words. Silence transforms the discourse into experience, and the experience of silence carries the seeker more profoundly into the inner divine presence. Silence, like recollection, is both active and passive: in active silence, the seeker puts aside all that intrudes and demands attention except the divine presence; in passive silence, the seeker basks in the glory of resting in the divine presence and rejoices. The silent state, induced as it is by habitual recollection, moves the seeker into a direct apprehension and experience of the divine presence.

From this silence comes a holy ignorance. The discursive categories so essential to building the habitual state of recollection of the divine presence seem to fall away, to be silenced, and to dissipate before the direct experience of the divine. A holy ignorance descends upon the seeker, who no longer clings to the categories and the knowledge achieved over many years of struggle to become holy and divinized. Now the seeker clings to the divine alone. The ignorance that follows upon discursive knowledge leads the seeker into an experience of the divine that defies human categorization and rationalization, so that the seeker not only basks in the silence of the divine presence, but also enters into deep union with the divine presence and impulse and finds rest and solace there.

This same progression of recollection, silence, and holy ignorance operates in communities that begin to live more and more out of the center of their contemplative life. The community discourse, so often oriented toward the remembrance of the divine presence and impulse in their presence, seeks to experience the deep silence of people centering their attention in the divine presence. That community discourse, which strives to manifest the divine presence and impulse in its activity and relationship with others outside the community, begins to reflect on the magnitude and majesty of a divine presence that drives them to restore relationships throughout the world. The community seeks to renew itself in the silence and to find in the silence of the divine presence a revived energy for action. Then the silence leads the community to discard the categories, to move beyond what they know and understand, to an apprehension and service of the divine in unexpected and unusual circumstances. The contemplative progression guides the community to understand the deep well of the divine presence living in silence in the heart of the community. It encourages the community to move beyond its own understanding to risk service and relationship in ways that have never been considered before. Communal holy ignorance inspires prophetic and bold actions reflective of the divine presence, actions that defy common wisdom and that fly in the face of the received practice of the day. The contemplative community is the most prophetic community — healing the sick, restoring the disenfranchised, embracing those whom the world refuses to embrace, and in every way acting beyond the given categories of society. The contemplative community acts out of a holy and defiant ignorance deeply rooted in the silence of the divine presence and built up over years of corporate recollection of the divine presence in activities and thought.

100 / The Final Restoration

D IVINIZATION IS a complex, changeable, mysterious, and comprehensive phenomenon. Gathering the energies and incremental
motions toward personal divinization, as well as the intentional and
devoted work of communities seeking to manifest the divine presence
in life and labor, divinization embraces more and more human individual and corporate effort in order to transfigure it into the divine itself.
Divinization embraces the disparate and conflicting, as well as the cohesive and harmonious. Divinization embraces the religious and the
doggedly nonreligious, the political and the social, the powerful and the
weak, the rich and the poor, and even the believers in various faiths
who seem continually to be at war with one another. The divine, who
gathers and embraces all these fragmentary and momentary efforts toward complete union and participation with the divine presence, seems
ever just beyond comprehension and understanding. Divinization in
that sense is a mystery, a mysterious unfolding of a divine plan for
restoration that confounds human efforts at categorizing and rational-
izing and yet calls for the most creative and intentional use of human
skills at categorizing and thinking.

This divinization has been going on for generations, for millennia,
and throughout the physical universe from its inception. Divinization
implicates in its restorative project everything, everyone, and every circumstance. No thing, no person, no circumstance, no element of the
physical universe, no star, no galaxy, no community, no event stands
outside the impulse toward divinization. The divine embraces it all, as
the divine has done from the beginning of creation until now. Divinization is truly universal, gathering and dispersing, creating categories and
destroying them, thinking with words and moving completely beyond
words into the direct experience and intuition of the divine. Divinization cannot be stopped, hindered, or thwarted even by the most serious
injustice, the most devastating personal experience, the most horren-
dous acts of evil and destruction. Nothing can prevent it, nothing can
hinder it, because the divine embraces now and has embraced always
everything, every one, every circumstance in order to restore them to
the fullness of the divine life that both inheres and transcends creation.

Mystics mostly, but some saints as well, have pointed to this final
restoration as the most compelling reason to begin to cooperate with
the transfiguration and divinization of all life. This final restoration
has provided for them the impetus to strive, to struggle, to create,

to think, and then to rest; to destroy, to acknowledge simply, and to pass beyond thinking into direct experience of the divine. In glimpsing this final restoration of all things in the divine, they have pointed the way to those around them, to those seekers who succeed them, and to those who might pick up their writings (either the text of their lives written into their bodies or the texts of their thoughts inscribed in pen and ink) in order to look into the far distance and to be drawn more fervently into the process. Holy seekers have pointed the way from the beginning of time, experiencing in themselves the incarnate divinity, instantiating the divine in their own lives, and seeking to honor and cherish the physical world about them as the very stuff of the divine. They have looked to the same future restoration that awaits all creation.

It is more difficult in the postmodern world to have such a vision of restoration. Postmodern seekers see the pollution of the air by relentless expansion of the capacity to build larger and less fuel-efficient automobiles; they see the waters polluted by industrial waste and chemicals; they smell the large waste pits filled with the garbage and the horror of nonbiodegradable plastics, which have become the hallmarks of postmodern living; and when they see all this, they think it is impossible. There is no divinization; the powers of the universe are aligned against anything so glorious. Communities of faith as well look around them at the disregard for the poor and weak, the inability of fabulously rich nations to provide simple food, shelter, and health care to their poorest and most vulnerable members, or, for that matter, for the majority of their citizens. Communities of faith look around them at the warring between religions, between communities within religions, between people of good will, and they despair at the enormity of the problems that face them. There seems no end to selfishness, destructiveness, and the capacity to evil and sin. And individual seekers look at their own lives, at how easy it is to forget the divine presence, how quickly they revert to the old patterns that seem out of step with divinization, how facilely old debilitating structures emerge; they consider the task of divinization too large, too complicated, too difficult. In all these, however, the final restoration of all things to the divine takes deep root.

The final vision may not ever be accomplished in one person's lifetime, or in the course of one community's life and labor, or even in the life of the galaxy in which postmodern seekers live, but the final restoration will happen. Slowly, incrementally, and in the smallest and most imperceptible movement of the person toward the divine, the final restoration becomes concrete and real. The vision takes hold of the smallest remembrance of the divine presence and the most insignificant cooperation with the divine impulse and the most fledgling of instantiations of the divine presence. The stuff of the universe — human, social, and cosmic — yearns for the final restoration and moves toward it. Nothing ultimately has the capability of exorcising that divine presence or thwarting the divine impulse toward restoration. The mystery is that it succeeds even in failure, it grows even in stagnation, it emerges even when progress is not evident. In the end, God will be all in all, and every element of this universe and every other universe will be gathered into the divinity that has called it into being. In this, we all may find our hope.

Table of Suggested Daily Readings

ADVENT

First Week of Advent

Sunday: Century 3, Starting Out
Monday: Century 5, Bodies
Tuesday: Century 70, Seeing Double
Wednesday: Century 89, World and Self
Thursday: Century 57, Living in Community
Friday: Century 59, Sodalities
Saturday: Century 33, Ascetical Eschatology

Second Week of Advent

Sunday: Century 34, Mary, the Mother of God
Monday: Century 13, The Society of the Godly
Tuesday: Century 86, Representation
Wednesday: Century 29, Ghostly Converse
Thursday: Century 20, Reading the Signs
Friday: Century 76, Temptation
Saturday: Century 87, Receiving the Mystery

Third Week of Advent

Sunday: Century 61, Generosity and Hospitality
Monday: Century 96, Visions of Deification
Tuesday: Century 85, Divine Virtue
Wednesday: Century 38, Anticipated Joy
Thursday: Century 68, Attention
Friday: Century 11, Revelation
Saturday: Century 35, Progress

Fourth Week of Advent

Sunday: Century 98, Divine Energy
Monday: Century 66, Study and Curiosity
Tuesday: Century 94, Contemplation
Wednesday: Century 77, Consolations
Thursday: Century 40, Mystic Communion
Friday: Century 32, Union with God

Christmas Eve: Century 100, The Final Restoration
Christmas Day: Century 4, Incarnate Living

LENT

Ash Wednesday: Century 62, Penance

> Thursday: Century 39, Self-Examination
> Friday: Century 20, Reading the Signs
> Saturday: Century 1, Conversion

First Week of Lent

> Sunday: Century 12, Living in the Present
> Monday: Century 54, The Divine Mystery
> Tuesday: Century 9, Vision of God, Reign of God
> Wednesday: Century 2, Sanctification
> Thursday: Century 31, Virtues
> Friday: Century, 53 Withdrawal
> Saturday: Century 60, Stages

Second Week of Lent

> Sunday: Century 67, The Deadly Sins
> Monday: Century 14, The Detriment of Idealization
> Tuesday: Century 75, Holiness of Resources
> Wednesday: Century 78, Aridity
> Thursday: Century 15, Knowing the Mind of God
> Friday: Century 22, Worldview
> Saturday: Century 35, Progress

Third Week of Lent

> Sunday: Century 8, The Memory of God
> Monday: Century 43, Cultivation and Avoidance
> Tuesday: Century 21, Mortification Reconsidered
> Wednesday: Century 6, Discernment
> Thursday: Century 53, Withdrawal
> Friday: Century 56, Exercises
> Saturday: Century 58, Spiritual Direction

Fourth Week of Lent

> Sunday: Century 9, Vision of God, Reign of God
> Monday: Century 55, Charting a Way

Tuesday: Century 71, Sin
Wednesday: Century 15, Knowing the Mind of God
Thursday: Century 96, Visions of Deification
Friday: Century 89, World and Self
Saturday: Century 57, Living in Community

Fifth Week of Lent

Sunday: Century 11, Revelation
Monday: Century 37, Thorns and Impediments
Tuesday: Century 76, Temptation
Wednesday: Century 26, Striving
Thursday: Century 93, Simultaneity
Friday: Century 86, Representation
Saturday: Century 19, Divine Indwelling

Holy Week

Palm Sunday: Century 79, Discerning the Divine Mind
Monday in Holy Week: Century 64, The Body Transparent
Tuesday in Holy Week: Century 91, Faith, Hope, and Love
Wednesday in Holy Week: Century 27, Oblation
Maundy Thursday: Century 16, Communion
Good Friday: Century 24, Holy Dying
Holy Saturday: Century 99, Recollection, Silence, and Ignorance

EASTERTIDE

Easter Week

Easter Sunday: Century 2, Sanctification
Monday in Easter Week: Century 52, Utopia
Tuesday in Easter Week: Century 69, Engaging the Tradition
Wednesday in Easter Week: Century 82, Illumination
Thursday in Easter Week: Century 57, Living in Community
Friday in Easter Week: Century 94, Contemplation
Saturday in Easter Week: Century 42, Assembling the Social Body

Second Week of Easter

Sunday: Century 18, Reality
Monday: Century 36, Empowerment
Tuesday: Century 49, Praying the Bodies

Wednesday: Century 30, Ennui and Steps
Thursday: Century 47, Embracing Difference
Friday: Century 70, Seeing Double
Saturday: Century 1, Conversion

Third Week of Easter

Sunday: Century 44, Baptism
Monday: Century 74, Holy Energy
Tuesday: Century 96, Visions of Deification
Wednesday: Century 23, Confession
Thursday: Century 50, Sacraments and Life
Friday: Century 93, Simultaneity
Saturday: Century 16, Communion

Fourth Week of Easter

Sunday: Century 73, Emotional Ecology
Monday: Century 92, Humility
Tuesday: Century 12, Living in the Present
Wednesday: Century 85, Divine Virtue
Thursday: Century 77, Consolations
Friday: Century 25, Disappointment
Saturday: Century 28, Perfection

Fifth Week of Easter

Sunday: Century 72, Playfulness
Monday: Century 84, Affective Contemplation
Tuesday: Century 33, Ascetical Eschatology
Wednesday: Century 42, Assembling the Social Body
Thursday: Century 48, Demons and the Ascetic Life
Friday: Century 65, Passions
Saturday: Century 91, Faith, Hope, and Love

Sixth Week of Easter

Sunday: Century 83, From Discourse to Affection
Monday: Century 27, Oblation
Tuesday: Century 98, Divine Energy
Wednesday: Century 32, Union with God
Thursday (Ascension Day): Century 87, Receiving the Mystery
Friday: Century 82, Illumination
Saturday: Century 90, Rest

Seventh Week of Easter

Sunday: Century 41, Habitual Prayer
Monday: Century 63, Renunciation and Reconstruction
Tuesday: Century 71, Sin
Wednesday: Century 88, Singularity and Integration
Thursday: Century 97, Prayer Beyond Words
Friday: Century 95, Transparency
Saturday: Century 99, Recollection, Silence, and Ignorance

The Day of Pentecost: Century 81, A Living God

THREE-DAY RETREAT

Day One: Century 12, Living in the Present
Day Two: Century 54, The Divine Mystery
Day Three: Century 96, Visions of Deification

SEVEN-DAY RETREAT

Day One: Century 4, Incarnate Living
Day Two: Century 32, Union with God
Day Three: Century 37, Thorns and Impediments
Day Four: Century 49, Praying the Bodies
Day Five: Century 75, Holiness of Resources
Day Six: Century 87, Receiving the Mystery
Day Seven: Century 100, The Final Restoration